D1095587

The Adventuress

TRUE CRIME HISTORY SERIES

Twilight of Innocence: The Disappearance of Beverly Potts
    James Jessen Badal
Tracks to Murder
    Jonathan Goodman
Terrorism for Self-Glorification: The Herostratos Syndrome
    Albert Borowitz
Ripperology: A Study of the World's First Serial Killer and a Literary Phenomenon
    Robin Odell
The Good-bye Door: The Incredible True Story of America's First Female Serial Killer to Die in the Chair
    Diana Britt Franklin
Murder on Several Occasions
    Jonathan Goodman
The Murder of Mary Bean and Other Stories
    Elizabeth A. De Wolfe
Lethal Witness: Sir Bernard Spilsbury, Honorary Pathologist
    Andrew Rose
Murder of a Journalist: The True Story of the Death of Donald Ring Mellett
    Thomas Crowl
Musical Mysteries: From Mozart to John Lennon
    Albert Borowitz
The Adventuress: Murder, Blackmail, and Confidence Games in the Gilded Age
    Virginia A. McConnell

The
Adventuress

Murder, Blackmail,
and Confidence Games
in the Gilded Age

Virginia A. McConnell

The Kent State University Press
Kent, Ohio

Library of Congress Catalog Card Number 2009047060

ISBN 978-1-60635-034-8

Manufactured in the United States of America

Designed by Christine Brooks and set in Cycles.

Printed by Sheridan Books, Inc., of Ann Arbor, Michigan.

Library of Congress Cataloging-in-Publication Data

McConnell, Virginia A.

The adventuress : murder, blackmail, and confidence games in the Gilded Age /
Virginia A. McConnell

p.   cm. — (True crime history series)

Includes bibliographical references and index.

ISBN 978-1-60635-034-8 (hardback : alk. paper) ∞

1. Walkup, Minnie Wallace, 1869–1957. 2. Women murderers—United States—
Biography. 3. Husbands—Crimes against. 4. Murder—United States—Case studies.
I. Title.

HV6248.W188M33 2010

364.152'3092—dc22   2009047060

British Library Cataloging-in-Publication data are available.

14 13 12 11 10   5 4 3 2 1

This one is for "the girls": my sisters-in-law Patty McConnell, Victoria Beckner, and the late Jill McConnell; my niece Kristin McConnell; and my good friends Lisa Greenville and Laurie Austin.

Contents

Acknowledgments   ix
Introduction   xi
Dramatis Personae   xv

Part 1: New Orleans
1. A Shootout and a World's Fair   1
2. The Visitor from Kansas   11

Part 2: Emporia
3. The Mayor Takes a Wife   21
4. Minnie Goes Downtown   29
5. The Death of a Mayor   45
6. A Sensation in Emporia   62
7. Defending Minnie Walkup   75
8. Starring Minnie Walkup   89
9. The Rise and Fall of Minnie Walkup   103
10. Intermission   116

Part 3: Chicago, 1893–1902
11. The Levee   127
12. The Death of a Club Man   134
13. Hansen versus Ketcham   152
14. Billy, Baby Jo, and the Prince   159

Contents

Part 4: Chicago, 1902–1915
  15. The Robber Baron's Partner   181
  16. Death from Afar   188

Part 5: Lagniappe
  17. Where Are They Now?   201

Notes   217
Bibliography   234
Index   236

Acknowledgments

⟜

Thanks to all those who provided me with information I could not have accessed otherwise: the family members of some of the people involved in this story for information and pictures; Robert Loerzel, author of *Alchemy of Bones* (on the Luetgert case), for the interview of Dethlef Hansen; and Cook County Archives for the Ketcham and Louderback probate files.

My sister, Martha Greer, and her lawyer friend, Sherry Chancellor, were loyal editors throughout, giving me feedback, encouragement, suggestions, and requests for clarification.

Barbara Blasey, Ph.D., provided this math-challenged author with the information on the size of a dose of twenty grains of arsenic so that readers (and I) could visualize it.

My student Steve Skinner's early involvement with this case for an English research assignment was so thorough that he succeeded in piquing my interest.

Our college librarian, Jackson Vance Matthews, not only did yeoman service in ordering all that microfilm for me, but provided a patient (and kind) ear as I ranted, exulted, and sulked over triumphs and disappointments. She, along with my other friends, is no doubt glad to have an end—finally—to my numerous tales of Minnie's antics.

The Lyon County Historical Society, Emporia, Kansas, graciously provided a copy of the picture of Minnie that she had taken after her trial, and also one of William Jay.

Robert Hodge of Emporia sent me some copies of his own research on the Walkup case, and his generosity is much appreciated.

Finally, a very large thank you to Joanna Hildebrand Craig, Joyce Harrison, Mary Young, and the folks at Kent State University Press for taking a chance on this very quirky project.

Introduction

What started out as mild curiosity about a woman put on trial for the murder of her husband, the acting mayor of Emporia, Kansas, soon turned into a four-year obsession as the facts unfolded—the most startling of which was that she was only sixteen at the time.

Each aspect of the search, each backgrounding of other characters in the drama revealed new scandals, new layers of venality— on the part not just of Minnie Wallace Walkup Ketcham Keating, but of those connected with her, as well. It was like pulling a loose thread from an old wool sweater: One thread led to another and another, and there was just no end to it. As an example, when I was writing the last chapter and tried once more to find the date of death for one of the characters, the avenue I took resulted in the discovery of yet another scam, this one by that character's husband and with her knowledge.

Scalawags, scoundrels, scamps, women of easy virtue preying on rich men, a carpetbagger governor, sleazy lawyers, lustful judges, partying rich boys, dueling politicians, wealthy womanizers, a classic robber baron—all of these revolve around the central unifying figure of this black widow from New Orleans like a loosely knit band of Irish Travelers. If you saw these folks in a movie, you would scorn the director for presenting such improbable plot lines with characters right out of Central Casting. Yet they were real, and these events actually happened.

I began to realize that, while Minnie Walkup was the main character, the story went beyond her. To leave out some of those events would be to deprive the book of some very entertaining moments. Hence, *The Adventuress* is not just about Minnie, although it is mostly so. She is the fixed foot of the compass, to paraphrase John Donne, to which we always return no matter how far afield we roam.

For the most part, these were not nice people, not even those who were murdered. Although they certainly did not deserve to die, they cannot be considered completely innocent victims. And those who were schemed against for blackmail or confidence games all had a hand in their own destruction.

Another revealing aspect of this story is how we in the twenty-first century can learn about the mores and customs of the past. It is not the law that reflects this: It's the newspapers and the people in a courtroom. If you want to learn how people were expected to behave in an earlier era, read a newspaper account of a high-profile trial and it will tell you everything you need to know about what was considered humorous, what was considered shocking, and what was considered indecorous, inappropriate behavior—not just in the reporters' commentaries, but in their descriptions of the observers' reactions.

Even if it's not legal proof, people will always feel that certain things must be done in a certain way. It is expected that a widow will grieve for her husband, and when she does not do so visibly—whatever she might feel inside—she is judged as lacking in wifely devotion and therefore possibly guilty of the crime imputed to her. It is expected that women are by nature retiring and modest, and when they boldly put themselves forward and stare back at those staring at them, they are no better than streetwalkers, whatever their station in life.

In fact, in our story, it is primarily the actions of women that are the subject of intense scrutiny, whether they are victims, perpetrators, courtroom observers, or merely peripheral players. How they dressed, how they acted, how they talked, where they went, whom they went with, what they failed to do—all of these were analyzed and criticized, by women as well as men. For example, in explaining to a reporter why Minnie Walkup changed from her housedress to another dress before going to purchase arsenic with which to poison her husband, a female neighbor informed him that "ladies in Emporia do not go out on the street in a Mother Hubbard."

Ever a favorite nineteenth-century murder-trial topic was the unseemly presence of women in the audience, especially if "unsuitable" topics such as sex were discussed. Reporters and editors were critical, sarcastic, amused, and outraged in turn, never failing to give the daily report of how many women were in attendance when they should have been home doing the laundry or preparing meals instead of listening to testimony of a shocking nature. There were definite double standards of behavior, and by far the stricter was applied to women.

Notice, for example, the difference in treatment of two con artists, one male and one female: Dethlef Hansen and Josephine Moffitt, both of whom made their living by preying on rich people. While Hansen is made the subject of ridicule, Moffitt is portrayed as evil and beneath contempt. The imposter, "Count Gregory," who was much more successful at his thievery than Josephine Moffitt ever was, is regarded with bemusement even as he is being hauled off to jail.

A related topic is that of what is considered appropriate material to include in a newspaper read by women and children. Although there were plenty of both at the Walkup trial, some newspapers refused to include any testimony on topics constituting what was thought of as "smut." Today's reader would be astonished to know what was deemed unsuitable for publication in the Gilded Age.

In the end, though, it is the women who are the survivors in our story. Although we cannot condone their behavior, particularly the dispatching of rich husbands, it is just possible that they were rejecting the classical role of women as wives and mothers and carving out new "careers" for themselves that did not include millinery or stenography. In a telling bit of testimony at the Walkup trial, the prosecutor asks Minnie Walkup if she hadn't known that the highest fulfillment for a woman was as a wife and mother, insinuating that *of course* she must have been aware of this. Minnie's response is, "I don't know that I regarded it that way." Indeed, she did not.

The Gilded Age was one of extremes: extravagant wealth and abject poverty. Although some of the people in *The Adventuress* were rich, most were—while not really poor—way beneath that class, which they envied, emulated, and tried to access. They hung out on the fringes of the wealthy, gaining occasional admittance and taking advantage of their unsuspecting victims. The image of Josephine Moffitt, her nose pressed against the window of the restaurant as she watches the rich young men at their bachelor party before she enters to ply her trade is a visual representation of a major theme of *The Adventuress*.

This was an incredibly fascinating and yet incredibly frustrating project. The fascinating part should speak for itself in these pages. The frustration stemmed from the lack of answers to so many questions, and to make a smooth story I had no choice but to fill in some of the blanks with what was most likely the answer (with insignificant issues only), based on common sense and previous knowledge. In other cases, however, where the issues were of larger importance, I had to use qualifying terms such as "probably," "most likely," and "supposedly," because the written record provided no help. I apologize for the many times I had to do that.

When people are quoted, the words are their own in approximately 90 percent of those instances. For another 8 percent, I took indirect statements and made them direct for a more interesting read. For the remaining 2 percent, I put words into their mouths based on their actions and what was most logical to have been said under the circumstances.

The facts herein were gleaned from a vast array of sources: multiple newspapers from Emporia, New Orleans, and Chicago, plus a smattering of articles from others around the country; vital records from all the locales concerned; reports from descendants; books and Internet articles dealing with peripheral or background items; probate, cemetery, and census records; and city directories. All of these had to be pulled together into a meaningful whole and as a check against the other sources. Readers can be assured that I did not make any of this up!

Although my own opinions as to what Minnie Walkup did and didn't do are evident, I have provided the information you can use to make up your own mind. Whether you agree with me or not, I am hoping you will come to the conclusion that she and many of the people involved with her (whether directly or indirectly) were most interesting characters indeed and deserve to have their stories told.

Dramatis Personae

⟨⟶

New Orleans

The Houstons
JUDGE WILLIAM T. HOUSTON, Minnie's godfather; possible lover of Dora Findlay
JAMES D. HOUSTON, his brother, a politician and officeholder

WILLIAM PITT KELLOGG: former governor of Louisiana and U.S. senator; one of Minnie's lovers

The Wallace Family
JAMES E. WALLACE, a lawyer, divorced from Minnie's mother
ELIZABETH WALLACE, twice-married and twice-divorced; mother of Minnie and Dora and proprietor of various boardinghouses in New Orleans
DORA KIRBY FINDLAY, daughter of Elizabeth Wallace and Patrick Kirby (Elizabeth's first husband); Minnie's half-sister
MINNIE WALLACE WALKUP, Dora's half-sister and daughter of James E. and Elizabeth
EDWARD GEORGE FINDLAY, husband of Dora Kirby; portrait painter
MILTON HOWARD FINDLAY, son of Dora Findlay and possibly Edward Findlay
EDWARD "EDWIN" KIRBY GEORGE FINDLAY, son of Dora and Edward Findlay
MINNIE JAY FINDLAY, daughter of Dora and Edward Findlay
WILLIAM D. "WILLIE" WILLIS, Elizabeth Wallace's niece's son; Minnie's first cousin once removed and thought of by her as a brother

Dramatis Personae

Residents of Emporia, Kansas

EBEN BALDWIN: friend of James Walkup; traveled with him to the New Orleans Fair

DWIGHT BILL: friend and business partner of James Walkup

WILLIAM BORN: neighbor of the Walkups; claimed he drank poisoned beer during the reception for newlyweds James and Minnie Walkup

LINA BURNETT: former neighbor of the Walkups; one of James Walkup's lovers

DRUGSTORE PERSONNEL: Moses Bates (James Walkup's brother-in-law); William Irwin; R. B. Kelly; Frank McCulloch; John Moore; Charles Ryder; Ben Wheldon

J. R. GRAHAM: neighbor of the Walkups and editor of the *Emporia Daily Republican*

ED GUTEKUNST: teenaged employee (and former inmate) of the Emporia jail; claimed that he and the sheriff's son, Oscar Wilhite, had had sex with Minnie during her stay there

MAJOR CALVIN HOOD: chief citizen of Emporia; head of the bank; also Mattie Walkup Hood's father-in-law

HENRY PLATT "HARRY" HOOD: son of Major Hood and husband of James Walkup's daughter Mattie; paid for extra prosecuting attorneys at Minnie's trial

WILLIAM IRELAND: grocer and friend of James Walkup; tended to him during his last illness

DR. LUTHER JACOBS: neighbor of the Walkups and James's attending physician

Jay Family

WILLIAM JAY, age sixty-five, was the guardian ad litem for Minnie at her trial. He and his daughter Mary attended every day. Next to Major Hood, William Jay was Emporia's most influential citizen

MARY MOSS: nineteen-year-old African American servant in the Walkup household

NEIGHBORS: Sallie McKinney; Carrie Roberts; Julia Sommers; Fannie Vickery. These women lived on the same block as the Walkups and spent much of their time spying on and gossiping about Minnie

NEWMAN'S DEPARTMENT STORE PERSONNEL: George W. Newman,

owner; Eunice Bartlett and Maggie Evans, saleswomen; Johnnie
Samuel, delivery boy

LUTHER SEVERY: elderly neighbor of the Walkups; witness to Minnie's
spilling of the arsenic

REV. WINFIELD SNODGRASS: pastor of the church attended by the Walkups. Minnie told him the fake suicide story before James Walkup's
death

Walkup Family

JAMES REEVES WALKUP, acting mayor of Emporia

MINNIE WALLACE WALKUP, his bride of one month

WILLIAM WALKUP, James's son by his first wife, Annie

MARTHA "MATTIE" WALKUP HOOD, James's daughter by his second
wife, Hannah

ELIZABETH "LIBBIE" WALKUP, James's daughter by his second wife,
Hannah

SHERIFF JEFFERSON WILHITE: sheriff of Emporia. His family treated
Minnie as one of their own during her incarceration

OSCAR MILTON "MIT" WILHITE: teenaged son of the sheriff, employed
at the jail. He claimed, along with Ed Gutekunst, to have had sex with
Minnie in jail.

WALDO WOOSTER: deputy sheriff of Emporia

The Trial

ATTORNEYS FOR THE DEFENSE: George S. Dodds (from Mississippi);
Thomas P. Fenlon; William W. Scott

ATTORNEYS FOR THE PROSECUTION: Judge J. Jay Buck; Colonel John
Feighan; Isaac Lambert; Clinton N. Sterry

DOCTORS FOR THE DEFENSE: Dr. S. Emory Lanphear (expert witness); Dr.
A. N. Conaway (Walkup's sexual activities); Dr. John Filkins (Walkup's
sexual activities); Dr. Charles W. Scott (Walkup's sexual activities, arsenic use, and syphilis); Dr. H. W. Stover (Walkup's sexual activities)

DOCTORS FOR THE PROSECUTION: Dr. Charles Gardiner; Dr. William
Jones

JUDGE CHARLES B. GRAVES: presiding judge

BILL GREER: pseudonym given to unidentified reporter from New Orleans *Daily Picayune*

MISS LANE: court stenographer at trial who kept newspapers supplied with transcripts

FRANKIE MORRIS: notorious Kansas woman accused of poisoning her mother; a visitor at Minnie's trial and introduced to her by their lawyer Thomas Fenlon

"SMUT" WITNESSES: H. R. Fleetwood; Nathaniel Benjamin Morton; Asa Smith. Their testimony about James Walkup's alleged sexual activities was of such a shocking nature that most newspapers declined to print it.

The Chicago Connection

WILLIAM BERMAN: friend of Billy Pike who showed Josephine Moffitt the anonymous note sent to Billy's father warning him about Josephine

ELMER BISHOP: Josephine Moffitt's attorney at the *Moffitt v. Pike* trial

GLADYS FORBES: notorious courtesan and procuress; a friend of Minnie's (also known as Gladys Hitt and Gladys Shannon)

"COUNT" BERNARD FRANCIS GREGORY: pseudonym of Bernard Greenbaum, a scam artist who tricked Lida Nicolls into giving him money

DETHLEF C. HANSEN: attorney who helped Minnie in her quest for the estate of John B. Ketcham; he later sued her for unpaid fees

ROBERT "PONY BOB" HASLAM: famed Pony Express rider and friend of John B. Ketcham

ALONZO H. HILL: wealthy Chicago banker and real estate magnate

HARVEY HILL: ne'er-do-well son of Alonzo; along with Agnes Sowka, tried to blackmail DeLancey Louderback

HOMER HITT: former husband of Gladys Forbes; spent his son's trust money on her

REV. WESLEY A. HUNSBERGER: the "marrying parson" who churned out a record number of marriages in Milwaukee; Minnie took John Ketcham here but had to settle for a substitute minister instead

JOE KELLER: Minnie's butler in Chicago; a witness to the will of John B. Ketcham

Ketcham Family

JOHN BERDAN KETCHAM, Minnie's second husband and second victim

GEORGE KETCHAM, his brother, who tried to rescue John from Minnie's home

NETTIE POE KETCHAM, John's second wife, who divorced him when he began dating Minnie and drinking to excess

DELANCEY HORTON LOUDERBACK: a financier and partner of Charles Tyson Yerkes in Chicago's and London's elevated railroad systems; friend of Minnie and possibly her third victim

VIRGINIA MIXSELL LOUDERBACK: DeLancey Louderback's wife

JOSEPHINE MOFFITT: notorious Chicago courtesan who tried to get money from rich men by claiming to be their common-law wife; a friend of Minnie (real name: Josephine Guillemet)

J. WESTLEY MOFFITT: Josephine's former lover; although she was never married to him, she took his name and called herself "Mrs. Moffitt"

ALICE MORRIS: Chicago prostitute; roommate of Josephine Moffitt

LIDA NICOLLS: also known as Princess Victor of Thurn and Taxis; sued Josephine Moffitt for claiming to be Princess Victor

HUGO PAM: attorney for Dethlef Hansen in *Hansen v. Ketcham* trial

EVERETT PEACOCK: husband of Bertha Schneider, DeLancey Louderback's secretary; Peacock took a million dollars from various banks through Ponzi and check-kiting schemes

JOHN BARTON PAYNE: attorney for Billy Pike in the *Moffitt v. Pike* trial; would eventually serve as secretary of the interior under President Woodrow Wilson

Pike Family

EUGENE S. PIKE, wealthy and influential Chicago magnate

CHARLES BURRALL "CHARLEY" PIKE, EUGENE ROCKWELL "GENE" PIKE, and WILLIAM WALLACE "BILLY" PIKE: his sons; Billy was sued by Josephine Moffitt for "separate maintenance"

Ritter Family

SARAH "SALLIE" ECKERT LOUDERBACK RITTER, DeLancey Louderback's half-sister

HENRY APP RITTER SR., her deceased husband

HENRY APP RITTER JR., her son, living with her in DeLancey's home

REV. I. P ROBERTS: minister who married Minnie and John Ketcham in Milwaukee

BERTHA SCHNEIDER: secretary to DeLancey H. Louderback

THOMAS P. SHANNON: Chicago alderman and live-in lover of Gladys Forbes

AGNES SOWKA: attempted to blackmail DeLancey Louderback for alleged sexual assault, a scheme she cooked up with Harvey Hill

Thompson Family

WILLIAM HALE "BIG BILL" THOMPSON: Chicago politician and friend of Billy Pike

GALE THOMPSON: his brother, whose bachelor party was the cause of the introduction of Billy and Josephine Moffitt

PERCY THOMPSON: another brother and also friend of Billy Pike

MARGARET THORPE: orphan living with Gladys Forbes and Thomas Shannon; though never formally adopted, she would later take the name of Forbes

SENA TORREY: Minnie's older cousin and her housekeeper at 3421 Indiana Street; a witness to the will of John B. Ketcham

TRUDE BROTHERS: Alfred and George, attorneys who represented Minnie at various times. Alfred was also on Billy Pike's defense team in *Moffitt v. Pike.*

VICTOR, PRINCE OF THURN AND TAXIS: a scam artist himself, he was almost scammed by Josephine Moffitt, who alleged a common-law marriage with him

THOMAS F. WALSH: wealthy Colorado mine owner being blackmailed by Violette Watson

VIOLETTE WATSON: a "casino girl" blackmailing Thomas Walsh and represented by Dethlef Hansen; she later settled with Walsh and refused to pay Hansen

FRANK WING: proprietor of a notorious bar and brothel in the Levee district of Chicago; site of a party attended by Josephine Moffitt and Billy Pike

CHARLES TYSON YERKES: famous robber baron and architect of Chicago's commuter railway system; onetime partner of DeLancey Louderback

Part One

New Orleans

Chapter 1

A Shootout and a World's Fair

⌒

The person who believes he can rise to a position of wealth and power in the state of Louisiana and not do business with the devil knows nothing about the devil and even less about Louisiana.
—*James Lee Burke,* Crusader's Cross *(2005)*

New Orleans may have been a big city in 1884, but people noticed things. They noticed how beautiful Dora Kirby was and they were especially cognizant of her half-sister Minnie Wallace's breathtaking loveliness. Even at fifteen, young Minnie stood out in a crowd: Taller than most girls at five feet, seven inches, with a husky voice and alabaster skin, she seemed to cast a spell on any male within her radius.[1] It was a common sight to see Minnie strolling through the streets of New Orleans in company with her cousin Willie or her godfather, forty-year-old Judge William T. Houston.

Yes, people noticed, all right. Judge Houston, a married man, paid a lot of attention to those Wallace girls and squired them to balls and restaurants and carnivals. He was none too discreet about it, either. He was constantly pestering their mother, Elizabeth, to allow Minnie to live with him and his wife. "She's too beautiful to be stuck in a boardinghouse," he would say.[2]

With Dora, Judge Houston was prone to public displays of affection, no doubt thinking (wrongly) that his lofty position as district court judge would shield him from criticism. Dora herself should have known better, as by Mardi Gras of 1884, when she attended one of the balls with Houston, she was a married woman of twenty-six with two children. A weekly newspaper, the *New Orleans Mascot,* reminded the judge of his obligations as an officer of the court in a most humiliating way.

The *Mascot* was founded in 1882 as a gadfly newspaper that would not hesitate to expose political and moral chicanery wherever it was found. While the more staid daily newspapers, the *Daily Picayune* and the *Times-Democrat* (later merging into today's *Times-Picayune*), often ignored the underworld or political corruption, the *Mascot* exposed it with demonic glee—and at the same time criticized its rivals for not doing so. Readers loved the gossip they found in the pages of their weekly *Mascot.*[3]

When, in late December 1884, Judge Houston got on a bandwagon advocating moral reform, "Bridget Magee" took him to task in "her" column. The "Bridget Magee" column comprised a mishmash of gossip and commentary related in an Irish brogue that rendered it somewhat humorous, but also difficult to read. In the *Mascot* of January 10, 1885, the Magee column ended this way: "Judge Houston should be the lasht man in the city to attimpt the role av moril raformer. . . . His intimate relations wid the Wallace family, ishpishally wid Miss Dora, are notorious, an' it's only his position on the binch that has kipt him from bein' publicly denounced on more than wan occasion, notably at a carnival ball last Mardi Gras, fur his open an' shameless asshociation wid her."

And so the matter would have rested had it not been for the southern sense of honor that goaded Houston's thirty-seven-year-old brother, James, into taking it upon himself to defend the family name against its detractors. Two days after the column came out, he armed himself with a gun, a knife, a blackthorn stick, and a former sheriff, and went calling on the editor of the *Mascot,* George Osmond, to "chastise" him (Houston's word) for the insult to his brother.[4]

Houston and ex-sheriff (now registrar of voters) Robert Brewster climbed the stairs to the *Mascot* office and stopped at the first desk they came to, that of engraver Adolph Zennecke. "Where is George Osmond?" Houston asked, and Zennecke pointed to a desk at the other end of the room. Houston and Brewster approached and inquired of the next man, "Are you George Osmond?" When he told them he was, Houston—without asking whether Osmond had written the offending Bridget Magee column (he had not)—began pummeling him with the three-foot-long blackthorn walking stick. When Zennecke saw that his employer was being attacked, he

The shooting at the *Mascot* newspaper office (sketch from the *Mascot*)

ran to his aid, but before he could get there, Brewster drew his .40-caliber Colt revolver and fired at him.

When Osmond saw Brewster shooting at Zennecke, he took his own weapon (a double-action .44 Tranter) out of his desk drawer. Before he could fire, however, James Houston pulled out *his* pistol (also a .44 Tranter) and shot at the editor. So at this point Brewster was shooting at Zennecke, and Houston and Osmond were shooting at each other. Osmond's first shot hit Houston in the hand, thereby putting him out of the fight. Having no weapon, Zennecke picked up a stove lid and flung it at Brewster like a Frisbee, whereupon Osmond and Brewster now emptied their pistols at each other.

Brewster later died in the hospital, but the amazing thing is that neither Osmond nor Houston was seriously injured, and Zennecke was not hit at all. The pistol-packing intruders were obviously terrible shots. Not so the defender Osmond, however: The coroner, Dr. Stanhope Jones, said that three bullets entered Brewster's chest, two of them fatal.[5]

Many New Orleanians were upset that the two men who had acted in self-defense, Osmond and Zennecke, were held without bond, while the aggressor Houston went free on $2,500 bail. But, then, Houston was no ordinary citizen.

James D. Houston was an ambitious man, a political mover and shaker who preferred working behind the scenes. Almost singlehandedly, as advisor and campaign manager, he was responsible for the election of Louisiana governor Samuel McEnery, and he also personally financed the Grover Cleveland presidential campaign in Louisiana. He was a former criminal sheriff of New Orleans and at the time of the *Mascot* shooting incident held the office of tax collector.[6]

Houston was no stranger to duels, fights, or assassinations. In 1882 he was the second for the state treasurer of Louisiana in his duel with the editor of the *New Orleans Daily Picayune*. By that time, Houston was said to have "filled a private graveyard in years gone by." In 1883 at a critical voting location, he shot and killed the leader of the campaign to elect McEnery's opponent, later claiming (falsely) that it was self-defense.[7] And there would be even more violence in his future.

Just before the *Mascot* shooting, that newspaper had printed a satirical series of hypothetical tombstones projected twenty-five years into the future and bearing the names of prominent politicians. James D. Houston's monument featured dueling pistols and a knife, with an inscription: "Here lies James D. Houston, who died happily with his boots on. He was a generous and devoted friend to himself." (Ironically, the now-dead Robert Brewster also had an entry, with a mourning dove that looked like a vulture on a broken column.)[8]

The *Mascot* claimed that its morals charge against William T. Houston regarding the Wallace girls wasn't James Houston's prime motive in seeking revenge, that he had been anxious to do so ever since he found that he couldn't bully that newspaper into backing McEnery. It defended its printing of the gossip by saying that it "simply made public what had been talked about for months" and that it had received complaints about the judge's behavior from citizens. (As we shall see, it is highly likely that some of these complaints came from James Wallace, Minnie's father.) Before printing the column, the *Mascot* investigated and had the information corroborated by what it termed "responsible people."[9]

Readers agreed with the newspaper in its criticism of the judge. "A Mother of a Family" wrote in to compliment the *Mascot* for not favoring the privileged. In other papers, she pointed out, no mention would be made of a young society woman's causing a scandal, but "if a poor working girl drinks too much lager," she would be fair game. The *Mascot* itself bragged that it was completely independent of influence and did not "bend the knee to moneyed aristocrats nor fear the murderous bullies of a corrupt government."[10]

Just who was this Wallace family at the center of such a sensational and scandalous sequence of events?

The Wallaces

When Minnie Wallace was born at 83 North Rampart Street in New Orleans on January 14, 1869, a temporary peace reigned in her family. Her parents, thirty-nine-year-old Elizabeth and forty-one-year-old James E. Wallace, had been married since July 1865, after Elizabeth's divorce from her first husband, Irish native Dr. Patrick Kirby. James Wallace was a successful attorney and also served as a U.S. commissioner, making more than enough to support Elizabeth, Minnie, and Elizabeth's eleven-year-old daughter, Dora Kirby.[11]

A couple of years after Minnie's birth, the family welcomed another addition: three-year-old William "Willie" Willis, the son of Elizabeth's niece, who had just died of consumption. Willie's father wasn't up to taking care of a little boy, so Elizabeth took him in and raised him like her own son. Minnie thought of him as a brother, since they were only eleven months apart in age, and the two were inseparable. When Willie was ten, his father died, too, leaving him officially an orphan.

But all too soon, cracks appeared in the façade of the Wallaces' life. James was drinking more and more, and funds were at a premium. An energetic and ambitious woman, Elizabeth began taking in boarders to support the family. She harped at James for his drinking, and he retaliated by accusing her of sleeping with the boarders. In 1873, the two separated.

Possibly as a result of her husband's position as commissioner, Elizabeth Wallace became acquainted with New Orleans district judge William T. Houston. Judge Houston was a married man, but he found himself increasingly drawn to the blooming and beautiful Dora Kirby, now a teenager. He began taking her around to various places and interesting himself in her upbringing. And, as little Minnie began to grow, everyone could see that she would be even more comely than her half-sister. Judge Houston noticed this, too.

The Wallace boardinghouse at 222 Canal Street in New Orleans (sketch from the *New Orleans Times-Democrat*)

Elizabeth Wallace may have decided at some point to raise her younger daughter in such a way as to assure her financial future as the wife of a wealthy man. She sent Minnie (and maybe Dora, too) to a convent school in New Orleans, the Ursuline Academy, where she learned the social graces and how to play the piano, as well as academic subjects. In 1882, Minnie transferred to the St. Louis Institute, another girls' school, although she left just two years later without graduating. Judge Houston more than likely paid her tuition.

On Minnie's thirteenth birthday, January 14, 1882, she was christened in New Orleans' Christ Church, with Judge Houston as her godfather. And, although her birth certificate, filed in 1869, shows her middle initial as A., she would now be known as Minnie Mabel Houston Wallace. James Wallace, her father, was not present at this ceremony, as ever since the official divorce in 1880, granted by none other than Judge Houston, Elizabeth had forbid him to see Minnie.[12]

Wallace worried about his daughter and the way she was being raised. There were tales of raucous revelries at his ex-wife's succession of boardinghouses, where men of questionable reputation gathered, men like "Handsome Charlie" Crushers and Jim Ruley, both of them gamblers and "fast men." Minnie played the piano for them, while Dora, who had a wonderful voice, sang. At these various establishments—44 Dauphine Street, 27 Bourbon Street at the corner of Customhouse (both addresses squarely within the confines of the legal prostitution section later called Storyville), and 222 Canal Street—the word spread as to the incredible beauty and accomplishments of the landlady's daughters.[13]

These boardinghouses run by Elizabeth and her daughters were prime watering holes for gamblers and politicians. Parties featured too much alcohol and too little restraint, and there was even a report (unsubstantiated) of a murder. The *Mascot* pointed a judgmental finger at members of the "Grand Old Party of morality and virtue" comprising the bulk of the partygoers. The food must have been pretty good, too, as local restaurants complained that their big spenders never patronized them again once they had a taste of the fare at the Wallace House—or maybe it was the atmosphere. Most of these rich and powerful men were infatuated with Minnie and her not inconsiderable charms.

On April 22, 1879, twenty-one-year-old Dora married portrait painter Edward George Findlay, nearly twenty years her senior. This was a hurry-up wedding, as their son Milton Howard Findlay was born just three months later—if, indeed, Milton was Edward's child at all.[14] Two years later, on June 8, 1881, Edward Kirby George Findlay, nicknamed Edwin, was born. And they all lived together at 44 Dauphine, 27 Bourbon, and 222 Canal Streets.

In 1884, the Wallace boardinghouse business got a welcome boost when New Orleans hosted the World's Industrial and Cotton Centennial Exposition, whose purpose was to showcase Louisiana's agricultural gifts and mark the end of the Reconstruction period that followed the Civil War, as well as to heal the rift between the North and the South by giving a bang-up party that northerners would want to attend.[15]

And attend they did, although not in the millions as originally—and optimistically—predicted: Between its opening on December 16, 1884, and its closing on June 1, 1885, a mere 1,158,840 attendees filed through the gates of the Cotton Exposition. This may have been the result of poor timing (a winter opening, which would not have made a difference to southerners, but would have influenced travel plans of northerners) or a lingering mistrust of the South. An example of the latter can be seen in the reluctant agreement of the City of Philadelphia to send the Liberty Bell to the fair on a railroad flatcar. The reluctance stemmed from Philadelphians' fears that the southerners would hijack the Bell and melt it down to make a statue of Jefferson Davis.[16]

Nonetheless, a Northerner from Emporia, Kansas, wanted to be among the first attendees at the fair. And with the entry of forty-eight-year-old James Reeves Walkup, our story properly begins.

Chapter 2

The Visitor from Kansas

‿‿⟶

He was a man who was quite determined when he had his mind made up.

—Minnie Wallace Walkup (1885)

At age forty-eight, James Reeves Walkup, a large man with large appetites, had already worn out two wives. He stood six feet, two inches tall, weighed well over two hundred pounds, and was what one might call "rough around the edges." Walkup ate, drank, smoked, and fornicated to excess, frequently visiting both black and white houses of prostitution and also indulging in sexual liaisons with women he encountered in his neighborhood and on his many business trips. His friend Eben Baldwin euphemistically called him "vigorous."[1]

If two separate physicians in Emporia can be believed (and they divulged this information only reluctantly and under oath), Walkup not only had a sexually transmitted disease himself (gonorrhea), once in 1883 and again in May 1885, but had twice employed these doctors to treat prostitutes for STDs as well.[2] And it was no secret that he was a frequent visitor at the home of Mrs. Lina Burnett, a divorcée fifteen years his junior with three children, who once lived on the same street as the Walkups (Merchants Street). Now that she had moved to Topeka, he was visiting her there, too.[3]

Despite his sexual proclivities, the more salacious of which were hidden from his fellow Emporians, Walkup was well-respected and enormously

Eben Baldwin (photo cour-
tesy of the Baldwin family)

successful. A Civil War veteran, he had made money in West Virginia coal
mines before moving with his family to Kansas in 1867. There, he took
up farming and later moved into the city of Emporia, where he became a
contractor for the Atchison, Topeka, & Santa Fe and the Missouri & Pacific
Railroad companies, engaged primarily in figuring out the taxes along the
routes that touched public highways. Walkup was not the only railroad
contractor in the state of Kansas, but he was definitely at the top of the
list. He also owned a 160-acre farm outside Emporia, had recently entered
into a partnership for the sale of wood and coal, and was active in buying
and selling grocery stores.[4]

Benevolent fraternities were popular in the nineteenth century, and
Walkup belonged to two of them: the Knights of Honor and the Ancient
Order of United Workmen (AOUW). And he was politically involved in the
government of Emporia as well, holding office as city councilman from the
First Ward and being elected president of that council. As president, he was
also acting mayor whenever Mayor Nelson Whittlesey was away. Later,
he would be appointed by Governor Martin to be a delegate at the River

Improvement convention in St. Paul, Minnesota. "Vigorous" sums up his working and public lives as well. The man never seemed to slow down.

Walkup had first married back in West Virginia, and when his wife Annie died a few short months after giving birth to their first child, William, in 1857, he waited exactly one year and then married Welsh-born Hannah Maddock. Their daughter Martha (called "Mattie") came along in 1861, followed by Elizabeth Ann ("Libbie" or "Lizzie") in 1866. In Kansas, Walkup had Hannah and the girls working hard for his various enterprises, primarily cooking for the men who worked for him on the railroad and keeping the books. When Hannah died in May 1884 at age forty-three, probably from cancer, there were many in Emporia who felt she had been worked to death.[5]

Now, a mere seven months after Hannah's death, James Walkup was on his way to New Orleans, ostensibly to see the World's Fair, but also to indulge himself in the city's legendary brothels.[6] Consciously or unconsciously, he chose as his traveling companion the very man who would do his best to keep him out of trouble: Eben Baldwin, a forty-three-year-old farmer who had a large spread near Lawrence, Kansas. The two had been friends for almost ten years.

On December 16, 1884—the day the Cotton Exposition opened in New Orleans—Walkup and Baldwin boarded an Atchison, Topeka, & Santa Fe train for Kansas City, then took a Missouri & Pacific train to St. Louis (Walkup's passage was probably free because of his employment with both companies). There, they would take the Anchor Line boat *Baton Rouge* into New Orleans, by way of Memphis. The *Baton Rouge* was scheduled to leave St. Louis at 5:00 A.M. but did not depart until noon. The two men strolled around St. Louis, and Walkup took advantage of the delay to get a prescription filled. Although Baldwin was with him in the drugstore, he wasn't close enough to see exactly what the medicine was. He would later wish that he had been.[7]

It would take them nearly two weeks to reach New Orleans, and somewhere between Cairo, Illinois, and Memphis, Tennessee—about a week into the trip—Walkup became quite ill with vomiting and stomach pains that came and went. Baldwin could do nothing for him but bring water and help him change his position in the bed. There was a doctor on board the boat, but Walkup refused to let Baldwin send for him, saying he had experienced this illness before, knew what it was, and was confident it would soon abate. During this time, he was taking the medicine he had purchased in St. Louis, which Baldwin blamed for the terrible smell of his urine in that very close space. ("It was so bad it would nearly drive you out of the room," he said later.)

This went on for two full days, until Walkup had a bowel movement at the end of the second day. From that point on, he was completely fine. He told Baldwin that these bouts were caused by excessive smoking, but the more likely cause of the problem, one that would account for the intermittent pain in the lower stomach, the vomiting, and the foul-smelling urine, was kidney stones.[8]

On board the *Baton Rouge* was a man named Green from Jacksonville, Illinois, whom neither Baldwin nor Walkup knew, but when he found out the two men were also headed for the World's Fair, he recommended the boardinghouse where he would be staying, run by a Mrs. Elizabeth Wallace. Green had a letter of introduction to her from a former boarder and instructions to the house at 222 Canal Street.

They arrived in New Orleans a few days after Christmas: Sunday, December 28. Instead of going to Mrs. Wallace's, however, Walkup and Baldwin went first to a lodging house. Given the propensities of both men, what probably really happened here is that Walkup wanted to stay somewhere a little more anonymous and a little less respectable than the Wallace place was represented to be. But when Baldwin saw how seedy the lodging house was, he insisted they go elsewhere. To the Wallaces' they went, then.[9]

Until he met Minnie Wallace later that evening, James Walkup was probably secretly cursing Eben Baldwin for making him leave the comfort of the lodging house. The Wallace boardinghouse was very cramped, with six men assigned to the same room and Walkup and Baldwin sharing a bed. But when Baldwin introduced his friend Jim to fifteen-year-old Minnie Wallace that first night (Baldwin had met her first, so would properly do the honors here), Walkup was clearly smitten right from the start. He found himself babbling about nonsense, about birds, about whatever came into his head—as long as this adorable creature would consent to stay and talk with him. He found out she played the piano and got her to play for him, with her sister, Dora, singing in accompaniment.

The very next morning, Walkup approached Mrs. Wallace and told her he was in love with her daughter and wanted to marry her. She just laughed at him. "Minnie has *many* such admirers," she told him. But Walkup—who never took "no" for an answer—would not give up. Every time he saw

Minnie, he corralled her for a private talk, something no well-brought-up young lady of that era should have tolerated.

Eben Baldwin was becoming alarmed. Although he himself was spending most of his days at the Exposition, he did not think Jim was. His friend was drinking quite a bit, hanging out at the brothels in the neighborhood of the Wallace house, and becoming more and more indiscreet regarding this young girl. For example, because she said she liked birds, Walkup got Willie Willis to go with him to the local bird fancier's and pick out a canary for Minnie. To make it appear more legitimate, he also bought a parrot for his daughter Libbie (who was three years older than Minnie).

Baldwin resolved to get Walkup away from the Wallace house as soon as he could, before he did something completely rash, such as marry Minnie, a totally unsuitable match, given their ages. It did not appear to Eben that either Minnie or her mother was pressing this match in any way or acting inappropriately, but Minnie's own version reveals a flirtatious attitude on her part that did more to tease Walkup than discourage him: For example, when he told her he wanted to marry her, instead of turning him down, she kept him dangling by saying she'd never thought of marriage before.

About five or six days into their stay, Walkup encountered Minnie on the stairs. He was quite drunk at this time, although neither Minnie nor her mother ever acknowledged that fact, as it might appear that they were taking advantage of him.

"I was just coming downstairs to look for you," he told her.

"Were you?" she answered coyly. "What did you want to say?"

"I wanted to ask if I might write to you. I'll write the first letter. I will not be able to live away from you."

Again, instead of nipping it in the bud, Minnie mused aloud about never having corresponded with a man before and not knowing the proprieties of it. The two of them went to Elizabeth Wallace, who immediately squelched that scheme. But Walkup insisted and, in order to get her to relent, said he would write to *her* instead, and she could pass the letters on to Minnie after reading them first. Elizabeth said that would be acceptable, and Walkup was beside himself with joy—although, as it turned out, there were only a few token letters to Mrs. Wallace after that, with the remainder of a somewhat voluminous correspondence (at least on Walkup's side) being conducted directly between the two parties.

Eben Baldwin had heard the conversation on the stairs and knew that his friend Jim was fairly deep in his cups. He had to get him away and did so that afternoon. And so, six days after their arrival in New Orleans, the two men headed back to Emporia, Kansas, one hoping he could convince a fifteen-year-old to be his third wife, and the other hoping that the Midwest air of reality would blow away the spell cast on his friend by the encounter in New Orleans. They got back to Emporia on January 12, two days before Minnie's sixteenth birthday.

But James Walkup did not forget his little Minnie. He was completely besotted with her and—according to her, anyway—found it difficult to concentrate on his work. (Minnie was given to lavish quotations wherein Walkup tended to gush over her, but it's hard to imagine this hardheaded businessman doing that, so she was probably embellishing.) He wrote to her frequently, constantly asking her to consent to marry him. He wanted her to meet his daughter Libbie, who still lived at home (Mattie had gotten married in 1882) and arranged to bring her to New Orleans that April, along with a friend of the Walkup family, Mrs. Nettie Fisher. When they showed up at the Wallace doorstep, Walkup said that Libbie and Mrs. Fisher wanted to see the fair.

There followed a week of walks, visits to the fair (all with Dora and Edward Findlay, their five-year-old son Milton, and Mrs. Wallace), and more private conversations all over the house. Walkup offered Mrs. Wallace $4,000 if she would let Minnie marry him. "There is no flesh and blood sold now," she replied. "If my daughter likes you, she will take you."

Finally, the desperate man aimed his bribery at Minnie: "Look here," he told her, "your mother works hard, your brother-in-law doesn't have very much money, and your cousin Willie hasn't had a chance to go to school. If you marry me, I'll buy your mother a house and she will never have to work again. I have five or six enterprises and your brother-in-law can take his pick of them. And I'll send Willie to school." Minnie would admit later, "That pleased me very much."

Walkup returned to Emporia, but on May 16, he was back in New Orleans to press his suit again. Minnie, more kindly disposed toward him because of his promises to take care of her family and his constant representations of how wealthy he was, conditionally agreed to a wedding in New Orleans in October—the condition being that she and her mother were to see the Emporia setup for themselves first. They decided on a July trip. Mrs. Wallace wanted to visit her sick sister in Cincinnati, so they would go first to Emporia and then on to Ohio.

In the end, young Milton Findlay went along, too. Dora was seven months pregnant, and Willie had his job as assistant record clerk at the district court (procured for him by Judge Houston), so they stayed behind, as did Edward Findlay. But before they left, Minnie wrote to James Walkup and teased him with, "When I come [in July], I may *stay*. How do you like that?" It looked as if she was wangling for an earlier wedding than October.[10]

A benign interpretation of all this would be that presented by Elizabeth Wallace, that she did not intend to allow her daughter to go off to a strange land with a strange man without assuring herself that Minnie would be well cared for. Discretion would seem to dictate this. An unkind view, however—and there were many of these over the next several months—had the Wallaces, mère et fille, embarking on a scouting party to make sure that James Walkup was as wealthy as he claimed he was.

Despite Walkup's shortcomings, he seems to have been very generous: he paid for the Wallaces' travel expenses, met them at the boat in St. Louis and brought them to Emporia, purchased (on spec as a wedding present, to be returned if Minnie refused him) a horse and buggy for Minnie to ride about in, and squired them all around the county. Minnie saw what she had come to see and agreed to marry James Walkup, who was so excited, he sat down and wrote a letter to Edward Findlay: "Minnie has said 'yes!'"[11]

Now that James Walkup had what he wanted (and he usually got what he wanted), he pressed his advantage. "I can't wait until October," he told his bride-to-be. "Let's get married now, here, in the Methodist church." Minnie *claimed* she told him she wanted to be married in New Orleans, where her friends could attend—but there was that letter, inconveniently kept by Walkup, wherein she hinted she would not be averse to an earlier marriage, and one in Emporia, at that.

Elizabeth Wallace at first refused to agree to the moving up of the wedding, especially since it was not to take place in New Orleans. But Walkup was insistent, so she finally agreed to it, *if* it could be done in Cincinnati so she could visit her sick sister and at least have some family in attendance. Walkup agreed but imposed his rather formidable will once again, insisting that the marriage be performed by a Methodist minister, even though the Wallaces were Episcopalians.

And so it was settled: Minnie, her mother, and little Milton were to go to Cincinnati, and James Walkup was to follow with Libbie as soon as he took care of some business.

Part Two

Emporia

Chapter 3

The Mayor Takes a Wife

‿⟶

To call you father don't seem natural any more, as I feel as if something had come between us.
—*Mattie Walkup Hood (1885)*

Founded in 1857, the city of Emporia, Kansas, had 12,000 inhabitants in 1885 (today there are 30,000). Located a little over halfway between Wichita and Topeka, and relatively close to Kansas City, it could hardly be considered the Wild West—not like Dodge City or some other Kansas towns. Moreover, it boasted a teachers' college (today Emporia State University), several newspapers, and a thriving agricultural and commercial center. The Atchison, Topeka, & Santa Fe Railway ran right through town, giving Emporians access to larger cities. But it wasn't New Orleans, not by a long shot.

It is not to be supposed that James Reeves Walkup's family and friends sat idly by while he indulged himself in his courtship of a teenager younger than his youngest child. When he returned in January 1885 from his visit to the Exposition, raving about the charms of the lovely Miss Wallace, his friends humored him for a while but then grew alarmed, as it dawned on them that he was really serious about pursuing this.[1]

Two men, whose names were never revealed, did what most astute people do today: They did a background check on the Wallaces by going down to New Orleans and asking around. They heard about the *Mascot*

21

shooting incident and immediately went to that newspaper's offices to find out whether the Wallaces who were the subject of the fracas were the same ones who lived at 222 Canal Street. Indeed, they were.

These men revealed to the editor that they were in New Orleans to get information that would help discourage a friend of theirs ("an old man with grown children") from making a terrible mistake because of his infatuation with Minnie. They believed he was being encouraged in this by Minnie's mother. The *Mascot* editor sent them to James Wallace for further information.

Sometime later, another man called at the *Mascot* offices, claiming to be a relative of James Walkup and wanting information on the Wallace family. "The happiness and honor of my family depend on this," he told them. But in this case, we can surmise who the likeliest "relative" was: Harry Hood, the husband of Walkup's daughter Mattie.

Henry Platt "Harry" Hood was the son of Major Calvin Hood, the most influential citizen of Emporia. Almost nothing happened of a political or economic nature in which Major Hood (a Civil War veteran who was never referred to as anything but "Major Hood," usually in tones of awe) was not in some way involved. He had made his fortune primarily in cattle but had also invested successfully in mines, beef contracts, and real estate. In 1885 he was the president of the Emporia National Bank. He loaned money both as a banker and as a private individual, and many there were in Emporia who owed money and favors to Major Hood.[2]

Mattie Hood was extremely upset at the news that her father wanted to marry the teenager from New Orleans. After the girls' mother died, Walkup promised her he would not get married again until after Libbie left home. Now he was not only going back on his promise but jeopardizing their inheritance. Why would such a young girl consent to marry a man thirty-two years older than she, and after such a short acquaintance, unless she was after his money? Mattie's heart broke as she thought of her dead mother, who had worked so hard for James Walkup and probably died as a result of it. She thought her father was being terribly disloyal.[3]

So the inquirer in New Orleans had to be Harry Hood, and we have further proof of this in Mattie's scolding letter to her father, in which she reveals something that nobody else ever mentioned: the murder in the Wallace boardinghouse. Only someone on the scene in New Orleans could have dug up that rumor, which may, in fact, refer to the *Mascot* shooting.

Minnie and J. R. Walkup (sketch from the *Mascot*)

At the time of Walkup's marriage, Mattie and Harry Hood were on an extended vacation in Wagon Wheel Gap, Colorado, so there was no question of their attending the wedding even if they had wanted to (and they clearly did not). But what about Libbie? She had gone down to New Orleans with her father to meet the prospective bride and, from all accounts, was quite taken with her. The two girls went shopping together and seemed to get along famously. And when Minnie went to Emporia to check out the situation there, she and Libbie spent many hours together riding around in Minnie's new horse and buggy.

But somewhere between that first visit and the wedding, Libbie changed her mind and turned against Minnie, making up an excuse as to why she couldn't attend the ceremony after all. What happened? Was she astute enough to see through Minnie? Probably not. Libbie appears to have been a naïve girl, overly influenced by her older sister, Mattie. Mattie would have chided her for disloyalty to their mother and told her they had to present a united front against this intruder. In a revealing gesture, Libbie left for Wagon Wheel Gap within a few days of the return of the newlyweds and would not be back to Emporia for three weeks.

In Cincinnati, the wedding party discovered that, since neither Minnie nor James was a resident of Ohio, no marriage could be performed. They went across the river to Covington, Kentucky, found a Methodist minister

Libbie Walkup (sketch from
the *New Orleans Times-
Democrat*)

(after more wrangling on Walkup's part over which religious denomination
would prevail), and—on July 22, 1885—were pronounced man and wife.
The bride gave her age as seventeen (she was sixteen), and the groom gave
his as forty-four (he would be forty-nine in August).[4]

There was no honeymoon. While there was some talk of Niagara Falls,
no serious effort was made to get there. James Walkup seemed anxious to
get back to Emporia: Not only was he acting mayor while Whittlesey was
on his own honeymoon, but he couldn't wait to show off his new trophy
wife to his friends. He wired ahead and made sure that everyone knew
when they would be arriving.

Minnie was overwhelmed by the reception at the train station in Emporia and at the wedding/welcome party held at the Walkup house for the
whole town to meet the new bride. The beer and wine flowed freely, and
things got fairly raucous. (Mattie wrote to her father that she had heard
"that the night you came home there was a crowd, Tom, Dick, and Harry
come up and brought beer and all got drunk; and I don't know what all.")
As for Minnie, she bragged to her family that it was the biggest party ever
seen in Emporia.[5]

And so Minnie settled into her new life. On the way back to Emporia, on
their wedding night, she had complained of a headache (to avoid sex?), but
she could not have headaches forever, and her mother, her main support

system, had gone back to New Orleans. In spite of the friendly neighbors, she must have felt somewhat frightened and alone. She could see that Libbie was now cold and aloof, and on her way to Colorado, leaving Minnie with James and their nineteen-year-old African American servant, Mary Moss.

Minnie had not been raised to be a housewife. Despite her mother's needing help around the boardinghouse, the only jobs she seems to have had there were entertaining the guests and being beautiful. She once let it slip to a reporter that she had never learned to do housework, leaving him to wonder why her mother had not prepared her for marriage.[6] Two possible answers present themselves, given Minnie's later history: She was raised to be a courtesan; or she was raised to be the wife of a man with money and servants.

Mary Moss had been hired by James Walkup in May 1885, and there were rumors that she was also his mistress. After Minnie came to live with him, Walkup got angry at Mary and fired her because she had a habit of staying out late at night, usually not returning to the home until 4:00 A.M. (Mary said she was fired because his dinner was late.) But Minnie, no doubt wanting some female companionship and decidedly *not* wanting to do the housework herself, got her husband to reverse his decision.[7]

True to his word, James Walkup wanted to follow through on his promises to help Minnie's family. He kept offering to send money to Mrs. Wallace or to buy her clothing or a house, but both Minnie and her mother claimed these were refused out of pride. He sent $25 to Willie Willis to come to Emporia, which was only $5 less than Willie made in a month at his court job, and the young man—unlike his cousin and his aunt—was not proud: He arrived in Emporia on August 7. Walkup would be sending him to school in the fall, but before then he put him to work in his downtown office as a clerk and errand boy.[8]

Although Mrs. Wallace would claim otherwise, Willie was undisciplined, irascible, and profane. He did not hesitate to speak his mind, often not thinking it through before he did so. He irreverently referred to James Walkup as "the old man" and bragged that if he himself ever left Emporia, Minnie would, too, married or not. But he seems to have been a good worker, nonetheless, and Walkup often took him when he inspected his various properties.[9]

As for Walkup's promise to better Edward Findlay's lot in life, it can only be said that he did his best, offering him ownership of a grocery store, a coal mine, or a farm. But, while Findlay expressed mild (and unenthu-siastic) interest in the coal mine, he turned down the other two: "I'm no farmer and I'm no grocer."[10]

And what of Minnie? How was she faring in married life? We know very little behind the scenes except that she said—untruthfully—that her husband was away frequently during that month. Surely, Minnie must have seen the signs of Walkup's stubborn nature before she married him, signs evident to readers nearly 125 years later. He wanted what he wanted when he wanted it. Despite his generosity, he was crude and overbearing, not at all genteel and refined like the cultured gentlemen of New Orleans. Did she think he would change after the wedding? And there were those reports of his almost insatiable sexual appetite, which might have been exaggerated but almost certainly were at least partially true. All in all, it might have been a lot more than Minnie bargained for, notwithstanding her desire to help her family.

But, in the meantime, Minnie busied herself with what she liked to do best: shop. She was incredibly vain and was constantly looking for ways to present herself to the best advantage, to hear the "oohs" and "ahs" she was so used to in New Orleans. (She even complained to a neighbor that people in Emporia were not as complimentary of her beauty as they had been in New Orleans.)[11]

The best place to shop in Emporia was G. W. Newman's Department Store on Commercial Street, the street that ran one block over from and parallel to their home on Merchants Street. James Walkup had an account at Newman's and Minnie took full advantage of it. In the month of August alone, and only two weeks into it, she had charged $180 worth of clothing and other items, the equivalent of over $4,100 today.[12]

On August 10, Minnie asked saleswoman Eunice Bartlett how often Walkup paid his bill. Eunice told her the bills were sent out the first of the month. "Has it been sent out for this month yet?" Minnie asked her. When told it had been, she asked if what she purchased that day would not appear on the bill until the following month. When Eunice told her that was correct, Minnie said, "Well, I'll go ahead and get that piece of silk, after all." Just a few days after this transaction, she was back at Newman's to purchase over $100 worth of goods from another saleswoman, Maggie Evans.

Some of these purchases were put in shipping crates and sent to New Orleans: There were cloaks and dresses and scarves and shawls and china

Mattie Walkup (sketch from the *New Orleans Times-Democrat*)

cups, among other things. And once, possibly, a cloak or two belonging to the Walkup girls.[13]

Minnie seemed to want to have things both ways: She wanted to be noticed and praised by her neighbors, but she also wanted to be able to move in privacy when it suited her. Now, this might have been possible in New Orleans, but it was certainly not the case in Emporia. She had no idea that Argus-eyed neighbor women were watching her closely and sending on information to Mattie Hood in Colorado. They were the ones who noticed those big boxes being picked up by Wells Fargo Express for shipping.[14]

Although James Walkup hadn't yet received his bill for August, he must have had an inkling that his account at Newman's was turning into a runaway train. When Minnie tried to get the Wells Fargo Express man to put the latest shipping charges on the Newman's account, it was the last straw. Walkup took Minnie down to the Express office to see what was going on. The driver, H. V. Brown, told him that he had picked up the box at the Walkup residence and was told by Minnie to take it to Newman's, get the express charges put on the account, then ship it to St. Louis. Brown took it to the office but did not go to Newman's for the money.[15]

Minnie and James left the Wells Fargo office and had a heated exchange on the sidewalk. Several minutes later, Walkup came back in by himself, asked agent James Collard for a hatchet, and opened the box. Collard could see a cloak, a scarf, and a cup, but that was all before Walkup replaced the cover and stalked out. The box sat there for another ten days before Willie Willis came by with the Bill & Walkup Company wagon to take it back to the Wallace home.

For Minnie, this public humiliation may have been the final straw.

Chapter 4
Minnie Goes Downtown

If you tell the truth, you don't have to remember anything.
—*Mark Twain (1894)*

Did Minnie Wallace intend to murder James Walkup when she married him? At her trial, the prosecution would claim that she—in a conspiracy with her mother—had planned to do so from the start, but it is not likely. Why kill the goose that laid the golden egg? In Kansas, the widow's portion (assuming she could get away with murder) was one-third of her husband's estate if he died without a will, whereas if she remained married to him, she could have access to the whole thing.

No, Minnie was a cunning schemer, but she would not have resorted to such drastic measures unless she felt she had no other option. Of course, most people would look to separation or divorce as a civilized option to an intolerable marriage, but Minnie had married him for his money and she had no intention of giving it up. Neither did she intend to stay married to this boorish lout who insisted on having sex frequently, was possibly physically rough with her, and—more to the point—would not let her spend money whenever she wanted to.

That James Walkup did not view his marriage in the same negative shades as his wife is evident in a letter he wrote to her mother on August 13, just nine days before his death, while he was on a business trip to Topeka.

Minnie (sketch
from the *Mascot*)

He seems to have been very happy with his wife and enthusiastic about
being able to provide for her and her family:

> Willie arrived all right, and is delighted with the city and country. . . .
> He is going to start to school next month. I want him to go nine months
> steady. Minnie is perfectly satisfied. She appears as well satisfied as
> if she was at home in New Orleans, and you may rest assured that I
> will leave nothing undone to make her happy. We are going next to
> Omaha, Neb., for a few days. *I have not been away from home but
> one day since we were married.* You may rest assured that Minnie is
> well contented and happy. Thanking you for giving me as good and
> affectionate wife as Minnie is, I will close.[1]

While Minnie would later say that James Walkup was away quite a bit on
business, he writes in his letter that the trip to Topeka was his first one. It
would make more sense that he did *not* go away before this, as his frequent
absence might have made the marriage more tolerable for her, at least for

a longer time than one month. She would lie about the absences to gain sympathy as an abandoned wife and possibly to take away the imputed motive of familiarity breeding contempt.

The only clue we have as to a possible premarriage plan to get rid of her husband is Minnie's story, told offhandedly to a druggist, about trying to buy strychnine in Cincinnati. Did she think she might eventually need to use it on her husband? Did she really ask for strychnine? And if she made it all up, to what end did she do so? She said she had gone to a drugstore for strychnine, but it turned out that the clerk had given her quinine instead.[2]

What would make Minnie suspect that she had not been sold the strychnine she asked for? The only answer can be that she gave it to her husband and he didn't die! She was determined to get it analyzed so she could know for sure what she had. After all, he was a big man, and maybe she just needed to give him a bigger dose. And so began her almost daily forays to Emporia's drugstores.

On Wednesday, August 12, 1885, Minnie went to Kelly's Drugstore on Commercial Street. She could hardly tell the druggist that the strychnine she bought in Cincinnati hadn't done its job, so she made up a story about getting a paper of calomel from a lady friend in New Orleans. She wanted Kelly to tell her if it was, indeed, calomel (used for constipation). She did not tell him why she suspected it was not.

The druggist, R. B. Kelly, did not analyze Minnie's powder, but put some on his tongue. He told her it was definitely not calomel, but rather morphine, quinine, or strychnine, and from the bitter taste of it, most likely the last. He advised her to throw it away. When Kelly felt sick later, he was sure it must have been strychnine.

The next day, Thursday, James Walkup left for a two-day business trip to Topeka and Atchison. Minnie went to Dr. John A. Moore's Drugstore, also on Commercial Street, and asked the clerk to analyze the powder, telling him the same story she had used at Kelly's. This time the testing was done, and the powder was proved to be harmless quinine.

Minnie eventually concocted a completely different story as to why she needed the powder analyzed: When she was in Cincinnati, her cousin Dora Bowers had given her some face powder called "snowflake." Minnie also had with her some calomel, which looked very similar to the snowflake. In an unbelievably stupid move, she took a sheet of pale pink stationery, cut it in two, and put the snowflake and the calomel in separate pieces—without labeling them! When she got to Emporia, she couldn't remember which was which—hence, the need for analysis.[3]

Since she now had no poison, but was stuck with quinine instead, Minnie went to yet another drugstore, that of forty-five-year-old Moses H. Bates, and asked for ten grains of strychnine, half a grain of which is sufficient to kill most people. Bates, who was also Walkup's brother-in-law (he was married to the late Hannah Walkup's sister Betsey), would only sell her eight grains, as that was all he had left in the opened bottle, and while he went to get it, he assumed she was filling out the legally mandated information in the poison book: name and purpose of purchase. He could see her writing something in this register, so it was a logical assumption.

Although Minnie expressed concern that someone would find out about her purchase, Bates assured her that the register would only be looked at if there were "an accident." After she left, however, he noticed she had not put anything in the "purpose" column.

Minnie must have wanted to stockpile her poison supply, because the next day—Friday, August 14—she was back downtown trying to buy more strychnine. At Irwin's Drugstore, she asked for ten cents worth but refused to put down the reason after signing the register. She would only tell him it was for a private preparation she was mixing. Irwin said he couldn't sell her the strychnine unless she indicated the purpose. "I'm sorry to trouble you, but I have already got my name signed," she told him, probably thinking he'd say, "Oh, go ahead and take it, then." But he didn't. He said it was no trouble to remove her name.

It was William Irwin whom Minnie told about trying to buy strychnine in Cincinnati and the clerk's giving her quinine instead. "He probably did it on purpose," Irwin commented, "thinking you would put it to bad use." "No," Minnie told him, "he was a young clerk, and he just made a mistake." This Cincinnati purchase must have been the powder she took to Kelly's and Moore's for analysis.

Undaunted by her failure at Irwin's, Minnie next tried Ryder's but came up against the same legal problem: no signing, no poison. "Why do I have to do that?" she asked Charles Ryder. "Do you think I'm going to commit suicide or something?" The druggist explained that it was the law, and everyone had to follow it.

At this point, it must be asked: How did Minnie think she could get away with poisoning her husband when she was trying to buy strychnine all over town? And why didn't she just make up a purpose as to why she wanted it instead of refusing to sign the register? The answer is that she had not thought she would be questioned about it and had not had time to think up an unimpeachable reason if anyone should connect her purchase with her husband's death. She couldn't say "rats," for example, if it turned out there were no rats on the premises at 157 Merchants Street. Moreover, she thought her youth, beauty, and status would insulate her from suspicion.

By the time she got to Irwin's, however, she realized she'd have to think of something, so she came up with the "private preparation," undoubtedly hoping that the druggist would assume it was some embarrassing feminine problem that was none of his business. Because if she really had what she would later claim was a special recipe for stain removal—strychnine combined with urine—she could have gotten the poison merely by putting "stain removal" in the purpose column. Obviously, then, she didn't think of the urine (or, indeed, the stain remover) until later, when she realized that she would need to come up with something embarrassing enough to account for her reluctance to indicate the purpose.

At 4:00 A.M. on Saturday, August 15, James Walkup returned from Topeka. That night he was taken ill with a combination of symptoms he said he had never before experienced: nausea, diarrhea, and a stretching and tightening feeling in his legs—the classic symptoms of strychnine poisoning. Minnie called Dr. Luther Jacobs, who gave Walkup a solution of morphine. Because the illness had come on so suddenly, Dr. Jacobs thought it might be either indigestion or cholera.[4]

Like James Walkup, Luther D. Jacobs, forty-three, a Pennsylvania native and a University of Pennsylvania Medical College graduate, had jumped into Emporia life with both feet once he arrived there. He was an officer in the Emporia Lodge, president of the Board of Health, and a member of other Emporia and Lyon County organizations. And he was also affiliated with the Atchison, Topeka, & Santa Fe Railway Company—as surgeon. He had been practicing medicine for twenty years.[5]

By Sunday morning, as a result of Dr. Jacobs's ministrations, Walkup was much better, able to be up and around. Minnie must have been mightily disappointed, so she took Mary Moss aside and gave her a note to take to Bates's Drugstore. "Don't tell any of the family where you're going," Minnie admonished her. "If anyone asks, say you're going downtown for butter."[6]

The note asked the druggist to give the servant more strychnine, as Minnie had dropped the bottle she had bought there on Thursday, spilling its contents. (The strychnine was in crystal form. If she were telling

33

Sketch of Minnie done from a photograph (*New Orleans Times-Democrat*)

the truth—which she was not—she could easily have salvaged most of it and put it in a new container herself.) She wrote that she would stop by on Monday to pay for the new bottle. But Mary Moss, who was ignorant of the note's contents, was unable to tell the druggist the purpose of the strychnine, so had to come away without it.

When Mary returned to the Merchants Street house, the family was at dinner. She told Minnie she was unable to get the "butter," and Minnie immediately got up from the table, took Mary into the hallway, and had a whispered conversation with her about what the druggist had said.

That afternoon, as soon as Walkup and Willie had driven off in the wagon to inspect one of the farms, Minnie hurried upstairs to take off her Mother Hubbard and don her going-to-town outfit.[7] Walking toward Commercial Street at her usual double-time pace, she stopped long enough to tell neighbors Sallie McKinney and Julia Sommers she was going down to get her husband some medicine.

Seeing their pastor, the Reverend Winfield Snodgrass, crossing Merchants Street, she hailed him and asked if he could stop by the house at 4:00 the next day to talk about a sensitive matter: "I'm in trouble," she told him, "and don't know who else to turn to. I don't really know anyone here well enough and I'm afraid the neighborhood ladies might gossip. But I know I can safely confide in you."[8]

Minnie asked Snodgrass not to let on to James Walkup that she had talked to him, but said that he should say he was stopping by to inquire about Walkup's health after his bout with sickness on Saturday night. When they parted, the minister was confused as to whether Walkup was going to be present at this talk or even in the house at all. He and his wife discussed what Minnie might possibly be going to reveal at their meeting.

Possibly disillusioned over the failure of the strychnine to dispatch her husband, as well as her inability to get more of it, Minnie decided to switch to arsenic on that Sunday trip downtown. (She did not know it, but it is much easier to recover from strychnine than from arsenic.)[9] Her first stop was Kelly's, where she had initially taken her paper of powders to be analyzed the previous Wednesday. Kelly asked her if she were the same woman who had come in with the unknown powder and, when Minnie admitted she was, he inquired whether she had thrown it out as he advised. "I burned it," she told him. But that, of course, was a lie.

Arsenic was an easier purchase than strychnine because everyone knew ladies used it to whiten the complexion. And Minnie's complexion was as white as could be, albeit naturally. Some people thought she was addicted to opium because of her extreme pallor, but her face had been that way her whole life.[10] She had no need of artificial aids. So Minnie was able to sign the register and purchase twenty cents worth of arsenic (half an ounce). As she had with Bates and the strychnine, she urged Kelly not to tell anyone what she had bought.

Kelly carefully packaged the arsenic so there could be no mistaking what it was: First, he wrapped it in manila paper and labeled it "Arsenic." Then he put this into a cardboard box, again labeled "Arsenic—Poison," and wrapped this entire package with more manila paper, also labeled "Poison."

Minnie scurried home, changed back to her Mother Hubbard, and was sitting on the porch in the exact same clothes she had on that morning just as her husband and Willie drove up. She must have been pleased to have timed it so well, thus avoiding having to answer questions and also at her success in getting "medicine" for her husband.

On Monday, August 17, Minnie went back downtown to explain to Bates why she had sent the servant girl to get more strychnine on Sunday: She

Panorama of Emporia, Kansas, 1909 (photo courtesy of the Library of Congress, LC-USZ62–58682)

had gone to Newman's Department Store after leaving Bates's drugstore on Thursday and left the package on the counter there. She must have forgotten what she had said in her note about breaking the bottle. Minnie would soon tell yet another story about the "disappearance" of the Bates strychnine.

After Minnie finished explaining to Bates, she did not ask him for more poison, and he did not offer to sell her any. Nor did he have her sign the register for the Thursday purchase, since she said she no longer had it.

That afternoon, Reverend Snodgrass, as promised, stopped by the Walkup house to see Minnie. She told him a disturbing story and said she wanted his advice, but in reality, she was setting him up to be a reliable witness who would later attest that James Reeves Walkup had already attempted suicide at least once.

On Friday, August 7, Walkup was in his room cleaning his gun when he dropped it and it went off, putting a hole in the wall. Downstairs, Minnie heard the shot and—afraid to check it out herself—sent Willie Willis up to see what had happened. He came back with the assurance that it had been an accident and Walkup was all right. This much, at least, was factual.

But, Minnie now told Reverend Snodgrass, when she went upstairs, Walkup confessed to her that he had tried to shoot himself in the head and missed. How can someone miss his own head? And in this case, he would have to have been a contortionist to have succeeded, based on the bullet's final location in relation to where he was sitting. It was possible, but not probable. The purported motive for this action by a man who indulged

himself in every possible way throughout his whole life and did not take "no" for an answer from anyone? He was depressed at a letter from his daughter Mattie in which she objected to his marrying a sixteen-year-old girl only a year after the death of his second wife.

The Reverend believed the story and was properly aghast at this revelation—which had not been divulged to anyone for an entire ten days after its occurrence. But when Walkup was later asked by his friends about the possible suicide attempt, he scoffed at the idea. It was nothing but a careless accident, he told them: "I damn near shot my hand off!"[11]

On the night that Minnie "confided" in the Reverend, Walkup was feeling so much better that he went downtown for the city council meeting, over which he was presiding as president and acting mayor. He took Minnie with him and sat her down in Moore's Drugstore to wait until the meeting was over. (He had a tendency to treat her as if she were a doll or a child, often referring to her as his "little wife.")

But Tuesday afternoon, Walkup was deathly ill again with vomiting, diarrhea, and pains in his stomach. He had no fever, which Dr. Jacobs thought was strange. The physician came back four times the following day, Wednesday, and finally convinced Walkup to submit to an injection of morphine to ease his symptoms. (The sick man's reluctance is more readily understood when it is known that the injection was to go into his eye.) "I'll give you $20 if this is any more painful than a fly bite," Dr. Jacobs told him.

As her husband lay ill all day Wednesday, Minnie made up a list of items she wanted from Newman's (naturally, to be charged to Walkup's account) and sent it down with Mary Moss. But Newman's either couldn't or wouldn't fill the order and sent back a note saying so with their young messenger boy, Johnnie Samuel.[12]

By Thursday, August 20, Walkup was much improved. He felt like eating some "cove" (canned) oysters and sent Mary Moss down to Davis and Hughes's grocery to get them.[13] The preferred method of eating cove oysters was to pour vinegar on them, which Mary did, but not without tasting some first. She confessed to taking two or three but may have been reluctant to admit to more. The vinegar they had in the house wasn't strong enough, so Mary left the oysters on the counter—unattended—while she left to borrow a stronger version from a neighbor. When the new vinegar was added, Minnie took the oysters to her husband.

Willie Willis had told them all to stay away from canned oysters, as he knew of some cases of poisoning, but his warning fell on deaf ears: Walkup wanted his oysters, and when he finished them, he wanted some soft drinks ("pop"). It was a hot day and Mary Moss refused to go back downtown for the pop, so Minnie said she'd go herself.

In fact, Minnie was glad to have an excuse to go downtown. She got the pop, all right, but she also stopped by yet another drugstore, that of thirty-year-old Ben Wheldon. She bought a glass of soda water and then said she wanted some arsenic. "Do I have to tell you what it's for?" she asked him. When Wheldon said she did, she said it was for her complexion, but that she didn't want to state that. He told her she had to.

Wheldon sold her four ounces of very poisonous commercial-grade arsenic for twenty-five cents. He told her that ladies did not buy this kind for their complexion, but instead used the less dangerous Fowler's Solution, which was highly diluted. As had Kelly, Wheldon carefully wrapped the arsenic in labeled paper. He put the package on the counter and went to get the poison register for Minnie to sign. But when he came back, she had taken the arsenic and left. Since she had stated the purpose, however, he signed it for her.

Afterward, Ben Wheldon remembered his wife's saying that James Walkup had been sick off and on with some mysterious illness, and the druggist thought Minnie's arsenic purchase, under those circumstances, was odd. He went down to see Walkup's partner, Dwight Bill, and told him about it. Bill said he would talk to Dr. Jacobs.

Meanwhile, Minnie had returned back home with the pop, and Walkup drank two bottles. Shortly after that, he vomited the oysters and proceeded to become ill again with many of the same symptoms he had before. Willie felt that his warning about the oysters should have been heeded: "Minnie and the old man should have listened to me," he told neighbors. But Mary Moss, who had sampled at least two (and probably more) of the oysters, had suffered no ill effects.

Dr. Jacobs was beginning to suspect arsenic poisoning and had already consulted with a medical colleague about it. He was reluctant to act without being sure of his diagnosis, and had even surreptitiously carried away some of the liquid that came up from the patient when he tried to vomit. (He had tried to get a urine sample, but by then Walkup's kidneys had ceased functioning.) However, an analysis of the vomit did not show any arsenic (because it had already passed out of his stomach), so Dr. Jacobs said nothing. But when Dwight Bill contacted him with Ben Wheldon's information, he knew he had been right.

That night, sick again, Walkup told Dr. Jacobs that he did not want any more medicinal powders but preferred to take liquid solutions instead. Did he suspect the powders his wife was giving him? Minnie was refusing to let anyone else give him his medicine or take him his food. Although Walkup did not say why he did not want powdered prescriptions, Minnie told Dr. Jacobs that her husband was complaining of a scratchy feeling in his throat. Jacobs knew that the reliable Squibb's product he was using—subnitrate of bismuth—could never cause scratchiness but that arsenic could.

By now, Libbie had returned from her trip to Colorado, arriving at the Walkup home on Tuesday, August 18. She was alarmed at her father's state of health and at odds with her new stepmother. She was missing some cloaks that belonged to her and Mattie, and asked Minnie if she had seen them. When Minnie said she hadn't, Libbie pointedly remarked that maybe they should look in some of those boxes that had been sent to New Orleans. Later, Mary Moss found some of the missing clothing inside Minnie's closet in the master bedroom.[14]

On Wednesday night, an abominably hot one, Libbie went up to bed early and lit a smoke concoction called "Persian Insect Powders" in the hallway to rid the upstairs of mosquitoes. It had burned out before she fell asleep, had never caused flames to begin with, and was at least eight feet from her bed, but Libbie woke up a few hours later to find her bed clothes on fire at her feet and next to her head. She went into her father's room across the hall to get some water from the basin and heard Walkup and Minnie snoring. The fire extinguished, Libbie went back to sleep.

Libbie always suspected that Minnie had set fire to her bed—whether to kill her or to get her to move out of the house, she didn't know. Or maybe it was for revenge: Because Libbie accused Minnie of stealing her clothes, it was possible that setting the bed on fire was Minnie's way of saying "Don't mess with me." Otherwise, the fire incident makes no sense. If Minnie were trying to eliminate heirs to Walkup's fortune, there were two more—William and Mattie—she would have no access to. But sometimes evil has no rational motive.

An interesting side note to this incident is that Mary Moss was sleeping in the hallway between the two bedrooms, so anyone crossing from one bedroom to the other (as Libbie had to do to get the water and Minnie would have if she had set the bed on fire) or going up or down the stairs would have had to step over her. Mary said she did not wake up at all and knew nothing about the fire until the next morning. Libbie's bedroom had another door, so it is possible that Willie Willis could have come up from his cot in the living room to set fire to her bed, but this seems very far-fetched. Libbie could have set fire to her own bed, but it seems unlikely that she would put herself in such danger or want to destroy her grandmother's homemade quilt, which was completely ruined. In the end, it might have been merely an unfortunate accident, made more sinister in light of the poisoning that would soon follow.[15]

At noon on Friday, August 21, Dwight Bill went to warn his partner about his suspicions that Minnie was poisoning him and to make sure she stayed out of the sickroom.[16] If it were not already too late, perhaps Walkup could recover from the latest dose. Minnie met Bill at the door. "What do you think is the matter with him?" she asked. "I think it's peritonitis," he told her. "Don't they die very suddenly when they have that disease?" "Yes," Bill said, "there is usually no hope for them." Minnie asked him not to let Walkup know what was wrong with him, so as not to worry him, and Bill assured her he would not, a promise he had no intention of keeping.

Bill found Libbie with James Walkup's mother in the sickroom and asked them to leave, as he needed to talk to his partner in private. Libbie and her grandmother left, and Bill began by saying that he didn't want to offend Walkup, but hoped to be able to speak freely.

"You can say anything you wish to me," Walkup assured him.

"The doctor and some of the rest of us are suspicious that you have been poisoned, and we mistrust your wife."

"I have mistrusted her, too."

"Why?" Bill asked, surprised.

"She told me she had bought some strychnine to take out stains from her dresses." (Why would Minnie volunteer this information unless possibly Walkup began to be suspicious about being poisoned and confronted her about it?)

"You were getting better Thursday evening, were you not?" Bill asked.

"Yes, I thought I was going to be well enough to come down to the council meeting this morning."

"You had a very bad night last night, didn't you?"

"Yes, I was very sick," Walkup told him.

"Your wife bought twenty-five cents worth of arsenic at Ben Wheldon's drug store yesterday afternoon."

"My God, is that so? Let us have her arrested!"

Bill told his friend that they wanted to be absolutely sure before they did anything so drastic as to arrest his wife, but they also didn't want him taking any more medicine from her. Walkup replied that he wouldn't even take a glass of water from her. He assured Bill that he wanted to live and hoped it was not too late to reverse the poisoning (thereby scotching Minnie's suicide story). He was completely nonplussed, though, and couldn't think why Minnie would want to kill him. He had thought they were getting along fine.

From that point on, Libbie was put in charge of giving him his medicine (the subnitrate of bismuth powders dissolved in water), and Minnie was not allowed to be in his room without someone else there as well.

By one o'clock that afternoon, Minnie was aware of their suspicions, as she had to be told why she was forbidden to tend to her husband. While Libbie was in the sickroom, Minnie went in, and Walkup told her to sit down. When she sat on the edge of the bed, he told her to sit on a chair instead. "You don't want me near you; you think I'm guilty," she said. "No, I don't say either way, but evidence is very strong against you," he told her. At this, Minnie began to cry and protest her innocence.

James Walkup's next visitor was a neighbor, fifty-seven-year-old Luther Severy, director of the Atchison, Topeka, & Santa Fe Railway and another extremely successful Kansas capitalist with extensive landholdings. It was Severy who had earlier urged Walkup to get his affairs in order and had sent a telegram to the Hoods in Colorado that Mattie's father was dying. (Walkup said he'd make out his will, but he never did.)

"I suppose you've heard of the suspicion surrounding my sickness," Walkup told Severy. Severy said he had. The sick man told him that Minnie had bought arsenic at Wheldon's for her complexion and put it in a box. Maybe they should weigh it and see if it was all there. Severy thought that was probably a good idea.

Grocer William Ireland, thirty-three, spent most of Friday afternoon with his friend James. "Walkup, what is the matter with you?" was his greeting as he entered the sickroom. "The doctor says I'm poisoned." Ireland was shocked. "Where did you get your poison?" "I don't know," Walkup told him.

Later, Minnie came into the room, walked dramatically to the window, then slowly turned to face Ireland and another visitor. "Gentlemen, do I look like a person who could do such a thing?" Ireland, who had not been told of the suspicions against her, asked, "Mrs. Walkup, what do you mean?" "I am accused of poisoning Mr. Walkup." Walkup muttered, "I guess not," and Ireland told Minnie he had not heard such a thing, nor did he think she could do it. "I didn't, but I'm accused of it," Minnie told him. Again, Walkup murmured, "I think not." "Yes, the doctors accuse me of it," Minnie repeated, began to cry, and left the room.

After Minnie was gone, Walkup told Ireland that if he recovered from his illness, he would always have his suspicions.

Down in the parlor at 3:00 P.M., Minnie was called to meet with Dwight Bill, Luther Severy, and Dr. Jacobs. She scolded Bill, saying he was very cruel to accuse her of poisoning her husband, as Walkup was "the very best friend I have in the world." The men asked her to account for her purchase of all that poison, and she told them about the "special recipe" for removing stains: strychnine mixed with urine, a recipe she had been given by "a colored woman in New Orleans." She had never tried it before and had no idea how much to use of either ingredient (the "colored woman," whom she later gave the name of Annie, not having thought to give her this vital information along with the recipe). As for what happened to the strychnine she bought at Bates's, she now thought it had been removed from her handbag while it was hanging on her dressing case. (This, of course, would implicate either Libbie or Mary Moss. Minnie was thinking ahead.)

Minnie had a dress with a stain on it, she explained (for once she was telling the truth), and wanted to try the special mixture on it. She had purchased enough strychnine "to clean all the dresses in Christendom," yet had only one stained dress and no immediate plans to use it.[17] She was nearly frantic in her many attempts to get strychnine *right now*, yet switched abruptly to arsenic and abandoned all thoughts of cleaning her dress.

So Minnie bought the arsenic, she said, to change her complexion (which was already snow white). Later, she would say she wanted to get rid of pimples, which nobody else could see on her face. As to what happened to the first batch she bought at Kelly's (thereby necessitating the purchase at Wheldon's), she said she had been in the process of transferring it from all that protective labeled packaging into an unlabeled face-powder box. Now, this was a task that could be accomplished in a few seconds, yet she told the men that, *as she was pouring the arsenic into the face-powder box,* she heard her husband coming up the stairs. Fearing he would not approve of her using it for her complexion, she—illogically, as most of it should have been in the powder box by then—threw the whole batch into a chamber pot, conveniently located right next to her.

Even more illogical was Minnie's "prescription" for using the arsenic: She had no idea how it worked, so she guessed she'd just dissolve some in water and drink it, using her own judgment as to how much. Later, she would come up with a "friend in New Orleans" who used arsenic all the time, but this woman, as did the "colored woman" with the strychnine, neglected to give Minnie the correct proportions of poison to liquid.[18] And, once again, she didn't think to ask. But there was no mention of the existence of the "friend in New Orleans" in the Walkup parlor on that Friday afternoon. She was making all this up as she went along and would later refine her various versions, hoping nobody would remember that they contradicted each other. Minnie was a liar, but she was not yet an accomplished one.

Dr. Jacobs decided to test her, so he told her that it was possible Walkup had been poisoned by the oysters, as he had known "a score of people" who had been poisoned from eating canned fish. Minnie immediately turned to someone in the room and said, "Do you hear what Dr. Jacobs said? He has known of an entire family having been poisoned by canned fish. It must have been those oysters that poisoned him."

Luther Severy remembered Walkup's suggestion about weighing the arsenic, and he now presented this to Minnie. She claimed to have all four ounces of the Wheldon arsenic—as with the Kelly arsenic, transferred from its warning wrappings to the unmarked face-powder box—and went to get it for Dr. Jacobs, who was just leaving.

Severy and Dr. Jacobs were standing out on the walkway when Minnie came out with the arsenic, holding the box by its lid. As she went to step off the porch, it fell out of her hands, the lid already off and still in her hand, spilling its contents on her dress and onto the stairs. Minnie said nothing—not "Oh, my!" or "Oh, no!" or "Oh, dear!" or anything else that most people would have used at the accidental destruction of their chance at exoneration, although even Severy cried out as he looked on. She simply walked into the house, came back with a table knife, and began scraping what she could back into the box.

Dr. Jacobs took some of the spilled powder and tested it. It was, indeed, arsenic. Severy was under the impression that, before being spilled, the little box was only three-quarters full. Later, druggist Charles Ryder tried to put four ounces of arsenic into a box of exactly the same dimensions as the one Minnie had, and he found that a quarter of it would not fit.[19] If Severy's impression were correct as to the box's not being full to start with, this left approximately two ounces of arsenic unaccounted for.

Throughout that Friday and into Saturday morning, as James Walkup lay dying, Dr. Jacobs was more than a little surprised at Minnie's demeanor. She was one cool customer, completely composed and stoic about her husband's condition and the town's suspicions of her. The only time he saw her anywhere close to being upset was when he informed both Minnie and Libbie that, in his opinion, Walkup would die. While Libbie burst into tears, Minnie just let out "a distinct sigh of distress." Or maybe it was relief.

By Saturday morning, August 22, 1885, James Reeves Walkup's system was shutting down. He had pain in his bowels, from which emitted bloody mucus, and he could not urinate, his bladder having collapsed. At 10:50 that morning, surrounded by friends and family—including Minnie, who kissed him and begged him to show that he recognized her—he died, his eyes fixed on the face of his young wife.

It was exactly one month to the day since his wedding to Minnie Wallace.

Chapter 5

The Death of a Mayor

⟨⎯⟩

I never turn back from anything I attempt.
—Minnie Wallace Walkup (1885)

Everything might have been up to date in Emporia City in August of 1885, but as far as the rest of the world was concerned, it was the Walkup case that put it on the map. From the very beginning, this case grabbed the nation's imagination and would not let go. In the state of Kansas, it would remain the number one murder case in its annals until, possibly, the Clutter family massacre in Holcomb in 1959, the subject of Truman Capote's seminal true crime work, *In Cold Blood.*

The appeal of the poisoning of a forty-nine-year-old mayor by his beautiful sixteen-year-old bride of one month was irresistible. Newspapers either sent representatives to cover the developments firsthand or hired reporters already on the scene. One man, who had never written a line before this, was sending stories to no fewer than twenty-one newspapers! J. R. Graham, the editor of the *Emporia Daily Republican* and a neighbor of the Walkups, was also being paid by the *St. Louis Post-Dispatch* for the bulletins he sent it.

The *New Orleans Daily Picayune* sent a young, enthusiastic Bill Greer, who bragged that he and the man from the *Topeka Daily Capital* were the only reporters on the ground who wrote exclusively for their own papers. All the other papers across the nation relied on temporary stringers.[1]

Greer spoke to everyone everywhere, from Minnie to the presiding judge to the neighbors to the sheriff, exhibiting a boundless energy at all times. Although he was on occasion susceptible to the era's "purple prose" disease ("she who kissed the blanching and chilling lips of the strong man in agony ere they closed upon the last poisoned breath"), his reports are mostly clear and straightforward.[2] In reading them, one has no doubt that Bill Greer was very excited to have received this assignment and eager to do a good job of it. And, because he was a stranger in a strange land, it is he who provides us with our most complete portrait of the spectators, the trappings, and the atmosphere of the trial.

In what was a sign of things to come, Minnie was placed under house arrest while her cousin Willie, who was somewhat unreasonably suspected of being her accomplice, was taken to jail, where he remained for ten days. Minnie was the one who brought the poisons into the house and even acknowledged doing so. Minnie was the one who had tended James Walkup constantly until approximately twenty-four hours before his death. Nothing implicated Willie except for his relationship to the prime suspect. Yet Minnie was allowed to stay in the home, while Willie was arrested. Evidence was completely against her, but nobody wanted to incarcerate a young and beautiful girl, so they settled on Willie (who was only seventeen himself). The crime cried out for an arrest.

From start to finish, there was one constant, and that was Minnie's remarkable behavior. She acted as if she were completely unaffected by it all. She shed no tears for her husband, showed no fear for her future, and much of the time acted as if she were receiving guests in her home instead of being under suspicion of murder. In an example of her extreme aplomb (many called it cold-bloodedness), Minnie showed no reluctance in going into her husband's room to change her clothes after the autopsy had been completed. There were organs and body fluids scattered all around, yet she closed the door and remained there for some time.[3]

And almost immediately, Minnie began damage control. She told a *New Orleans Times-Democrat* reporter that James Walkup had confessed on his deathbed to having a "colored mistress" in Topeka (a confession heard by no one else in the room). Minnie thought this woman had poisoned him out of jealousy for his having gotten married. Concurrent with this was her story that Walkup had become ill in Topeka and was still quite sick when he got home. She wrote to her sister, Dora, and told her she had purchased *not* strychnine but oxalic acid for stain removal, but then she told Sallie McKinney and Julia Sommers that she bought the strychnine to remove menstrual stains from underwear. She made no mention of a stain on a dress. She complained to neighbor Fannie Vickery that she couldn't understand why she was suspected, as even a twelve-year-old child would know better than to buy poison in the town where she lived if she intended to use it on someone.[4]

Bill Greer of the *Picayune* lost no time in getting an interview with Minnie. Was she "an unscrupulous adventuress of the worst class" or "an innocent and much injured woman"? Opinion was about equally divided. After Greer saw with what perfect equanimity she was taking the death of her husband and her own legal predicament, he took her measure carefully and declared that, "innocent or guilty, she is a woman well calculated to win in any ordeal to which she may be subjected."[5]

Things were going well for the interview until Greer happened to ask her if she knew J. D. Houston, the judge's brother (the one involved in the *Mascot* shooting). Immediately, Minnie shut down and would answer no more questions. Neither did he have any luck down at the jail when he tried to question Willie Willis: Instead of giving information, Willis "answer[ed] all questions with a flood of profanity."

In the resort town of Long Branch, New Jersey, Judge William T. Houston got a shock when he picked up the *New York Herald* that Sunday: James Walkup of Emporia, Kansas, was dead, and his wife, Minnie Wallace Walkup, was suspected of poisoning him. He immediately sent his godchild a telegram offering his assistance, and she replied, "Yes, please come." (When Greer commented that Houston said he would be coming "as fast as steam could carry him," the judge objected. Nonetheless, he headed out to Kansas right away.)[6]

During the next few days, there were neighbors, officials, and family members wandering all over the house and grounds, while the rest of the town milled around on the sidewalk. Through it all, Minnie "sat with folded arms and exhibited her charms, unmindful of the remarks made by strangers."[7]

Sallie McKinney, looking for a writing desk for Libbie, happened to come across the empty Bates strychnine bottle in the latter's room—so it had not been broken or left at Newman's, after all.[8] The bottle was obviously placed there to implicate Libbie (Minnie had earlier suggested that someone stole it from her handbag), but she couldn't have used it: She didn't get home from Colorado until Tuesday afternoon, and by then her father was suffering from symptoms of arsenic poisoning, not strychnine. And if she *had* used it on James Walkup, her best move would have been to dispose of the bottle, not leave it in her room.

Back in New Orleans, the *Mascot* gloated with a "we told you so" attitude: The Wallace family was bad news, and once again there was a death connected with it. And there was Judge Houston rushing to Minnie's rescue. The *Mascot* revealed many of the skeletons in the Wallace family closet, and the source of these was Minnie's father.[9]

James Wallace was not only upset about this turn of affairs, but bitterly resentful at his ex-wife's part in it. She had cut him off from all contact with Minnie when he tried to remove her from the boardinghouse, which he saw as a bad influence, and expressed his desire to send her to New York State to live with his relatives and finish high school. Moreover, Elizabeth had not consulted him about Minnie's marriage, and Wallace said he never would have given permission for it. He suggested that the marriage was not even a legitimate one, as he was unable to obtain a marriage certificate. (The Kentucky authorities produced one later.)

In his rant to the *Mascot,* James Wallace dropped another bomb: He wasn't even sure that Minnie was his child. Elizabeth had told him she was not but instead was the offspring of a man named Reynolds, the surname supposedly used when Minnie attended the Ursuline Academy. Wallace later recanted, saying he had been very angry and upset, but no one seems to have checked to see if it were true.

As for Elizabeth Wallace (who would not know of the *Mascot* article until she got to Emporia), she was so shocked at Walkup's death and the suspicions leveled at Minnie that she became hysterical and physically ill, unable to leave for Emporia until she had sufficiently recovered. Her reaction seems genuine, so if she conspired with her daughter at all, it was probably to milk Walkup for everything she could—not to murder him.

Elizabeth Wallace had another motive for championing Minnie's marriage to James Walkup, one she would later wish she had not divulged (thereby making it more likely to be true), and that was to get her out of the clutches of the importunate Judge Houston.[10] So it would seem that she would probably not have counseled her daughter to kill off Walkup as soon as she could, as this would have resulted in Minnie's return to New Orleans and the further advances of Judge Houston—assuming Minnie didn't end up on death row for murder.

Mrs. Wallace must have realized that the whole marriage setup looked bad for both herself and her daughter, that the logical interpretation was that they were gold diggers out for Walkup's money, so she put her own spin on the facts. She told a *New Orleans Times-Democrat* reporter that she had known "General" Walkup (she was the only one who ever referred to him in this way, as it was a rank he had never achieved) for ten years and he first saw Minnie in Cincinnati in 1878, both statements complete fabrications.[11] Once Elizabeth Wallace reached Emporia, she never again brought up this previous relationship with James Walkup.

The Funeral

James Walkup's funeral was held on Monday, August 24. Before then, Minnie blithely worked on sewing a mourning dress (having probably decided it would have been imprudent to get one from Newman's), even as she was being interviewed by reporters. The Walkup girls, however, said they did not want Minnie to attend the funeral, as they were convinced she had murdered their father.

Minnie seemed more concerned about Willie Willis's comfort in the Emporia jail than about plans for the funeral, and sent Willie some money to buy tobacco and anything else he needed. When Mattie and Libbie withdrew their objections to Minnie's presence at the funeral, she declined to attend, saying she did not want to become a spectacle.[12]

Walkup's funeral was the largest ever seen in Emporia, with 3,000 people attempting to squeeze themselves into the Methodist Episcopal Church (three-fourths of them were turned away) and a hundred horse-drawn vehicles to accompany the casket to the cemetery. Before the service, the casket was placed for viewing in the vestibule.[13]

The funeral began with the 90th Psalm, then continued with the choir's rendition of "A Few More Years Shall Roll." Reverend Snodgrass gave a eulogy, there was a second hymn, and then it seemed as if the entire city of Emporia proceeded to the cemetery.

As the funeral procession passed by the Walkup residence, a large crowd stopped to see if they could see Minnie. Sheriff Jefferson Wilhite, in charge of guarding the fair prisoner, thought that the only way to disperse the hundreds of people outside the home would be to give them what they wanted: a glimpse of Minnie. He brought her out to the balcony and said, "Ladies and gentlemen, this is Mrs. Walkup." Sure enough, the crowd moved on.[14]

However, it seemed to most people in that crowd that Minnie herself had done the introducing and they felt it was an unseemly attempt at getting attention. Sheriff Wilhite said later that he had laryngitis and his voice was higher than usual, possibly sounding like a woman's. And Minnie did have a husky voice, so perhaps this was legitimate, not an attempt to spin the incident in her favor. (Why would a law enforcement officer want to present a prisoner in a favorable light? Because he was, as one reporter put it, "mashed on the girl from New Orleans.")

Bill Born's Beer

Neighbor William Born came forward with a strange—and pointless—story.[15] As he was never asked to testify about it, the tale was obviously not considered probative. On the night of the reception for the new bride and groom back in July, Born showed up late and then drank a few glasses of beer. Something of a connoisseur, he declared the beer inferior to what he had in his house. "Prove it!" the partygoers said.

So Born sent for some bottles of the beer he kept on hand, and this was, indeed, declared superior. He drank one of the bottles, then headed for home. Soon he was crippled with nausea and stomach pains. When Dr. Jacobs was called in the next day, he diagnosed Born with poisoning. Born said that shortly after his attack, Minnie went down to have her white powder analyzed, implying, of course, that she had used it in beer possibly meant for Walkup but accidentally given to *him* instead.

However, Minnie's trip to town was actually at least two weeks after Born's poisoning, and the white powder she had at that time was not poison. Also, it's highly doubtful that as early as July 27, the night of the party, having been married for all of five days, she would have decided to get rid of her husband—or would have done it in such a randomly careless way. As no one else at the party became ill, and lots had drunk much more of the beer than Born, the real answer to his poisoning probably lies in his own product.

What this anecdote does illustrate, however, is how much people wanted to be a part of this incredible story.

The Inquest

The coroner's jury, made up of six citizens, the coroner, and the county attorney, began its inquiries right in the Walkup home at 3:00 P.M. on the day the victim died: August 22, 1885.[16] Minnie, just three years younger than Libbie, told her that going through the inquest would be much easier for Libbie, as she herself was "just a young girl." But, as it turned out, Minnie's lawyer refused to let her testify at all.

On the first day of the inquest, the witnesses consisted of Libbie Walkup, who testified about her father's health since she returned from Colorado and to the fact that there were no poisons in the house; the druggists Minnie had visited to obtain, or attempt to obtain, the various poisons; Luther Severy, who told of the spilling of the arsenic box; and Sallie McKinney, who had found the empty strychnine bottle. Then they adjourned until after the funeral on Monday.

Day two of the inquest was entirely devoted to Dr. Jacobs, who had attended James Walkup that last week of his life and had also been a witness to the arsenic spilling incident. He told the jury what Minnie had said about why she purchased all this poison.

As it progressed, the inquest was frequently reshaped to fit new discoveries. In New Orleans, a reporter found some chemists who claimed that inferior grades of bismuth contained arsenic, which prompted a stout defense of the bismuth by Emporia doctors. While it was possible that some arsenic could remain in bismuth if it were not processed correctly, the product put out by Dr. Squibb of Brooklyn was the purest and contained no poison whatsoever.[17] No doctor had ever had a patient complain about it.

Dr. Jacobs and John Feighan, the county attorney, undertook an experiment. They had druggist Charles Ryder, who had sold the Squibb bismuth to Dr. Jacobs, dissolve a large spoonful from that very same package in a glass of water. Both men drank the mixture, suffered no ill effects, and experienced none of the grittiness Walkup had complained of. They went back to the inquest proceedings and testified as to the results of their experiment.

Another refocus occurred when Minnie claimed that James Walkup was already sick when he got home from Topeka. Witnesses were brought forward to confirm or deny that: Some said he was, some said he wasn't. His partner Dwight Bill said Walkup was downtown at the office early on Saturday morning after having gotten into Emporia at 4:00 A.M., acting hale and hearty and saying nothing about having been ill. But Dr. Jacobs admitted that Walkup had told him of feeling sick in Topeka. These two were highly reliable witnesses, so it is possible that both statements were true, that Walkup had been feeling poorly in Topeka but then had recovered. Perhaps it was another bout of kidney stones or whatever had ailed him on the trip to New Orleans. Whatever the case, it is clear that any illness in Topeka was unrelated to what killed him, but Minnie's defense attorneys would use this in an attempt to cloud the issue and create reasonable doubt.

Editorials in Emporia and New Orleans at this time counseled caution: Let's not jump to conclusions here; let's wait until the evidence is in before passing judgment on Minnie. Everyone seemed to want to find something that would exonerate this young girl. And her lawyer thought maybe he had done just that.

Dr. Scott of Kansas City

Forty-four-year-old defense attorney William W. Scott was a rising star in Kansas politics.[18] A Columbia Law School graduate, he had at one time been a Minnesota county attorney and a Republican delegate to the National Convention. Scott moved to Emporia in 1874, where he had a thriving practice and three years before the Walkup case had been elected to the Kansas State legislature. He was a gifted orator in an era that prized such talent, and he agreed to take on Minnie's defense.[19]

Either Scott himself or a detective hired by him uncovered a physician in Kansas City who had a sensational story to tell. An astute reporter for the *Kansas City Journal* saw Scott go into the office of Dr. Charles W. Scott (no relation to the defense attorney), waited until the lawyer came out, then went in and got a tremendous scoop: James Walkup was an arsenic eater. Attorney-client privilege be damned, the doctor felt it was his duty to make this known.

Here was the story told by Dr. Scott: In late November or early December of 1884 (which would be just before Walkup left for New Orleans), two drunk men came to his office late one afternoon. One man remained in a corner, silent, while the other came forward and complained of cramps and pains in his stomach and groin area. This man gave his name as James Walkup, and it was such an unusual one that Dr. Scott assumed it was a fake. "Oh, call yourself Jones. You might just as well," he reportedly told

Minnie's main defense attorney, William W. Scott (sketch from the *New Orleans Times-Democrat*)

the patient. At that, the man became indignant, insisted it was his real name, and said he was an alderman in Emporia.

Dr. Scott asked Walkup if his pains were from drinking, because he was so clearly under the influence. Walkup said he didn't know, but he had had the pains before. Dr. Scott didn't want to advise him while he was drunk, so he told him to come back when he was sober. At this point, Walkup volunteered that he was taking arsenic in pill form and also in a solution. He produced a vial that he said contained arsenic. The pills, for which he had a prescription, were a combination of arsenious acid and opium.

Walkup told Dr. Scott he was taking the arsenic for two reasons: first, because he had a chronic disease (for which he was also taking mercury) and second, because he thought it worked as a male enhancement drug. How did Walkup know this about arsenic? He had read an article, a report from the Edinburgh Surgical Commission, contained in Head's textbook on toxicology.

So Dr. Scott had advised Walkup to stop taking arsenic, as it could be causing those stomach pains. Walkup said he had no intention of doing so, as it made him sexually strong. He never went back to see Dr. Scott. (At this point in the interview, Dr. Scott went into great technical detail for the reporter, explaining how autopsy tests were conducted for the presence of arsenic, all completely over the head of the beleaguered writer. "Thank you. That is very plain," the reporter said sarcastically when the doctor finally finished. "Don't mention it," Dr. Scott replied.)

Dr. Scott had no idea how the defense attorney had found out about him, as he had not come forward himself, hoping something else would surface to prove Minnie's innocence. On the day the lawyer visited, he brought a set of fifteen photographs, from which the doctor had no trouble picking out James Walkup.

When Attorney Scott got back to Emporia after this interview, he immediately began trying to influence future jurors.[20] First, he called Minnie "an open, guileless girl" who "bears the stamp of innocence on her countenance" (and, he added, she was "decidedly interesting," probably one of the case's great understatements). Next, he excoriated Emporia druggists, calling them "pusillanimous" for not coming forward and admitting that James Walkup had bought arsenic from them—conveniently ignoring the fact that the poison registers were public records. If he didn't search them himself, he did his client a big disservice, but he was much too good an attorney to have overlooked that. It can be assumed that he *did* look at the poison registers, failed to find James Walkup's name, and declined to mention that fact.

What about the arsenic story? Could it be true? Could James Walkup have purchased arsenic in other cities? It certainly did present the defense with the element of reasonable doubt it was looking for. And it was not outside the bounds of reason that Walkup, an aging ladies' man, would seek out something to help him in the "vigorous" department. But how likely is it that this untutored businessman would be reading something called *Head's Toxicology*?

Another factor to consider is the "testimony" of James Walkup himself. Look how interested he was in getting better. Look how concerned he was that his wife be proven innocent (it was his suggestion, after all, that the Wheldon arsenic be weighed). If he knew he was the author of his own demise by taking too much arsenic, wouldn't he have said so? An antidote that could have been given early on probably would have saved him. And he knew that if he died, his wife would be arrested. He said himself that he was surprised she would try to kill him because he thought they were getting along fine (and further said so in his letter to Minnie's mother), so he wasn't holding any grudges against her for which he would seek post-humous revenge by overdosing himself and letting her be hanged for it.

Who was this doctor, then, who had given the defense so much am-munition? Charles Scott had "graduated" in 1870 from something called the Eclectic Medical College of Pennsylvania, a fraudulent diploma mill run by a "Dr." Buchanan.[21] Buchanan was indicted for his fake diplomas, and Scott said he himself had to go before a board and pass further ex-aminations because his degree meant nothing. Supposedly, he passed with flying colors. However, he later taught anatomy at another substandard school—the Kansas City Hospital Medical College, founded in 1882. And, while he later testified that he specialized in "diseases of the mind and the nervous system," his card said nothing of the sort. Instead, it seems that Dr. Scott was a urologist.

Why would a man suffering stomach and groin pains, looking for a doc-tor in a strange city, enter the office of a urinary specialist unless he knew his specific problem? Thus, if James Walkup really did consult Dr. Scott for anything, it would have been for those kidney stones, which would explain how the doctor could pick him out of the photo lineup—assuming he didn't have any "help" with the identification from Attorney Scott. As for the arsenic story, that could have been a collaboration between the two Scotts or the result of the doctor's desire to make himself a player in this most famous case. Bill Greer noticed that many doctors, both local and from out of the area, tried to cash in on the Walkup sensation. He blamed the other reporters for encouraging them by giving them so much ink, but, of course, Dr. Scott's testimony—whether true or not—would be a linchpin for the defense. Scott would not be the last surprise witness unearthed by Minnie's team.[22]

The Autopsy

The autopsy results, as expected, showed the cause of death to be a lethal dose of arsenic.[23] Once the Dr. Scott interview came out, the examining physicians looked for signs of chronic arsenic usage, but found none. There are clear indications that point to an arsenic eater, and not one of those could be detected in the victim's organs. All the signs were of recent ingestion. For example, the fatty condition of the liver, most likely caused by the arsenic, could only have been effected by recent dosages. Long-term usage would have made the liver hard, not fatty.

And, because of the rumors, the doctors looked for indications that he had syphilis, as well, and found no signs of any stage of that disease. Dr. Scott had said that Walkup told him he was taking mercury, presumably for syphilis, but no traces of that were found, either. It was never stated, however, whether there were any traces of gonorrhea, which Walkup was said to have had as recently as May 1885.

A surprise find, probably unnoticed by Walkup, was that one lung showed an incipient state of tuberculosis. It would have been many years down the road, however, before that would have amounted to anything.

Judge Houston Scorned

Judge William T. Houston arrived on August 27 and immediately wanted to take over the case for his godchild.[24] Minnie's brother-in-law, Edward Findlay, had arrived a couple of days before that, and Houston enlisted him in the hunt for evidence. The two would travel to Topeka, Lawrence, Kansas City, and other of James Walkup's haunts to see what they could dig up.

In an interview with the *Winfield Courier,* Judge Houston admitted to being completely puzzled by the case. He had talked to Minnie, and she had told him she was innocent. He was inclined to believe this, knowing her as he did since she was a child, but he also said that strong evidence could sway him the other way. If she *had* done this, he told the reporter, she would lie to him about it. Maybe they could somehow show that Walkup took the poison accidentally or got it from someone else.[25]

A telling point here is that Judge Houston was being interviewed on September 2 and Dr. Scott's "arsenic eating" claim wasn't published until September 5. Although after the fifth, Minnie would say that her husband had told her to get some arsenic for her complexion and even gave her money for it, she did not before this say anything about that to Judge Houston, although it would definitely have helped establish her innocence. In fact, after the Dr. Scott interview, Minnie told a reporter that she had once discovered a vial of brown liquid in her husband's desk and he told her to leave it alone.[26] This tidbit had never been raised before this and was never raised again.

Minnie's mother didn't arrive in Emporia until August 29, two days after Judge Houston. She was delayed by her own illness and by Dora's advanced state of pregnancy. Mrs. Wallace must have been dismayed to arrive and find Judge Houston on the scene and very much in charge, just the same as he had been in New Orleans. It probably seemed as if they could never get away from this man and his influence.

Elizabeth thought that Minnie would be best served by the appointment of a local guardian to look after her legal affairs (and help her reputation with the people of Emporia), since Minnie was still a minor. Judge Houston was adamant in his objection to this: Minnie did not need any guardian, as her marriage made her an emancipated minor; *he* was perfectly capable of looking after her.

This, of course, was exactly what Elizabeth Wallace did not want. She refused to give in, and Judge Houston, thoroughly miffed, left town. The Wallace family had hoped to be able to count on Houston's money for Minnie's defense, but he refused to put forth a single penny unless he could do things his way. He suggested that Elizabeth sell her belongings to get defense funds. The parting between Judge Houston and the Wallaces was an acrimonious one, with much resentment on the family's part and wounded vanity on his.

Hence, a legal guardian was appointed by the court for Minnie, and with it the entry into the case of one of its most colorful individuals: William Jay.

William Jay

Second only in importance to Major Calvin Hood in the city of Emporia, sixty-five-year-old William Jay was the most ardent and protective of all Minnie Walkup's loyal janissaries. He had served two terms as mayor and had made his fortune in many enterprises, primarily lumber. Jay was tall and thin and craggy. Bill Greer thought he looked like William Tecumseh Sherman.[27]

Jay was energetic and irascible, never hesitating to speak his mind. His fierce protection and defense of Minnie, and his utter refusal to see any of her behavior—past or present—in any but the most favorable light, made him the butt of many jokes in those days. (For example, when a bothersome tooth necessitated Minnie's visit to the dentist to have it pulled, Jay

William Jay (photo
courtesy of the Lyon
County, Kansas, Histori-
cal Society)

reportedly held her hand as she sat in the chair, weeping in empathy for
the pain she felt.)[28]

William Jay cared for none of this. He did not alter his behavior one
whit after reading the many jibes printed about him or his characteriza-
tion as "the fanatical friend."[29] He was smitten with this girl, and his wife
(who, tellingly, never accompanied him to any of the legal functions) must
have wondered if he had lost his mind. He even had his picture taken to
present to his lovely ward.

In a lengthy letter to the editor of the *Emporia Daily News,* Jay criticized
the "sneak-thieving" that was being done by stealing Minnie's reputation
with nudges, winks, and innuendoes—she who was "friendless, houseless,
and homeless . . . with the hangman's rope constantly before her eyes."[30]
Those "gassy" gossipers should hold their tongues.

Jay provided the deep pockets Houston had taken away with him, and
agreed to front the money for the defense. The story was that Minnie was
to reimburse him from her widow's share, but as it was likely that she
would be convicted of murdering her husband, that share would probably

not be forthcoming, so he could not realistically have expected repayment. Jay immediately hired another successful defense attorney, fifty-year-old Thomas P. Fenlon of Leavenworth, Kansas, to join William Scott.

Minnie Goes to Jail

Minnie had been kept under house arrest, loosely watched by either Sheriff Wilhite or his deputy Waldo Wooster.[31] But when Major Hood was appointed executor of James Walkup's estate, he wanted her out, so Minnie had to go to jail . . . sort of. Although the sheriff fixed up a special cell for her and allowed her to bring her wardrobe, at first Minnie spent very little time there. Instead, she lived with the Wilhites, taking meals with them and sharing the bedroom of one of the daughters. However, when one of the children came down with typhoid fever, it was thought best that Minnie not stay there, so to her cell she went.

Willie Willis was released from jail on September 1, loudly profane and mightily aggrieved. He swore that someone would answer for this miscarriage of justice. If he had been as cantankerous during his ten days' stay as he was at the beginning and the end of it, his jailers were no doubt glad to be rid of him. He eventually went back to New Orleans with Mrs. Wallace, both returning for the trial in late October.[32]

Minnie's cell was ten by twenty feet, with a high ceiling, barred window, bare floor, bed, stove, and table. Still, it wasn't exactly like being in jail. She wasn't locked in, instead merely requested not to leave. From morning to night throughout the entire sixty-five days she was in custody, Minnie entertained visitors, both friends and strangers. People came from hundreds of miles away just to stand and gaze at her. ("Where's them dresses?" one elderly woman asked brusquely. She had heard of Minnie's spectacular wardrobe and wanted to see it.) They brought gifts of food, flowers, and fripperies and wrote her letters by the score. Minnie went buggy riding with the Wilhite children, and Mrs. Wilhite cooked her meals.

And Minnie devoured every word of print about herself. She had stacks of newspapers from all over the country and vowed to read every single one if it took the rest of her life.[33]

Soon something else would occupy her mind: the birth of her niece back in New Orleans. The black-haired, blue-eyed little girl was originally named in honor of her aunt—Minnie Wallace Findlay—but by trial's end her name had been modified to reflect the generosity and loyalty of Minnie's staunchest supporter: Minnie Jay Findlay.[34]

It was around this time that Minnie began throwing out subtle (and not so subtle) hints that she herself was pregnant ("enceinte," as it was euphemistically expressed). She coyly avoided an out-and-out statement one way or the other, possibly seeking to garner some sympathy, possibly hoping to chill the hearts of the Walkup children who were looking to deprive her of her share of the estate—for, even if she were to lose her own share, her child would not. And, although Minnie would keep this up for the next four months, disingenuously insisting she didn't know for sure (and how could she not know by four months?), she never bore children—and was probably never "enceinte"—in her entire life.[35]

Back in New Orleans, Elizabeth Wallace spun wild stories for a reporter, some of her own making and some undoubtedly from Minnie. She said Minnie had *not* been forced out of the Walkup home by Major Hood but that the move was necessitated by the sheriff's sick child. The sheriff went back to his home and a deputy would have had to take over Minnie's custody. (It was not explained why that would have been a problem, and, in fact, a deputy had sometimes been placed in charge.) Elizabeth thought it was best for Minnie to move to the jail (although in reality, Minnie had wept bitterly at the move and Elizabeth had complained loudly about it). The jail cell was quite nice, she said, and even had a carpeted floor (it did not).[36]

Walkup, claimed Mrs. Wallace, had been taking arsenic for eight or ten years and "probably told Minnie to buy some for him." "Probably" told her? Wouldn't Minnie have said something to her mother if he had? And Libbie Walkup supposedly spread a rumor that Elizabeth Wallace wrote a letter to Minnie directing her to kill James Walkup by October (there was no such rumor). When Elizabeth was leaving Emporia, she told the reporter, the authorities were just getting ready to arrest Mary Moss for James Walkup's murder. (Mary Moss was never a serious suspect. Only in the minds of the defense was she one at all.)

According to Minnie, she was constantly getting bouquets of flowers, including a huge basket of them from some Emporia women. The card read, "From the ladies of Emporia, who recognize your noble qualities and firmly believe in your innocence." Now, while it is possible that this event really happened in some form, it is equally likely that Minnie was embellishing.[37]

Both Minnie and her mother seemed unaware of the fact that newspaper articles written in New Orleans could also be read in Kansas. Minnie told Bill Greer that Walkup's twenty-seven-year-old son, William, not only was on her side but even brought his children to visit her in jail. The son called her "mother," and the children called her "grandmother." Given the circumstances and given William's duty of loyalty to his family—whatever his personal feelings about Minnie—this encounter must have taken place only in Minnie's mind. Such a meeting would certainly have been written up in all the Emporia newspapers (William Jay would have seen to that), but this little flight of Minnie's imagination appeared only in the *New Orleans Daily Picayune.*[38]

Ultimately, of course, Minnie was found guilty by the coroner's jury and entered a "not guilty" plea at her arraignment. According to her, the majority of the jurors changed their minds after their verdict and decided she was innocent, after all. Not only that, but the entire city of Emporia now believed in her.[39] Nonetheless, she still sat in jail.

The stage was set for the trial in the biggest murder case in Emporia's history: *The State of Kansas v. Minnie Wallace Walkup.*

Chapter 6

A Sensation in Emporia

⁓

*If one material fact would come to light convincing me of her in-
nocence, I would not press this case if the whole country was behind
my back howling for her blood.*
            —*Colonel John Feighan, Attorney for Lyon County (1885)*

Preparing for Trial

Lyon County authorities were well aware that the Walkup trial would be
a big one. Not only would there be newspaper correspondents from all
over the country, but the crush of people wanting to attend was liable to
be staggering. Sheriff Wilhite's task was to find room for three hundred
seats in the main courtroom area and also to build a witness platform so
everyone could see those testifying.[1]

Female attendees were limited to the east gallery, overlooking the
courtroom. No daily newspaper account of the trial (all by male reporters) was complete without an accounting of the number of women present, their behavior, and the appropriateness, or (mostly) lack thereof, of
their presence on that particular day. Usually, there were about 200–250
women in attendance, and often they brought their children—some quite
small. The bailiffs had a hard time controlling the antics of bored children
who amused themselves by running up and down the gallery stairs, and
testimony was sometimes drowned out by the wailing of infants. (They

might not understand the rap of the gavel, a newspaper pointed out, but they would probably understand a rap on the head.)

The women figured out early on that to leave their seats at the lunch break was to lose them for the afternoon session. Consequently, many of them brought lunch baskets to court, while others merely stuffed their pockets with apples and gingerbread. The women seem to have been quite vocal as well, laughing or gasping in response to testimony and chatting among themselves or admonishing their children. Judge Graves frequently interrupted the session to say that he would have the bailiff evict those who could not control themselves, but he never followed through on these threats.

Most of the women in attendance had opera glasses, necessitated by their distance away from the action, but the binoculars were not always trained on the witnesses. They were used instead to look at Minnie, to note her appearance and her reaction to the testimony.

Another group relegated to the gallery section was African Americans, primarily men. Sometimes a reporter would comment on the number of "colored gentlemen" on a given day, but for the most part they were ignored.

Those who could not squeeze themselves into the seating on the main floor or the galleries had to stand. On the first day of the trial, which consisted of jury selection, the attendance figure was seven hundred, and this number was frequently repeated throughout the duration. There were schoolchildren and students from the Normal School (teachers' college) and visitors from out of town, primarily doctors and lawyers. One esteemed visitor was attorney Colonel Charles Crysler of Independence, Missouri, who had recently defended outlaw Frank James, brother of Jesse, for a train robbery in Gallatin. Court was held on Saturday and all the farm families from the outlying districts, in town to do their weekly shopping and trading, stopped in at the courthouse.

It is no surprise, then, that there was so much ongoing disorder in the courtroom. It was impossible to keep everyone quiet, and Judge Graves seems to have resigned himself to a somewhat acceptable level of noise, above which he would threaten to throw people out. Added to the human element was the deafening presence, within forty feet of the courthouse, of the Atchison, Topeka, & Santa Fe Railway.

To accommodate those who would not be able to attend the trial (and probably also those in attendance who wouldn't be able to hear anything over all the din in the courtroom), the *Emporia Daily Republican* promised its readers a verbatim transcript of the testimony each day. This transcript would be available only through a special subscription of seventy-five cents (equivalent to about twenty dollars today). And so, after every day's proceedings, the court stenographer, Miss Lane, produced a transcript for the *Daily Republican*.[2]

Bill Greer wanted a transcript, too, although his newspaper would not be printing a verbatim account. He approached Judge Graves, who told him he could have one the next morning. "No, your Honor, that won't do," the reporter told him. "I will be writing up my article and wiring it to New Orleans before your Honor goes to bed tonight." "We live in a fast age," Graves said. "All right, you've got your transcript." And so, Miss Lane (who was universally admired by the male reporters for her youth, beauty, and efficiency) had even more work after her day in court. Greer thought she was "the hardest-working person in the case."[3]

Greer did not forget Judge Graves's kindness ("His Honor is a most courteous and affable gentleman"). Every afternoon, when his bundle of *Daily Picayune* newspapers arrived, he saved one for the judge. The rest were quickly snapped up by the attorneys. To Greer's immense pride, "the *Picayune* is universally complimented on the fullness of its report."[4]

The Presiding Judge and the Attorneys

Judge Charles B. Graves, forty-three, was, like most of the attorneys in the case (and, in fact, like most of the men of James Walkup's generation in Emporia), a veteran of the Civil War. He had been a farmer, a city attorney, and a county attorney before his 1880 election as judge of the Fifth Judicial District. He was a kindly man, but also a no-nonsense one. Bill Greer observed an actual slugging match between two attorneys arguing before Judge Graves on another case. Graves came down from the bench, grabbed one of the combatants, and pitched him over the railing into the spectator section.[5]

Colonel John W. Feighan, forty, county attorney for Lyon County, was a graduate of Miami University of Ohio and the Cincinnati School of Law. His former partner, fifty-year-old J. Jay Buck (called "Judge Buck" because he had once been a justice of the peace), joined him as the trial went on.[6]

Ordinarily, Feighan would be the only prosecutor in the case, because that was his job, but William Jay had hired more defense counsel and Harry Hood wanted to even up the sides. Hood brought in his best friend, the

Judge Charles B. Graves (from Cutler's *History of Kansas*)

portly Clinton N. Sterry, forty-three, who had vowed to Hood that he would see to it that his father-in-law's poisoner would be punished; and Isaac E. Lambert, thirty-one, Major Hood's protégé and the youngest attorney at the trial. Sterry was actually a close personal friend of defense counsel William Scott (although it would be hard to tell that as the trial progressed). A brilliant cross-examiner, he went through the entire trial with an unlit cigar in his hand. Lambert had studied under the controversial Robert Ingersoll and had a very impressive 9–3 record in murder cases.[7]

Besides William Scott for the defense, there was Thomas P. Fenlon of Leavenworth, another noted trial attorney. Admitted under special permission was young (age thirty-one, the same as Lambert) George S. Dodds of Hazlehurst, Mississippi, whose stated motive in joining the defense was to help his childhood friend, Minnie Wallace. It is not known how exactly Dodds could have been a childhood friend, given their age difference and that Dodds does not seem to have ever left the town of Hazlehurst, 125 miles from New Orleans. But he was young and handsome and much admired as a "large, fine-looking man."[8]

Rounding out the defense was Edward C. Ward, forty-six, of Parsons, Kansas, whose services were obtained by Mrs. Augustus Wilson, Kansas Commissioner for the New Orleans Cotton Exposition and paid for by Minnie's father (see chapter 10, page 117).[9]

Jury Selection

Those living in the twenty-first century would be shocked at the nineteenth-century jury selection process. There were no women and no African Americans. As the process went on, prospective jurors' names, addresses, ages, and occupations were printed in the newspapers, along with the various reasons for their being excused. In the Walkup case, each candidate was asked for a short biography, then questioned as to whether he had heard about the case and formed an opinion. If he had no opinion, he was allowed to stay. If he had formed an opinion, he was excused for cause. In today's system, a prospective juror (sometimes referred to as a venireman) would not be excused for having formed an opinion unless it were determined that he or she could not or would not change it.[10]

Murder was a hanging offense in Kansas, and the veniremen were asked if they would be afraid to find a woman guilty. One man was a Quaker and against capital punishment, so he was gone. Another had conscientious scruples against serving as a juror. He was gone, too. Those in the jury pool were asked if they had known either James Walkup or Harry Hood. And that was it. A jury of twelve was obtained by 4:00 that afternoon, October 19, 1885. They were all farmers, all married, and their average age was forty-six.

For the duration of the trial, the jurors would be sequestered at the Park Place Hotel under the guardianship of Deputy Sheriff Waldo Wooster, who took them for an hour's walk each night, saying that he was "exercising his pets."[11]

Minnie, for her first day in court, was very stylishly dressed in an "ottoman silk jersey and cashmere dress, trimmed with chenille, all in a rich shade of black." Two minutes after the doors were opened that day, the courtroom and galleries were filled to capacity. Seven hundred people packed themselves inside, not to hear the boring jury selection, but to get a glimpse of Minnie.

Throughout the trial, Minnie's mother sometimes sat with or near her daughter and sometimes up in the ladies' gallery. William Jay nearly always sat somewhere close to his young ward and was each day accompanied by his unmarried thirty-four-year-old daughter, Mary. The most common verb used by the newspapers in describing Jay's behavior each day was "flitted": The old man had boundless energy and was everywhere in the courtroom, sometimes taking notes, sometimes talking to Minnie or to witnesses or audience members, sometimes consulting with the defense attorneys.

The Case for the Prosecution

The prosecution's opening statement was given by Colonel Feighan, who presented the story of a "powerful, vigorous man, somewhat uncouth, without any charms of person or deportment," who was then made the victim of a vicious conspiracy between Minnie and her mother to take him for everything they could, then murder him for the widow's portion.[12]

The first days were given to the druggists, the Newman's Department Store clerks, and the Walkup neighbors. Mary Moss's testimony caused some amusement for the audience when she was cross-examined about a buggy ride she had taken with "a redheaded white man." Mary seems to have been quite a sociable young woman, and when the handsome Mr. Landry begged her to walk around the park with him, she finally gave in. A few days later he asked her to go on the buggy ride.

It turned out that Landry was a detective hired by the defense, and his job was either to get information from Mary Moss that would help Minnie's case or get her to perjure herself. Landry went back to his employers and told them (falsely) that Mary said Libbie had told her to make up the story about "going for butter" when Minnie sent her to Bates's with the note. He also claimed that Mary told him that she saw James Walkup take some white powder out of a box, stir it in some water, and drink it down. Mary denied ever saying any of this, and as it was stated that Landry would be arrested for perjury if he took the stand and testified that she did, it is evident that nobody believed his story. He was probably trying to give his employers their money's worth. There was a rumor going around that he was "a Pinkerton man," but this was not true. Landry had disappeared completely from the scene before the trial began.

Mary Moss characterized Landry as "a little low man with a low mustache" and caused much laughter in the courtroom when she ruefully commented, "I didn't suppose anybody knew anything about it or I wouldn't have gone with him." As Scott was cross-examining her ad nauseam about the buggy ride, his friend (and now adversary) Sterry, who also had red hair, thought they had all had enough: "I object, your Honor; she has admitted going riding with my redheaded friend and is heartily ashamed of it." Scott immediately rejoined with, "And if you had been the redheaded white man, she would be still more ashamed of it." The bailiff had a hard time getting order back after that interchange. (Lawyers today are forbidden to address each other directly in court but must do so through the judge, a system designed to prevent them from wrangling and coming to blows.)

Two important additions to the druggists' testimony were Joseph Murphy and Frank McCulloch. Murphy had a stationery business inside William Irwin's drugstore and heard Minnie tell Irwin about purchasing what she thought was strychnine in Cincinnati. McCulloch, a clerk in Dr. Moore's drugstore, was present when Moore told Minnie that the powder was quinine. As Minnie would later deny all of this, the corroboration was important.

Neighbor Fannie Vickery revealed that Minnie had once asked her, "One poison kills another, doesn't it?" although the timing for this was not specified. After Walkup died on Saturday, Fannie told Minnie about Libbie's bed having been set on fire the previous Wednesday. Minnie seemed surprised by this and cried out, "My God, what next!" But Minnie had admitted knowing about the fire the next day, so her reaction here is a strange one.

Luther Severy related that, as Walkup lay dying, Minnie revealed to him the attempted suicide story she had told Reverend Snodgrass, enlarging on it a bit. She said that on August 7, designated to be President Grant's memorial day (he had just died), she and her husband were picnicking at Soden's Grove at the southern edge of town. James had been drinking and got to brooding on the letter he had received from Mattie. It was after their return home from this outing that he went upstairs and attempted to kill himself.

The remainder of the prosecution's lay testimony was the same as it had been at the inquest, with the addition of witnesses who said that James Walkup had either not said anything about having been ill in Topeka or that he had looked fine on that Saturday when he returned. However, as Walkup told his physician, Dr. Jacobs, that he had been feeling poorly either in Topeka or on the way home (Dr. Jacobs could not remember which), we can probably assume that he was sick to some degree at that time, but not seriously so.

The largest part of the prosecution's case consisted of an impressive array of medical experts, many of whom had either assisted at the autopsy or had analyzed Walkup's organs. The primary witness, of course, was Dr.

Luther D. Jacobs, who had attended Walkup throughout that last week, had witnessed Minnie's behavior during that time and also her spilling of the arsenic, had heard her explanations for purchasing the poisons, and had assisted at the autopsy. As the case progressed, Dr. Jacobs was frequently recalled regarding one of these issues.

During William Scott's cross-examination of Dr. Jacobs, one of the defense's theories was revealed: The victim had at some point long before his death (possibly in Topeka) ingested, either through his own actions or those of someone other than Minnie, a fatal dose of arsenic that had somehow become encysted in his stomach. Immediately prior to his death, something happened to act upon the protective casing that had grown up, pearl-like, around the poison, causing it to dissolve and kill him. It was a preposterous theory. Could they prove it?

Dr. Jacobs responded that, while it might theoretically be possible for this to happen with a small dose, it could never happen with a fatal dose. Well, then, how about the action of arsenic on organs "demoralized by prior disease" (i.e., syphilis): Could that cause the elimination of the poison to be delayed at all? Dr. Jacobs conceded that might be possible, since the organs couldn't do their jobs properly. And how about if he had that pocket of mucus surrounding his arsenic, then ate those oysters, drank that pop, and vomited: Could that dislodge it? Possibly.

Poor Dr. Jacobs was submitted throughout the trial to the defense's accusations of malpractice in not administering the arsenic antidote to James Walkup. Of course, by the time he realized that Walkup had been poisoned, the victim was too far gone for the antidote to be of any use. Still, Scott harped away on this and seemed to insinuate that if it hadn't been for Dr. Jacobs's failure in this regard Walkup would still be alive. Dr. Jacobs became extremely defensive about this after a while, probably wishing he had given his patient the antidote regardless.

The next witness, Dr. Charles Gardiner, who had taken charge of Walkup's organs for the autopsy, quickly disabused the defense of any notion of encystment, answering succinctly instead of giving a lot of "possibly"s and "might be"s:

Scott: If a man had syphilis and was taking mercury or arsenic to strengthen
his sexual powers and then got sick, couldn't the sickness set the mercury
or arsenic loose so the organs would look like Walkup's?
Dr. Gardiner: No.

Scott: If he was a habitual arsenic eater and took a medicinal dose of arsenic ten days before death that did not assimilate, then took something like cove oysters with vinegar and pop, wouldn't the dose set free the arsenic and produce the appearance as described?

Dr. Gardiner: No.

Dr. Gardiner explained that arsenic eaters never increase their usage to a fatal dose. Moreover, soluble arsenic cannot be encysted. Besides, mercury is the common remedy for syphilis, not arsenic. But all that was moot, as there was no sign in Walkup's organs either that he had syphilis or had taken any mercury.

The lesions in Walkup's bowels were fewer than ten days old, while those in his stomach could not have been made by syphilis in any stage. In fact, there were no syphilitic lesions anywhere in the body. Dr. Gardiner did concede, however, that the fatty degeneration of Walkup's liver could have happened within forty-eight hours or over the course of several weeks. Many things other than poison can cause this condition.

On redirect, Dr. Gardiner backed Dr. Jacobs in saying that by Friday it was already too late for the arsenic antidote to have done any good, although the doctor should have given it just to protect himself. Also, it is not possible for arsenic to be encysted in the stomach, as the poison could not remain there for ten days without corroding it.

Dr. William Jones, a professor at Kansas City Medical College, was in charge of analyzing the organs for poison. His report, which lasted for three or four hours, was extremely tedious and undoubtedly went right over the heads of many of the jurors. Dr. Jones seemed to think he was lecturing his medical students, as he made no attempt to make the material either interesting or understandable. He went into exhausting detail about how he prevented contamination of his instruments and how he went about analyzing each organ.

During the afternoon session, however, Dr. Jones must have come to his senses (or else someone had given him a tip) because he allowed the jurors to come forward and look at the arsenic crystals through his state-of-the-art Zentmayer microscope. Whether they knew what they were looking at or not, they enjoyed the show-and-tell and the chance to get out of the jury box. And, when later the professor let Bill Greer look through it to see the arsenious acid (this was in the box that Minnie dropped on the porch) and also to see the effects of arsenic on the liver and the kidneys, the reporter was both gratified and impressed. "The Emporia physicians and experts are fully informed in medical and microscopical science," he wrote. "And, for once, they all agree."[13]

The Hypothetical Questions

At a trial, hypothetical questions allow an expert witness to present an opinion on matters not yet proven. They say, in effect, "Let's pretend that these facts are true. In that case, what do you think?" They can go a long way toward clarifying difficult scientific matters for a jury of lay people. Unfortunately, the Walkup prosecution's hypotheticals did just the opposite, leading audience members to murmur among themselves, "What's it all about?" It may be assumed that the jurors echoed those sentiments.

There were ten questions asked of eleven doctors for the prosecution and one for the defense (the lone physician for the defense who was an expert only and not also a witness to other events). The rules regarding hypotheticals forced the prosecution to ask long, involved, convoluted, and repetitious questions based on a set of long, involved, convoluted, and repetitious supposed facts. And, as these same questions had to be repeated in their entirety for each physician and in the context of the hypothetical facts surrounding them, it can readily be imagined how tiresome it all was for everyone concerned. Here, boiled down to their absolute essence, are the hypotheticals and a composite of the answers for all except the defense's medical expert (and even his answers did not vary greatly, but, as he was being paid by the defense, he skewed his responses slightly; see Dr. S. Emory Lanphear's testimony, chapter 7, pages 86–87):

1. How long would it be possible for arsenic in the stomach to be kept there previous to death? [Answers varied between 1 and 5 days, with most falling in the 2–3 day range.]
2. Would it or would it not be possible that the arsenic that killed this [hypothetical] man was taken on the Saturday previous to his death or any time before that? [Not possible (unanimous).]
3. What caused his death? [Arsenic (unanimous).]
4. How long previous to death would it be probable that arsenic found

in his stomach contents had been taken? [Answers varied between less than sixteen hours and up to forty-eight hours, with most falling in the eighteen- to thirty-six-hour range.]

5. How many times previous to his death had arsenic been taken by this person between Saturday [August 15] and his death [August 22]? [Two or three doses (most said three or "over two"; one said three or four).]

6. Would it be possible that the death was caused by arsenic taken a week previous to his death in one or more doses? [No (unanimous).]

7. What was the amount of arsenic taken into the stomach and producing death so that after death four grains still remained? [Large dose (unanimous).]

8. When was the dose of arsenic given that caused death, as to the longest time before death? [From a low range of two hours to the majority answer of twenty-four to forty-eight hours.]

9. Would it be possible that the sickness commencing Tuesday noon [August 18] and the death that followed it, and the arsenic found in the body, was caused by and came from the arsenic he might have taken on the previous Friday [August 14] or Saturday [August 15]? [Here, the prosecution is saying to the defense, "OK, let's have it your way. Let's say he *was* given a dose of arsenic in Topeka, by himself or someone else. Did it cause his death?" Answer: No (unanimous).]

10. Would an antidote be of any benefit on Friday morning [August 21]? [No (unanimous; Dr. Jacobs, for whose benefit this question was included, was not asked the question).]

The doctors believed that the fatal dose was given to this hypothetical victim on Thursday of the week he died. Cross-examination failed to do anything to erode the strength of the state's case in this regard, and one physician even maintained that Walkup could not have been given arsenic in Topeka, or he would not have recovered from the poisoning of Saturday night. His system would have been too compromised at that point.

This, then, was the prosecution's case: Minnie Walkup had the means (one purchase of strychnine, two of arsenic), the motive (Walkup's money), and the opportunity (she was the only one who gave him his medicine that fateful week, until it was too late for him to recover). For there to be four grains of arsenic (two grains is a lethal dose) in some of his organs after death, when some of the poison had been vomited up or eliminated through diarrhea, James Walkup had to have been given a massive amount. Some physicians speculated that it was as much as twenty grains. Druggist Charles Ryder had said that a single dosage of ten grains of bismuth, as prescribed for Walkup by Dr. Jacobs, would resemble (in appearance and amount) about twenty-one grains of arsenic, a little over a quarter of a teaspoon.

How would the defense counteract this?

Sunday in Emporia

The indomitable Bill Greer walked around Emporia to see how those connected with the case were spending their Sunday. He found the lovely Miss Lane coming from church, "tripping down the street . . . bright as a new $20 gold piece." Colonel Feighan took a buggy ride with his family, William Scott went for a walk, and Judge Graves drank coffee and read (of course!) the *Picayune*.

Minnie, as usual, was surrounded by callers and her courtroom entourage (the Jays and her family members). The case was the single topic of conversation throughout Emporia, even as the subject of Sunday sermons. Arguments as to the fair defendant's guilt or innocence broke out everywhere.[14] Greer noticed that most of the newspaper correspondents seemed to be on Minnie's side and they were allowing their feelings to influence their reports. For example, during the state's case, some of the evidence prejudicial to Minnie was not included by these reporters. J. R. Graham, editor of the *Emporia Daily Republican*, declared that he was "hoodooed" by Minnie, then later denied it and said he just wanted to see her get justice because he thought she was innocent.[15]

The *Kansas City Times* began to suspect that its stringer, the man representing twenty-one newspapers, was submitting "cooked-up evidence," so it sent its own reporter to Emporia to check it out. He was shocked at the partiality being shown to Minnie by almost all the correspondents. After that, the stringer hired by the *Times* had "only" twenty papers to report to.[16]

The *Republican*'s promise to provide a daily verbatim transcript for an extra fee proved more problematic than at first imagined. It was a good idea, but almost impossible to carry out. Some of the testimony was so long (for example, Dr. Jacobs was on the stand for six hours one day) and so complicated that poor overworked Miss Lane could not complete it all by press time. Nobody was more delighted about this state of affairs than the *Republican*'s rival, the *Daily News*. At the beginning of the trial, it had sourly asserted that a verbatim report would be pretty dull to read. As the case went on, the *News* took many shots at its opponent for the so-called verbatim report, much of which was missing in each day's paper. (A perusal of other newspapers reveals the truth of the accusation, as these reports invariably include items left out by the *Republican*.)[17]

That Monday, October 26, the day of rest having ended all too soon, the defense would begin its case. And, while the prosecution had mostly repeated the testimony of the inquest witnesses, which everyone in the country was already familiar with, nobody knew for sure what Minnie's lawyers would present. What they came up with would shock Emporia to its core.

Chapter 7

Defending Minnie Walkup

⌒

*Of course, Minnie Wallace Walkup will be acquitted of the charge
of poisoning her husband. . . . Her neck was made for strings of
diamonds and pearls, and not for the hangman's circlet of hemp.*
                                        —Atlanta Constitution *(1885)*

The first day of the case for the defense saw another attendance figure of
seven hundred. One woman fainted. By 1:30 P.M., there was such a crowd
in the courtroom, the hallways, and the stairs that the sheriff had to close
the doors to the courthouse.[1]

Defense attorney William Scott's opening statement lasted an hour and
a half. In an age that valued oratory, long speeches were a given, expected
by audiences who often rated the performances of speakers. Even so, one
juror fell asleep during Scott's speech.

Scott presented a David versus Goliath situation, with the big bad
prosecution, paid for by Harry Hood's money, pitted against a poor girl of
sixteen who had only "one noble man" to help her "scrape up the evidence
in her defense." And he revealed a northerner's perception of southern
girls as maturing faster by saying that if she had been brought up in the
North, she would "hardly have been said to have arrived at the age of full
maturity and competent to take upon herself the duties and responsibilities of womanhood."

The defense attorney demeaned James Walkup by saying that he fell in love with Minnie, "so far as a man of his calibre [could] understand . . . love," and was "leading a low and disreputable life . . . cohabiting with lewd, debauched, and diseased women, both white and black" in dives in Kansas, New Orleans, and elsewhere. The defense theme of blaming the victim was evident in this opening statement. It would show that Walkup was the author of his own destruction and that he had had many similar attacks over the years, including the illness on the boat. These, Scott said, were all caused by his arsenic habit.

William Scott went on to relate the story of Walkup's meeting Minnie, the courtship, and the trip to Emporia in July, which included Minnie's five-year-old nephew Milton Findlay ("a fit member of a formidable conspiracy to take the life of a human being").

James Walkup's friend Eben Baldwin was called as a somewhat hostile witness on the first day of the defense's case. Baldwin had testified for the prosecution and now was asked to relate Walkup's drunkenness and debauchery while in New Orleans—which he did reluctantly. He retold the details of the illness his friend suffered on the boat going down and the prescriptions filled along the way, in St. Louis and in Cairo, Illinois. Baldwin didn't know what the prescriptions were, which left it open to the defense to suggest that they were arsenic preparations for the treatment of syphilis.

A witness named Van Holmes testified about the bullet hole in Walkup's room, saying that it was at a downward angle and the gun must have been held where a man's head would be. This man was on the inquest jury and had told Scott about the bullet hole because he had seen it himself. It seems odd, from a forensic point of view, that nobody thought to plot the trajectory of the bullet in any scientific way.

In cross-examining this witness, Clinton Sterry gave him a revolver and asked him to point it at his own head and demonstrate how it would be held so that, in missing the head, it would make a hole three feet from the floor. Holmes was clearly uncomfortable pointing a gun, empty or not, at his head, and the audience enjoyed his discomfiture. The witness eventually gave it up, saying he didn't know whether Walkup had been sitting or standing.

Sterry was a very aggressive and effective cross-examiner who pulled no punches. His out-of-court friend Scott labeled him a "human hyena thirsting for the blood of the young girl." As for Minnie, she seems to have alternated between crying at times and at other times showing little interest in what was happening. But, as many later spoke of her impassivity, the teary parts must have been minimal. One of her attorneys, Thomas Fenlon, made what could have been a tactical error in bringing to court with him that day another client of his, Frankie Morris, and introducing her to Minnie. The two women chatted for a long time, and they probably had much to chat about.

Frances Morris, thirty, had been convicted of the arsenic poisoning of her mother, Nancy Poinsette, for $15,000 in insurance money. It was thought that Frankie was in cahoots with her stepfather (divorced from Mrs. Poinsette) and her own ex-husband to do away with her mother and split the proceeds. At the time of the Walkup case, she had just been granted a new trial, which would begin later in the fall, and, although she was now married for the second time, she was always known as Frankie Morris (her maiden name).[2]

Because of the notoriety of Frankie Morris and the similarity of the two cases, there was a lot of negative comment about these two women being introduced to each other. Morris came back to the trial at least one more day. (The *Winfield [Kansas] Courier,* disgusted with the bad press these two were bringing to the state, suggested that they join another pair of female murderers and get P. T. Barnum to buy them for his circus.)[3]

Bill Greer reported that one of the witnesses for the defense would be Lina Burnett, there in court that day to talk about her affair with James Walkup in Emporia and Topeka. However, Mrs. Burnett was never called to the stand, possibly because of her arrest in September on a charge of grand larceny in Shawnee County, which would have compromised her credibility.[4]

"A Carnival of Filth"

The testimony presented on day two of the defense case was so lurid and shocking to the Emporians of 1885 that the *Daily Republican* refused to print even a summary—let alone the promised verbatim transcript—of the testimony of three of the witnesses, as it was "too obscene and vulgar for publication in a decent newspaper." One of the Emporia weeklies also declined to print it, saying that it didn't belong in a family-oriented publication.

But, luckily for modern readers, the *Daily News* had no such scruples, although it left out a good deal too much. ("Smut!" was the large title, in bold, given to this issue.) It did not miss out on the opportunity to scold its competitor who, after taking the extra seventy-five cents from its patrons and already giving them short shrift on the transcript, now went back entirely on the deal by not providing them with so much as a summary. Why was the *Republican* being so prudish when there were at least 250 women and way too many schoolgirls who had heard the testimony in its scandalous entirety? "We give it all," crowed the *News,* "and let the public discriminate if they want to."

The day began with Dr. Charles Scott on the stand, the urologist trying to pass himself off as a "mind specialist." He now identified Walkup's companion, Mr. Morton, as one of the "obscene" witnesses who would follow him on the stand.

Sterry's cross-examination could not elicit a definitive answer as to how attorney William Scott knew James Walkup had visited Dr. Scott. The physician said it might have been through a Mister or Colonel Butterfield (never identified, never produced by either side), to whom Dr. Scott had told the story a few days previously. Walkup and Morton stayed in the doctor's office for an hour, with Walkup apparently being quite entertaining in the stories he told. Dr. Scott didn't feel he could charge for the little bit of advice he had given ("stop taking arsenic"), so he never presented him with a bill. (Sterry sarcastically called him "a missionary.")

The next witness, Nathaniel Benjamin Morton of Vidalia, Louisiana, was the first of the trio of smut purveyors. He said he was the editor of the *Concordia Sentinel* in Vidalia and had been involved in printing and publishing newspapers in Indiana, New Mexico, and Texas, among other places, and that he had known James Walkup for quite a while. Walkup frequently took arsenic for syphilis, and Morton had once taken a bottle of Fowler's Solution from him in a Basin Street brothel in New Orleans.

Morton had been on the boat to New Orleans with Walkup in 1884 and said his sickness at that time was from the arsenic. But, although he claimed he also knew Eben Baldwin and had spoken with him on the boat, Baldwin said he had never seen the man before—on the boat or otherwise.

What Morton testified to that was so shocking was the incredible number of sprees he and Walkup went on together. These "jamborees," as he euphemistically called them, always involved a lot of drinking and a lot of sex. They were together with two girls at the Dodge House at the big Cattlemen's Convention in Dodge City in 1883. In Kansas City, when Walkup went to see Dr. Scott, the men stayed in a brothel called the Cable House. Whenever they were on one of these jamborees, Walkup used only his first and middle names (James Reeves), while Morton "threw out his banner" as Nathaniel Benjamin. (Apparently Morton had missed the part where Dr. Scott said that Walkup had told him his real name. Why give a fake name at the Cable House and his real name to the doctor?) And, although Morton said he was not a pimp ("procurer"), he performed this service for Walkup on occasion, sometimes even delivering women to him in Emporia.

The cross-examination of Morton lasted an hour and a half and provided much entertainment for the audience, who could barely be kept under control. Morton had a self-deprecating sense of humor that caused riotous outbreaks in the courtroom. He never got rattled, made no apologies for what he was, and had a "unique way of calling a spade a spade in the crowded court-room." Unfortunately, no newspaper shared this hilarious performance, and no transcript exists today.

Who, exactly, was Nathaniel Morton, and how did he get involved in the case? In January 1883, two steamboats, the *Laura Lee* and the *City of Greenville,* collided on the Mississippi River near New Orleans. The *Laura Lee* was being sued for $190,000 in damages. A man calling himself Colonel Ben Morton contacted the owners of the *Laura Lee,* saying he was a newspaper publisher and had been on board the *City of Greenville* at the time of the collision. Morton claimed that he had been drinking with the pilot and that the pilot, drunk, had not been paying attention to his duties. Naturally, the *Laura Lee* people were thrilled to be able to add this boost to their defense, and gave Morton several thousand dollars to come up with other witnesses who had seen the pilot drunk.[5]

Time went by, however, and the "colonel" had not contacted the *Laura Lee* representatives. Detectives tracked him down to Henderson, Kentucky, and found letters in his possession that indicated he had been pulling the same scheme with the owners of the *City of Greenville*! He was passing himself off to the *Greenville* as a planter named Pike who had been on board the *Laura Lee* and could attest to the drunken state of the pilot at the time of the collision.

In September 1885, Morton went to Vidalia as an itinerant printer, calling himself J. G. Martin, and got a job at the *Concordia Sentinel.* He was hired on for a week while another employee was sick. He claimed to know all about James Walkup and his habits, but he was such a liar that nobody in Vidalia believed him. Morton took some *Sentinel* letterhead stationery and wrote to Minnie and to Dora Findlay, offering his services as a witness to the depravity of James Walkup if they would pay his traveling expenses to Emporia. After his testimony, Nathaniel Morton disappeared from town, even though he was recalled to the stand the next day.

The second member of the "carnival of filth" trio was Asa Smith of Melvern, Kansas. In 1883 he had seen the victim in a store and, at that time, Walkup "bragged about making a new conquest." "Aren't you afraid you'll get caught?" Smith asked (this was code for catching a venereal disease). Walkup showed him a vial of something he was taking that would prevent his getting anything. Smith said Walkup was "always very boastful of his 'mashes' or conquests. [He] said he couldn't stay away from women more than a day; he had to have it."

The last member of the Smut Brothers was H. R. Fleetwood, an African American barber from Atchison who was suspected of being a pimp. He said he had seen Walkup at various times going into "negro houses of ill fame" in Atchison and Topeka. On cross-examination, he said he had gone into one of the houses with Walkup because Walkup asked him to.

It was no wonder, then, that Bill Greer would refer to this collective testimony as "a carnival of filth . . . of a character to satisfy those of the most prurient and depraved imaginations." Reporters unanimously criticized the women for staying through it all, writing that it should have been "ladies' day off" at the trial. And when they came back in even larger numbers the next day (no doubt hoping for more of the same), there was a universal journalistic outcry.

The *Picayune,* in reading Bill Greer's report of that day's testimony, published an editorial criticizing the women of Emporia for attending the trial: "No such scene could ever be made the occasion of criticism upon the ladies of New Orleans." But then the *Emporia Daily News* rebutted that most of the women in court that day were from New Orleans![6]

Tamer testimony on that second day included that of a man from Kansas City who supposedly witnessed Walkup and Morton together in April 1884, thereby providing further proof that the two were acquainted other than just Morton's say-so.

An Emporia resident named Parkman showed how desperate the defense was to prove that Walkup had received the fatal dose of poison in Topeka, and not in Emporia at Minnie's hand. Parkman said he had seen Walkup outside his house on Merchants Street on Saturday, August 15, at about 10:00 A.M. This was the same morning he had arrived from Topeka. Walkup supposedly told Parkman he had been sick in Topeka and all the way home, and that his "little wife" had rubbed his feet and put him to bed. That Monday, August 17, Parkman again saw the victim, who said he was still sick.

Unfortunately for poor Parkman, someone had seen Walkup going downtown at 7:30 A.M., and at 10:00—the time Parkman allegedly saw him—Walkup was meeting with Dwight Bill and some other men. On cross-examination, Sterry was merciless. He himself had talked with Parkman on the day Walkup died, and Parkman had said nothing about having seen the deceased on the previous Saturday. Moreover, he had told Sterry at that time that, on Monday the seventeenth, Walkup told him he felt as if he had an attack of paralysis on Saturday night. Parkman, backed into a corner, denied ever having said that.

Colonel Feighan had told Parkman on August 22, the day Walkup died, that he wished he could find some evidence that would make him believe Minnie was innocent, but Parkman never said a word about this Saturday conversation—which would have implicated someone in Topeka, rather than Minnie. Parkman claimed not to remember this, nor could he adequately explain why he had not appeared before the inquest jury.

Sterry gave Parkman the coup de grace by tricking him into saying he knew James Walkup was back from Topeka because he had seen it in the newspaper, and that's why he went to his house that Saturday morning. But news of Walkup's return wouldn't have been in the newspaper on Saturday (Parkman would have read it on Sunday or Monday). As soon as he spotted his mistake, Parkman tried to withdraw his statement. "What did you make it for?" Sterry badgered. "You explain it," countered the cornered witness, at which Lambert piped in, "I can't and I don't think you can. Was it a slip of the tongue?" Parkman stuck to his guns about seeing Walkup on Saturday as well as on Monday, but those guns were pretty well spiked by the time he left the stand.

A farmer named Miller from Hutchinson, Kansas, saw Walkup on a train in the spring of 1885 (which would have been after the victim met Minnie). James told him he'd been quite sick over the winter and was taking arsenic, which he thought had come close to killing him. The witness was not allowed to relate the reason Walkup gave him as to why he had to take the arsenic, which is strange, as all kinds of hearsay against the dead man had been allowed before this, including that from Morton on the same topic (that he was taking arsenic for syphilis).

Dr. John Filkins, formerly a doctor and presently a broker (he seemed surprised that the defense discovered he had once been a physician), said he saw James Walkup that Saturday, August 15, and they had a conversation about his having been sick in Topeka. Walkup had supposedly gone to Filkins a couple of years before that and complained of vomiting, pains, and a burning in his throat. While he was relating these symptoms in that earlier visit, he was eating a can of cove oysters, whereupon he threw them up and was sick for an hour.

Filkins was asked about the woman he treated for syphilis at Walkup's request, and he admitted it "under protest." He said Walkup was keeping the woman in a room over the doctor's office. On cross-examination, Filkins admitted that Walkup had never said he was taking arsenic, nor did he think the man was suffering from poisoning when he saw him. He did not know the name of the woman he was asked to treat.

After that, there were some witnesses as to Walkup's feeling ill, or saying so, when he got off the train in Emporia on his return from Topeka, and a doctor in Topeka who said that Walkup had consulted him—on Thursday, August 13—about his taking arsenic for syphilis for the past five or six years.

A deposition from the druggist in Cairo—the one who had filled Walkup's prescriptions on his trip back from New Orleans—revealed that the drugs were not arsenic and were not for syphilis. (They were for "certain disorders," but it was not stated what these were.)

Sheriff Jefferson Wilhite had to take the stand that day and admit to a serious breach of duty. Colonel Feighan and Isaac Lambert had told him to search the Walkup house for any evidence and turn it over to them. Wilhite now claimed he did not remember their telling him this. And he did find something: two bottles containing medicine, which he promptly turned over to . . . William Scott, Minnie's defense attorney. Even without having been specifically told to turn evidence over to the prosecution, common sense would seem to dictate that he do so. Certainly, no self-respecting law enforcement officer would turn it over to the defense. Yet, this is what Sheriff Wilhite did, and both the *Daily News* and the *Daily Republican*—rivals in other respects—joined forces in encouraging Emporia citizens not to reelect him.

As it turned out, the bottles contained a prescription for a "common private disease" (the name of which is maddeningly omitted from records), but it was not syphilis. Still, as the newspapers pointed out, the bottles were the kind of evidence that could have been used to avoid an expensive trial if they had contained arsenic (which they did not), which would have supported the theory that Walkup was taking the poison on his own.

Mr. Jay's Big Day

A Dr. A. N. Connaway of Toledo, Kansas, both a doctor and a farmer, started out the third day of the defense. He said he had known James Walkup since 1871 and had a conversation with him in the fall of 1880 regarding his relations with women and how he "kept up." Walkup said he had a preparation of arsenic that helped him "keep up."

But the defense had a problem with all these witnesses to Walkup's arsenic use: Not one of them was from Emporia. It is to be assumed that the lawyers and their detectives had searched the poison registers and interviewed Walkup's local associates regarding arsenic use, all in vain—until William Jay came forward with his outlandish story. Surely, he had heard Scott and the others bemoaning the lack of an Emporia witness and how essential it was to find one, so Jay found himself.

On the stand that third day, Minnie's staunchest defender was energetic, feisty, contentious, ungrammatical, immensely entertaining, and almost certainly a perjurer. Asked what his business was, he spoke about the lumber and farming, but then said his "business" for the past two months had been "devoting [my time] to the cause of this innocent girl." When the prosecution was successful in getting this remark stricken from the record, Jay was incensed. He supposed he was to tell the whole truth. "Is part of that to be suppressed?"

Jay's story was that one day in July 1885, prior to Walkup's marriage to Minnie, he encountered the victim on the street. The two went into Jay's office to transact some business, whereupon Walkup complained of not feeling well and asked Jay for some water and a knife. After this, Jay turned away for a moment, and when he turned back, he saw some white powder on the knife. Walkup put the powder in the glass and then drank it down. When he gave the knife back to Jay, he cautioned him to wipe off the blade. Jay asked, "Why, it ain't poison, is it?" "Yes, it's arsenic," Walkup told him. "What!" Jay supposedly exclaimed. "Arsenic," Walkup repeated with a smile.

Now, there are several things wrong with this story right from the start.

Sketch of William Jay (from the *New Orleans Times-Democrat*)

First, if the other arsenic witnesses are to be believed, the only forms of the poison seen in Walkup's possession were pills and vials of liquid, never powder. Next, why would someone used to taking powders be without his own knife, if that's what he used to measure the correct amount? And wouldn't he use the knife to stir the powder into the water? Assuming he did as Jay said—just dumped the powder into the glass and drank it without stirring it—the polite thing to do, especially when dealing with a venerable citizen like Jay, the second most important man in Emporia after Major Hood, would be to wipe off the blade before returning it.

Sterry's cross-examination immediately revealed the weakest flaw in William Jay's oh-so-timely story: He had not come forward with it before this when he knew there was even talk of getting together a lynch mob for Minnie. He was at the inquest, and the chatter all around Emporia was about nothing other than this case and whether Minnie could have done it, yet Jay kept this important piece of evidence to himself. Sterry did not even try to conceal his disbelief:

Sterry: Then it suddenly popped into your mind that the matter of his taking poison in your presence had occurred?

Jay: Will you be kind enough to define the definition of the word "popped"?
Sterry: Don't you understand English?

Sterry reminded Jay that he, Jay, had gone to Colonel Feighan shortly before the beginning of trial to lay out the facts that showed Minnie to be innocent. Why had he not brought up this evidence of Walkup's arsenic use at that time? Jay said that Scott had told him not to, but, Sterry pointed out, "Why? What harm could it do?"

Jay was then asked to take his knife and a bottle given to him by Sterry and put the same amount of white powder on the knife as he had seen Walkup use. When he had finished, affirming that this was the amount as he remembered it, Sterry informed him that it was four grains of arsenic—two more than the minimum lethal dose. Not even an arsenic eater would take that much at one time.

On redirect, William Jay concluded his testimony with the statement "Nothing will keep me from doing what I think is right," and therein probably lies the rationale behind his obvious perjury. He was absolutely convinced that Minnie was innocent and undoubtedly thought his tale was in the nature of a "white lie" designed to prevent a greater wrong. Jay seems otherwise to have been an honorable man, and, as we shall see, his fellow citizens considered him to be such.

It must be said at this point that, while perjury is regarded as a serious offense today, it does not seem to have been looked on in the same light in the nineteenth century. In fact, a perusal of cases indicates that it happened fairly often when a witness judged a piece of testimony to be irrelevant to the guilt or innocence of someone, wanted to put a defendant behind bars or prevent that from happening, or even wanted to prevent embarrassment to oneself. The main goal seemed to be the conviction or acquittal of the accused, and the means of accomplishing this was not nearly as important. Hence, all was fair in love, war, and criminal trials.

Dr. H. W. Stover, forty-four, an Emporia physician, told of treating Walkup for gonorrhea twice, once in 1883 and again in May of 1885, just before his marriage to Minnie. He had also, at Walkup's request, "doctored a lewd woman kept by him" for syphilis. He had never, however, doctored Walkup for syphilis—just gonorrhea. On cross-examination, Dr. Stover refused to divulge the name of the woman, insisting she was at that time married and now a respectable citizen. There followed a hot debate between the defense and the prosecution as to whether this question should be answered, but Stover continued to insist that he would not reveal the patient's name, and Scott ultimately withdrew the question.

There is, of course, the chance that the defense staged this entire testimony, knowing that the prosecution would want the name of a possibly nonexistent patient. Withdrawing the question would do no harm, because the jury would already have heard the testimony and "you can't unring a bell."

The sole expert witness for the defense was twenty-six-year-old Dr. S. Emory Lanphear of Kansas City, whose direct examination was long, tiring, and boring for everyone in the courtroom, but whose cross-examination provided many humorous moments. Dr. Lanphear, who had been in practice for "four years, six months, and twenty-six days," was also editing a medical journal. He spoke of the beneficial effects of arsenic, including as a booster of male sexual powers, citing many authorities for this. Although his testimony differed from that of the other physicians, it did not do so markedly in important areas, and he did no real harm to the state's case.

Here is how he answered the ten hypothetical questions: Arsenic could only stay in the stomach for, at most, a few days before death. It is possible that the arsenic that killed the hypothetical victim on a Saturday was ingested a week or more before that (an answer that directly contradicted his previous one). The cause of death would be acute arsenic poisoning, with the fatal dose being taken just before the final attack. The victim as described in the hypothetical would have taken a total of three doses of poison, although it was possible that he had taken the fatal dose a week or more before his death. The fatal dose would have to have been very large for there to be four grains still remaining in the victim after death. He could have been given the fatal dose several days before death, even as long ago as the previous week. Lanphear agreed with all the other physicians that the antidote would have been useless once the victim's system collapsed.

Dr. Lanphear, then, supported the prosecution's medical witnesses in all answers except for the ones that supported the defense's theory: questions 2, 6, and 9. He subscribed to the defense's encystment theory, which would be expected, as they were paying him to testify, but he couched his answers in so many qualifications that he was mostly in line with what the prosecution's doctors had said. For example, while he gave the defense its encystment with one hand, he took it away with the other when he said it could not happen with soluble arsenic, but only with powders (which no one other than William Jay had seen Walkup take). And when asked as to whether it would be possible that tertiary syphilis might not show up in an autopsy, Lanphear said it was entirely possible—if the examination were a superficial one (which, of course, the Walkup autopsy was not). On cross-examination, there were indications that Dr. Lanphear had legal troubles of his own regarding the selling of liquor from a drugstore he owned with some other people. Whatever the truth of this, he would definitely have run-ins with the law in the future (see chapter 17, page 206).

In giving the history of his pharmaceutical and medical careers, Dr. Lanphear could not recall when exactly he reached Hartford, Connecticut, where he began his practice, as "I was courting my wife and do not remember." Asked to draw a human stomach, he asked Sterry if he should "draw it hungry or full." When Dr. Lanphear spoke about the distention capabilities of the stomach and said it "is sometimes tolerant of considerable abuse," Sterry—who was very large—commented, "I know that myself."

After Sterry asked Dr. Lanphear if the inside of the stomach looked like tripe and he responded that he did not know what tripe was, the crowd's raucous laughter was too much for Judge Graves, who had put up with an almost constant uproar throughout the cross-examination of this witness: "There is too much disposition to levity in this court," he said sternly; "it must stop or I will cause the sheriff to eject those who are so full of laughter that they cannot control it in court."

Certainly, Judge Graves was aware that some of the hilarity was caused by the lawyers themselves. Earlier, Sterry and Fenlon had begun bantering back and forth, and Graves had to step in and break it up: "Gentlemen, I don't like this cross-firing between yourselves. Confine yourself to the business before you and let the case go on."

A Poem from the Gallery

The Emporia *Daily News* published a poem entitled "Experience of Ladies Attending the Walkup Trial" by a gallery-occupier named Naomi Nottingham. It began:

> There is something fascinating in the storm
>   And "war of words" which in this case we hear;
> So strange the court proceedings, and so new the legal form
>   That we stay to listen, 'spite of all we fear.

Plain language from the witnesses oft fills us with disgust,
   And our faith in humankind is sorely tried;
And in view of testimony, we feel 'twould be but just
     If James Reeves Walkup's friend [presumably Morton]
        had also died.[7]

The poem goes on to praise the wit and acumen of the attorneys on both sides, the quick thinking of Judge Graves in making decisions, and the "business-like stenographer . . . ladylike throughout [Miss Lane], though position, age and wealth give others [probably William Jay] an excuse for petulance and anger." That there is sympathy for Minnie's plight is obvious in the poem's reference to "the quiet, graceful manners of the prisoner at the bar, her child-like blooming face and lovely eyes."

The reporter for the *Kansas City Times,* however, did not think Minnie was very "child-like." He had been watching her throughout, and his judgment was harsh: "At no time during the trial was she forgetful of her personal beauty. The self-conscious use of her charms, her want of regard or even respect for the memory of the dead and her obtrusive vanity were at all times painfully noticeable and evidence a heartlessness and shallowness of nature."[8]

There was much excitement in the courtroom at the end of day three of the defense because everyone knew that the witnesses for the next day— Thursday, October 29—would be Mrs. Elizabeth Wallace and then Minnie herself. Since Minnie had not testified at the inquest and had been forbidden by her attorneys to talk about the case with anyone, there was much discussion as to what her explanations would be. And, after the voluminous testimony about James Walkup's licentious habits, the sympathy of most of the inhabitants of Emporia was most definitely with her. In the words of one of them, "[He] ought to have been killed."[9]

Chapter 8

Starring Minnie Walkup

⌒

The fair defendant's memory was a trifle at sea.
—*Bill Greer,* New Orleans Daily Picayune *(1885)*

As was to be expected, the court was more than filled to its capacity for the anticipated testimony of Minnie and her mother on Thursday, October 29. Spectators had begun showing up as early as 7:00 A.M. for the 9:00 session, and by 8:30 there was no more room—so people lined the hallways and the staircases just to be close to the action and maybe have a remote chance of being admitted at some point. Years later they would be able to say "I was there."

A hush fell over the crowded courtroom as Elizabeth Wallace took the stand.[1] Thomas Fenlon led her through her testimony, which she gave mostly in a loud, clear voice. However, she frequently sobbed, especially when the attorneys were wrangling about the admissibility of evidence. She gave some autobiographical background and presented the picture of a woman trying to do the best for her family.

Colonel Feighan did the cross-examination, and he tried to show that Mrs. Wallace was basically an unindicted coconspirator in the fleecing and murder of James Walkup by her daughter. "Have you any children?" she asked the county attorney at one point, trying to get him to sympathize with her desire to see her children well placed in life. But Feighan was having none of that: "Please leave all mention of my children out of this trial."

89

Minnie's mother claimed she had never seen Walkup intoxicated, but that can hardly have been true. His own friend Eben Baldwin said he was, and it can be assumed that Baldwin would have wanted to present him in the best possible light, so he would never have made that up. Moreover, an acknowledgment of Walkup's drunken state on Mrs. Wallace's part would have made it look as if she and Minnie had taken advantage of him while he was incapacitated, so she had a motive to lie about this.

When Feighan asked Elizabeth Wallace about Charlie Crushers and the other lowlifes, she became indignant. She said she had never associated with these people, and Minnie added a strong denial from the defense table. Gathering strength from her daughter's contribution, Mrs. Wallace said that that information had been reported by a detective sent to New Orleans, and Feighan hotly replied that he had sent no detective to that city. Elizabeth said she could produce a witness sitting in that very courtroom who could testify to the fact that there had been one. (It is not clear, however, how this disproves the truth of the statements about Mrs. Wallace's "business associates.")

Both Feighan and Mrs. Wallace were probably not being entirely truthful in this exchange. The county may not have sent a detective to New Orleans, but two separate groups of people had gone down there to do research on the Wallaces before James Walkup had even married Minnie. And it is entirely possible that Feighan sent someone who was not, by vocation, a detective. As for Mrs. Wallace, her answers regarding the gamblers and "fast men" seemed to be focused on 222 Canal Street and not on any of the boardinghouses she had run prior to that. After this heated exchange, Elizabeth Wallace was excused amid a buzz of commentary in the audience. Now it was Minnie's turn to tell her story.

Minnie's Direct Examination

When Minnie Walkup took the stand, it was clear to everyone in the courtroom that she was up to the task. She was calm, composed, and completely sure of herself. As she went through her direct testimony, she frequently turned to address the jury in explaining a point. She shed no tears and exhibited no nervousness. Her husky voice could not always be heard, and she was frequently admonished to speak up. She was on the stand for six hours that first day.[2] Thomas Fenlon seemed to have no organizational plan of attack but was all over the board with his questions, darting here and there. Perhaps he hoped by this to confuse the prosecution and distract the attorneys from focusing on certain issues vulnerable to cross-examination.

Minnie painted a picture of herself as an innocent maiden unexpectedly charmed by this rough rustic from Kansas and had never before that thought of marriage. As for the propriety of her behavior, "I never walked on the principal street, Canal Street, with a gentleman in my life" (leaving open the possibility of walks on other streets). She said she told Walkup in May, when he made his third visit, that she would marry him in October, but the letter he sent to Edward Findlay from Emporia, telling him "Minnie has said 'yes!'" put the lie to that: She had made sure he was rich before she married him.

As Fenlon was leading Minnie through the courtship and marriage, she suddenly stopped and asked, "May I tell you something?" "Yes, of course," he replied. Whether the interruption were really spontaneous or orchestrated by the defense wasn't evident. It is just as likely that Minnie thought her story about Walkup's daughter would make it look as if Libbie had not always objected to her father's marriage.

Minnie said that before they left for Cincinnati to get married, Libbie approached her and asked if she would get James to buy his daughter a diamond ring—without, however, letting him know that Libbie had put her up to it. When they were in Kansas City, on their way back to Emporia, Minnie suggested to James that he buy a ring for Libbie. "Did Libbie suggest that?" he asked. "No, it was my own idea," Minnie told him. She then picked out a $60 ring (equivalent to more than $1,300 today), but Walkup said he wasn't going to pay that much, so she found a $40 one instead ($924 today). Walkup wanted Minnie to give Libbie the ring, but she told him it would mean more to her if he presented it himself.

This is an interesting tale, if true—and we must assume it so, or at least the request and the purchase part of it, as Libbie never said it wasn't. It illustrates her own fear of being displaced by Minnie in her father's eyes and wanting some reassurance that he still loved her. It shows Minnie's tendency to extravagance, as even the less expensive ring would have been the equivalent of a week's pay for many people. And it shows Walkup's suspicion of Libbie and her intentions ("Did she suggest that?") and his reluctance to spend a lot of money on her. He doesn't seem to want to buy the ring at all, except that his "little wife" is asking the favor. And he doesn't want to give Libbie the ring as coming from him, possibly so as not to let her think he was acceding to her ploy for attention. He would have bought Minnie a $60 ring, though, if she had asked for it.

When James Walkup came home from Topeka early that Saturday morning, August 15, Minnie testified, he was quite sick with nausea and head pain and couldn't even undress himself. He seemed to be paralyzed. Minnie pulled his boots off, falling against the window in the process, then rubbed his legs for him. She wanted to get a doctor, but he said that he knew what was wrong with him, that this happened to him every summer, and that he would pull out of it. He told her he had been taken ill in Topeka.

This scene had probably happened, all right, as Clinton Sterry would later assert in his closing argument—at least the illness part of it—but not on Saturday morning. It would have happened Saturday evening when the strychnine Minnie had given him was kicking in. As for Walkup's statement that he knew what was wrong with him and would recover, by the time she gave her testimony, she had already heard Eben Baldwin's similar conversation with the victim on the way to New Orleans. We know that the "drawing and stretching of the limbs"—the classic sign of strychnine poisoning—did not "happen to him every summer" because he told Dr. Jacobs that he had never in his life experienced those feelings.

Now, for the first time, Minnie told the story of the two powders (calomel and snowflake) and of putting them in the lookalike pieces of pink stationery. She denied telling anyone about a woman in New Orleans who had given her calomel, despite the fact that three people heard her say it. And, she claimed, she had taken *both* powders to druggists Kelly and Moore for analysis, not just one.

Minnie testified that one day as James Walkup lay recuperating in bed and wanting the oysters and pop, she was looking in the mirror and despairing of all the pimples on her face, eruptions she had never before experienced. "That doesn't look very pretty, does it?" Walkup supposedly commented. "Do you know anything that would be good for it?" Minnie told him she thought arsenic might work, since it was good for the complexion. Although she had no idea whether it could cure acne, she wanted to give it a try.

Walkup asked if she was afraid to use it. "No," she told him, "not if I use a certain quantity." But she never said what quantity that was, and he—the great arsenic eater—never told her what might be a safe amount or made sure that she would use it correctly. Nor did he offer her any from his allegedly prodigious personal stash; he told her to buy some arsenic downtown when she went for the pop and gave her $2 for the purchases.

Prior to this scene, after her first purchase of arsenic at Kelly's, Minnie had dumped it all in the chamber pot when she heard him coming up the stairs, because "gentlemen are always averse to their wives using cosmetics," a statement that probably was a surprise to many a husband and wife sitting in the courtroom that day.

As for that Wells Fargo Express box that James Walkup got incensed about, here is Minnie's explanation: She had brought some blankets of her mother's from New Orleans and was shipping them back to her. However, Walkup told her he was planning to take her and Libbie to New Orleans in October, so the blankets could go then, and there was no need to ship them now. But why bring the blankets all the way to Emporia for just a couple of weeks (in the summer, at that), then send them back before the cold weather hit? And Minnie undoubtedly forgot that the Wells Fargo clerks testified that the box was to be shipped to St. Louis, not New Orleans (the addressee was never stated).

Over the course of her direct examination, Minnie denied many things already in evidence and claimed she did not remember many others:

- She did not remember that Kelly told her the powder could be strychnine or quinine; she only remembered the morphine possibility.
- She did not remember Kelly's asking her if she was the one who had brought the powder in earlier.
- She did not remember Bates asking her what she wanted strychnine for.
- She denied telling Bates that she didn't want to tell him the purpose. (How could she deny this when she didn't even remember that he *asked* her what the purpose was?)
- She denied telling any druggist that she would not reveal the purpose.
- She denied telling Mary Moss to say she was going for butter, if asked by any of the family. ("Never! Never!")
- She did not remember going to any drugstore on Friday or Saturday to get strychnine and not getting it.
- She did not remember asking Kelly not to tell anyone she had bought arsenic.

Minnie did, however, remember sitting up all night with her husband on Wednesday, Thursday, and Friday, and that she didn't go to bed at all, a statement that would later trip her up. And when Fenlon asked her if she had given Walkup either strychnine or arsenic, she forcefully replied, "So help me God, I did not."

In 1947, sixty-two years after Minnie's trial, John E. Reid, today considered by law enforcement professionals to be the top authority in interviewing and interrogation in criminal cases, developed a technique, named in his honor, to help police officers question suspects and determine when someone is being deceptive. One clue to deception is when a subject feels it necessary to add something to the answer to make it seem more believable, and invoking the deity is one of these. "So help me, God," "As God is my witness," and "This is the God's honest truth" are examples. "A truthful subject will allow his denial to stand on its own," Reid says. Hence, under this system, Minnie's "So help me God" indicated deception, whereas if she were telling the truth, a simple "No, I did not" would have sufficed.[3]

Cross-Examination

The words most often uttered by Minnie in her grueling cross-examination by Clinton Sterry were "I don't remember." She said this regarding at least forty-seven separate topics (not counting the seven "I don't remember"s on direct examination), and if the *Daily Republican* failed to print a complete transcript, then that number is higher. The word most frequently uttered by Sterry during this time was an incredulous "What?" He was a formidable questioner, but even he could not penetrate the wall of "I don't remember"s and "No, I did not"s.[4]

Sterry began the session, at the tail end of the direct examination, by going right to Minnie's statement about staying up all those nights with Walkup, even getting her to add Tuesday to the list. Then he showed that she was a liar because of the fire in Libbie's room on Wednesday night (Libbie had said her father and Minnie were snoring when she went into their room to get the water). Minnie's response to that was that she didn't remember which night the fire was, but if Libbie had arrived home on Tuesday, and Minnie was supposedly up that night and every night following, her lack of knowledge did not disprove her lie. (The newspapers said she "seemed confused at the question.")

After Minnie said she had not thought of marrying Walkup before October, Sterry produced her letter, dated June 2, in which she told him she might stay once she arrived in Emporia. Her response? "I don't remember writing this letter." He showed her the letter, she acknowledged that it was her handwriting, but "I don't remember writing it." So, of course, that prevented her from having to make up what she meant by it.

Possibly, by 1885, Clinton Sterry had figured out what John Reid would discover in the twentieth century about the invocation of the deity as indicative of deception. He asked her why she had used "So help me God," and she replied, "My heart prompted me to." "Is that the only way you can account for it?" "That is all," she said.

Sterry asked questions designed to show how ridiculously suspect it was for a city girl of such a young age to entertain the possibility of marriage with a significantly older man from the country after such a short time of acquaintance. And, if Sterry had anticipated Reid, he had evidently not anticipated the equality of women:

Sterry: You knew what marriage meant, didn't you? . . . You knew that it
    is the only real life to woman—did you not?
Minnie: Yes, sir.
Sterry: You knew that married life and motherhood was the one thing
    almost, that a young girl had in the future for herself?
Minnie: I don't know that I regarded it that way.

Sterry seemed to have been under the misconception that Minnie had caused the shootout at the *Mascot,* not Dora. When he realized his mistake, he nonetheless tried to implicate a relationship between Minnie and the much older Judge Houston:

Sterry: [The Judge] was constantly visiting you during the time you were
    [in jail]?
Minnie: Yes, all my friends visited me in that hour; I had very few friends.
Sterry: Yes, that is very nice. Did I ask you anything about that?
Minnie: You did not.
Sterry: Then confine yourself to answers to my questions, if you please.

Minnie had testified on direct examination that before Walkup left New Orleans on that first visit, he had asked if they could write letters to each other. In fact, Eben Baldwin had said the same thing, adding that Walkup was quite drunk during this exchange. But now, when Sterry broached the subject, she claimed she couldn't remember whether it was that visit or not! Sterry couldn't believe it:

Sterry: Didn't you testify in answer to Mr. Fenlon that you did arrange a
    correspondence with him on his first visit?
Minnie: I don't remember.
Sterry: Your memory is not bad, is it?
Minnie: No, not generally.
Sterry: You can't even recollect back during this examination of yourself as
    to whether you testified that it was on Mr. Walkup's first visit that you
    arranged to carry on a correspondence with him, is that correct?
Minnie: I don't know. I think it was, though.

Minnie tripped herself up by saying that she wanted to write to Walkup because she couldn't make up her mind whether to marry him, even though she'd only seen him a few times in her life, then telling Sterry that she wasn't very serious about the whole thing. Walkup hadn't made any promises about caring for her family until his second visit, so her supposed motive of marrying him to make that happen couldn't possibly have existed on this first visit. So, Sterry wondered, what other motive could she have? Her answers were vague and not responsive.

Further, Minnie said she had absolutely no idea of getting married before October, and she was adamant about this. Yet when Sterry asked her (prior to showing her the letter she had written to Walkup) if she had *suggested* to Walkup that she might do that, she said, "I don't remember." She must have suspected he would produce that letter, so she had to back down from her definitive stance.

When Sterry got to the papers of calomel and snowflake, and Minnie had gone through a litany of "I don't remember"s, she obviously felt she needed a time out. Claiming she was chilly and needed her shawl, she was allowed to go to her cell, adjacent to the courtroom, accompanied by Deputy Wooster.

On direct examination, Minnie had said she took both powders in for analysis, but now she told Sterry that she wasn't certain whether she had taken them both in:

Sterry: Didn't you state yesterday that you took them both?
Minnie: I don't remember.

Sterry: Did you take them both to Dr. Moore's drug store?

Minnie: I don't remember.

Sterry: You had no difficulty in answering the questions asked by Mr. Fenlon, had you?

Minnie: I don't know about that, either.

Sterry: You don't know about that; what would be your best guess as to whether you took them both to this place or not?

Minnie: I don't remember. I don't know that I care to guess at it.

Sterry went on to point out that there would have been no need to take both powders in: If she knew she had calomel and snowflake, she would only have to have one analyzed to know what the other was. Yet, when Kelly said it was morphine, quinine, or strychnine, Minnie never said, "It can't be any of those. It's either calomel or snowflake." And when Moore told her it was quinine, she never acted surprised, never said, "That's odd. I had only calomel and snowflake."

Another of Minnie's preposterous statements was that although she had known that both strychnine and arsenic were poisons, she had no idea they were *deadly* poisons. She had to say this, ridiculous as it sounds, because she had to have a reason why those purchases and the thing about signing the registers were not very memorable. For most people, purchasing poison and having to sign the register would be remarkable events, but Minnie was in the middle of an "I don't remember" litany, and it wasn't terribly believable.

Sterry: Did you suppose a person could take it without killing him, in a large quantity like a teaspoonful?

Minnie: I don't know that I ever thought about it.

Asked about the size of the strychnine bottle she got from Bates, Minnie said she didn't remember. Was it large? Was it small? How was it in relation to the size of the bottle shown to her (the one found in Libbie's room)? "I don't remember." Sterry must have been ready to tear his hair out at this point: "Haven't you memory sufficient to even form a judgment?"

Minnie told Sterry that she had unpacked her trunk when she got to Emporia, saw the dress with the stain on it, and decided right then that she would try the strychnine-and-urine recipe. Yet, a few minutes after that, she told him she never took the dress out of the trunk at all!

Sterry: What? . . . Didn't you tell me a little while ago that you unpacked your trunk after you got back from your marriage and then took it out?

Minnie: I don't remember. I suppose so.

Sterry: What?

Minnie: I don't remember.

Sterry: You don't remember whether you unpacked the trunk after you got home?

Minnie: I remember unpacking my trunk . . . I don't remember whether I took out this particular dress or not.

Sterry: You had taken it out on that day upon which you got this strychnine. Is that correct?

Minnie: I don't remember that.

Sterry: Didn't you just now say that you had taken it out that day?

Minnie: I don't remember.

Sterry: What?

Minnie: I don't know.

Sterry pressed her as to why she suddenly abandoned the quest for strychnine and switched to arsenic. Well, they were for different purposes, she told him blandly. Yes, of course, they were, but why not continue in the quest for the strychnine? Didn't she want it just as badly on Sunday afternoon, when she went downtown for the arsenic, as she had wanted it in the morning when she sent Mary Moss down to Bates for more? "I don't remember."

Minnie showed her cunning when Sterry began asking about the pimples on her face, which she gave as the reason for wanting the arsenic (although she had told Dr. Jacobs and the men in the parlor that she wanted it to change her complexion). She was able to anticipate where the attorney was going with his questions:

Sterry: How long had [the pimples] been there?

Minnie: I don't remember how long. After I came they commenced on my face.

Sterry: So that anybody could see them sitting off from you as far as I am sitting?

Minnie: Yes. I don't remember whether Mrs. Sommers saw them or not.

Sterry: I did not say anything about Mrs. Sommers, did I? What made you suggest that?

Minnie: Why, I thought of something that suggested it to me.
Sterry: You were afraid I was going to ask you about Mrs. Sommers.
Minnie: No, I was afraid of nothing of the kind.

Questioned about the "friend in New Orleans" who used arsenic all the time, Minnie must have realized that it was not believable that she didn't know the proper proportions and had not asked, so she threw out vague answers about a "pinch" added to a bottle of undetermined size. When Sterry asked her again how much arsenic she was supposed to use, she said it was a teaspoonful—thereby proving, if there was any doubt, that there was no friend in New Orleans who used arsenic: One-quarter teaspoonful of arsenic is approximately twenty grains. Two grains is considered a lethal dose. Minnie's imaginary friend would have her take eighty grains at one time to clear up her complexion.

Sterry: When you were at the drug store, did it occur to you to make any inquiries as to whether it was poison or not?
Minnie: No, it did not.
Sterry: Did it occur to you to make any inquiries as to how a person ought to use it and use it safely?
Minnie: I think not.

Minnie said that it had been so long she couldn't remember which days her husband was sick, which days he was well, and in what order many of the events took place. Sterry did not hide his disdain at a wife who claimed she had come to love her husband, yet could not keep in her mind the occurrences of the last week of his life. "Why can't you recollect that just as clearly as you can recollect all of his symptoms the day that he got home from Topeka?" he asked sarcastically.

As Minnie had said during her direct examination that Walkup told her he knew what was wrong with him when he was so sick coming home from Topeka, she repeated that when Sterry asked about it.

Sterry: Did he tell the physician he knew what was the matter with him?
Minnie: I don't remember hearing him.
Sterry: Did you tell the doctor . . . that Mr. Walkup had told you he knew what was the matter with him?"
Minnie: No, I don't remember that I did.

Reading the transcript of this cross-examination, the modern reader wishes that Sterry had followed through with some of Minnie's obvious inconsistencies instead of abandoning one issue and moving on to another. However, one can also sense what must have been a high level of frustration for him in the absolute stubbornness of this witness, in the face of all reason, to deny everything that incriminated her, to plead ignorance every time she got cornered, and to claim she could not even remember her own testimony given minutes or hours before. Sterry was right to push her as hard as he did, and it was impossible for him to rein in his disdain, his sarcasm, and his incredulity. Yet, to the audience, he came across—as one defense attorney would later say—as a "bar room bully."

Sterry was the big, bad prosecutor attacking the poor, defenseless little girl. One senses in the next day's newspaper reports the growing admiration and sympathy for Minnie. "Nerve!" shouted one headline. "The little lady [is] a brick!" And what spunk she had when she stuck up for her mother during Elizabeth Wallace's cross-examination. "Mrs. Walkup is the bravest of the brave. Is there another?" How many sixteen-year-olds could have stood up to that? Apparently, the spectators were more impressed with how Minnie handled herself, without tears, without breaking down, than with the myriad contradictions, nonsensical statements, and "I don't remember"s.

Even our New Orleans friend Bill Greer was impressed: "Her story was told with the accent of truth itself, and with all possible simplicity and innocence." Some of the prosecution attorneys told Greer that Minnie was "an exceptionally good witness."

The growing sympathy for Minnie can be seen in the lyrics of a song sung everywhere in Emporia at this time:

Oh, the judge and the jury
And the lawyers in a fury
  Are walking up the court house stairs;
For Mr. Walkup he got sick,
Because he took some arsenic,
  And now he's climbing up the golden stairs.
Chorus:
  Don't you hear the bailiff calling,
    He calls so mournfully,
  Don't you hear them lawyers pleading,
  Walking up the court house stairs.

Minnie had to go to jail,
'Cause she couldn't get the bail,
   Walking up the court house stairs.
But when they put her on the stand
She played a very cunning hand,
   Walking up the court house stairs.
Mr. Jay is her guardian,
And he's very often seen
   Walking up the court house stairs;
He hasn't much to say
But he's thinking every day
   'Bout taking Minnie down the court house stairs.[5]

It seems that everyone was "hoodooed" by the girl from New Orleans.

Rebuttal

The only testimony left was in the form of rebuttal and surrebuttal. Since Minnie said she had told Julia Sommers and Sallie McKinney she wanted the strychnine for a dress, not underpants, as they had testified, they came back to say that they were standing together when Minnie told them she wanted the poison for menstrual stains on underwear. Eben Baldwin denied ever seeing Nat Morton on the boat to New Orleans, and Dr. Charles Gardiner testified that arsenic would not make someone's urine smell bad.[6]

The defense came back with a New Orleans man named William Anderson, who claimed to know Nat Morton and said Morton also used the name G. W. Rigley, a name found in the Dodge House register during the Cattlemen's Convention in April 1884 and supposedly in Morton's handwriting. But Morton had never said he used this name, and he was nowhere to be found, so Feighan objected to this testimony: "This is the first time the name Rigley has wriggled into the case."

Anderson said he was a friend of the Wallace family and worked for a company that sold school furniture and other commission items. The name of the business was Ginerally & Company, so Sterry got a big laugh by asking, "Gineral what?"

Another man said that the name "T. H. Butler" of La Junta, Colorado, found in the Dodge House register at that same time, was in James Walkup's handwriting. But it turned out that Butler was known in Emporia, and even Clinton Sterry knew who he was: a claims adjuster for the AT&SF Railroad.

S. S. Warren, a former mayor of Emporia, was staying at the Dodge House for the 1884 Cattlemen's Convention. He never saw James Walkup at either the hotel or the convention. The secretary of the convention testified that it had begun on April 2 and closed April 4, and Emporia city council records showed that Walkup was there for the April 1 elections and at the council meetings on April 4 and April 7—so it was highly unlikely that he was on a "jamboree" with Nat Morton and a couple of girls in Dodge City at that time.

At last, on Saturday, October 31, testimony in the Walkup case came to a close. It had taken just two weeks.

Chapter 9

The Rise and Fall of Minnie Walkup

 ⌒

Is it a crime to dance upon the newly made grave of one suddenly stricken to the earth?

—Emporia Daily News *(1885)*

That Sunday, when a reporter visited Minnie in her cell, she complained of a headache and was miffed that a couple of jurors had fallen asleep every afternoon of the defense's case. The reporter told her they were probably just closing their eyes because the sun was shining on them, but Minnie said they were snoring.[1]

The *Kansas City Times* reported that witness William Anderson of New Orleans was going to propose to Minnie if she were acquitted, but the correspondent apparently made this up out of whole cloth. Anderson, a married man with two children, was so irate he went out looking for the man who had printed this.[2]

Minnie's lack of knowledge as to how much arsenic to use in clearing her complexion almost led to the deaths of two copycats who wanted to make themselves beautiful. The young women from Florence, Kansas, got arsenic from their local druggist and took too much because the correct dosage was never given in the newspaper reports. They got to a doctor in time and recovered.[3]

Bill Greer researched Kansas law to find out what would happen if Minnie were convicted. A conviction would mean an automatic death sentence, but hanging couldn't take place for at least a year. After the year was up, the governor could review the conviction and issue an order for execution. However, most governors never issued these orders, and so there were few executions in Kansas. Some people felt this unwillingness to hang convicted criminals was tantamount to encouraging lynch law, such as what had happened in the recent Vinegar case.[4]

Sis Vinegar was a fourteen-year-old black prostitute in Lawrence, Kansas, in 1882. One of her clients was a rich white farmer, and Sis conspired with two men to rob and kill him. She and the two men were taken to jail, along with Sis's innocent father, and the three men were eventually lynched by an angry mob of white men as the sheriff stood by and watched.[5]

Jury Instructions

Unlike in the twenty-first century's justice system, in 1885 Kansas the judge issued jury instructions before the attorneys gave their closing arguments.[6] Modern jury instructions are a combination of boilerplate models and those specially crafted by each side to fit the particular circumstances of the case. These special instructions are argued over in chambers, with the final decision as to wording and inclusion made by the judge. In 1885, however, it would seem that jury instructions were solely the province of the trial judge.

In that case, then, it is quite clear that Judge Charles Graves was in favor of an acquittal for Minnie. It is hard to imagine the prosecution consenting to some of them if objections had been allowed. In a nutshell, here are the instructions he gave Minnie's jury:

1. Poison is always first-degree murder.
2. "Malice" doesn't mean hatred, but a wicked condition of mind.
3. You must decide which witnesses are credible.
4. Don't be afraid of circumstantial evidence, but if there's another reasonable cause for Walkup's death, you must acquit.
5. The facts to be established beyond a reasonable doubt are these:
   a. James Reeves Walkup died from poison.
   b. The poison was administered by the defendant.
   c. The defendant intended to take Walkup's life.

  d. The victim died from the effects of poison the defendant gave him
     for the purpose of killing him.
6. Proof of motive is not necessary. Regarding extravagant purchases at
   Newman's, keep in mind that it is a husband's duty to provide for his
   wife and that includes the necessaries reflective of his and her stations
   in life. If the defendant thought her purchases were necessary for that,
   then they were justified.
7. If you think Walkup took arsenic at any time before his death, you must
   acquit. If you think someone else gave him arsenic, you must acquit.
   You can also consider the defendant's age and experience.

These last two instructions were definitely pro-defense and practically
directed the jury to issue a verdict of "not guilty."

Apparently, Judge Graves gave these instructions to the *Daily Republican* in advance for its verbatim transcript, because the reporter in charge
immediately sent them out to the other newspapers in Emporia. When
the judge discovered that his instructions had been printed in the newspapers before he had read them to the jury, he was furious and banned
the reporter from all further proceedings in the case. On top of that, the
hapless journalist was promptly fired by the *Republican* for scooping his
own paper![7]

Closing Arguments

Spectators were just as plentiful for the oratorical showmanship of the
closing arguments as they had been for the testimony.[8] Later, they would
evaluate the lawyers among themselves. If they could, they would have
held up scoring placards after each argument.

The usual system was that the prosecution would begin and end the
arguments, in this case, Clinton Sterry and Colonel John Feighan. In between would be defense attorneys and others on the prosecution team. So
that the orators could get into their stride without restriction, the counsel
tables were removed from the front of the courtroom.

Somewhere in here, two things happened to prevent the *Emporia Daily
Republican* from giving readers the complete transcript of the arguments:
First, there was a stacking-up effect: Things were happening so fast that the

transcript of some of the speeches often had to be completed the next day. For example, Sterry spoke for three and a half hours that first day, but the newspaper also wanted to give readers the benefit of reading what the other orators had to say, so it carried the conclusion of his argument over to the next day. Ultimately, the *Republican* was still presenting closing arguments in the newspaper when the jury had retired to deliberate. The second event was the illness of the court stenographer, Miss Lane, no doubt incredibly worn out by the end of the trial. There were no reports of some of the lawyers' speeches, and the transcripts of others' were incomplete. Eventually, the *Republican* just gave up on it and declared that it had fulfilled its promise of a verbatim transcript by doing so for the witness testimony.

Sterry argued the facts regarding the presence of poison in Walkup's system at the exact times following Minnie's purchases downtown, but most of his speech was directed at the inappropriateness of her behavior: her encouraging of "this old man," her cool composure on the stand, and her failure to shed a tear as her husband lay dying and after his death. Why didn't she produce the letters Walkup had written her? She had all those he had sent to her brother-in-law, Edward Findlay, because they showed her in a good light. So it seems the other letters must have somehow hurt her case or she would have made sure they were put into evidence.

Also, Sterry said that Minnie had to keep saying "I don't remember" because otherwise she would have had to contradict all those other witnesses (especially the druggists) who had no reason to lie, as she did. And then Sterry made a gross error: He postulated that Minnie switched from strychnine to arsenic because she knew that Walkup took arsenic. Since Judge Graves's instructions had already been given to the jury, and one of these was that an acquittal was automatic if it were determined that Walkup had *ever* taken arsenic before his death, this admission could have guaranteed a victory for Minnie.

Young defense attorney George Dodds of Mississippi followed Sterry and provided what Bill Greer characterized as "one hour of Southern eloquence" (although it was later reported that Dodds had spoken for *two* hours). The lawyer called Sterry a "bar room bully" and said Sterry was "not a gentleman," the ultimate southern insult. Harry Hood had hired Sterry, and so he was out for "private vengeance." Dodds's argument was very poetic and somewhat melodramatic ("this one lonely little soul transplanted from her Southern home"), with very little arguing of the facts of the case.

Judge J. Jay Buck for the prosecution
(from Cutler's *History of Kansas*)

Dodds insinuated that either Libbie Walkup or Mary Moss could have poisoned James Walkup, but it is hard to see what their motives would have been. If either was angry at being supplanted by Minnie, it would seem more logical to get rid of *her* rather than the object of their affection. Poison is not a heat-of-passion instrument of murder. While someone could be so angry at a loved one that she could shoot or stab him, it takes cold calculation to set up a poisoning.

Isaac Lambert decried the smearing of a good man's name by the defense, a man against whom nobody had had a bad thing to say for seventeen years. Now his family would have to bear that burden for the rest of their lives. The defense seemed to be focusing on returning this young defendant to her family rather than presenting any evidence to show she hadn't poisoned Walkup. What about the victim's family? Even though Libbie might not be as beautiful as Minnie, didn't she deserve sympathy, too? Lambert didn't mince words about "old man Jay," saying he had told a lie "from beginning to end." Calling him "our enthusiastic friend," he pointed out that Jay was the only one out of an entire county of 20,000 people to see Walkup take arsenic. Defense attorneys could not come up with a single druggist anywhere who had sold Walkup arsenic in any form, not even the fairly ubiquitous Fowler's Solution.

Judge J. Jay Buck for the prosecution gave a closing argument so mild that it was considered more helpful to Minnie than to the state. In fact, after he concluded, Minnie went to him, shook his hand, and thanked him! The newspapers commented that there had been two speeches for the defense and one for the prosecution that day, even though two prosecutors and one defense attorney had spoken.

Thomas Fenlon for the defense showed his strategic savvy when he began his argument, then feigned illness a few minutes into it. He realized that he would complete his speech at the close of the court session, then Feighan would begin the final prosecution argument the next day. Overnight, the jurors would have forgotten what Fenlon had said, and he wanted them to have his points fresh in their minds when they began their deliberations. When he showed up the next day, he was in perfect health.

Prosecution attorneys were unanimous in their denunciation of the defense witnesses regarding Walkup's arsenic use and debauchery as liars—with the possible exception of William Jay, who had obviously had a momentary lapse of reason. Some characterized him as crazy, while Feighan maintained that Jay was an honest man who had deluded himself into believing his own story about the arsenic powder on Walkup's knife, a story desperately needed by the defense, though merely a hallucination on his part. At that point, Jay interrupted with, "Is that in evidence?" "No," Feighan told him, "but it's a pretty good theory."

Deliberation

At the conclusion of the seemingly unending closing arguments, the jurors were taken to the Park Place Hotel for dinner, then brought back to the courthouse for deliberation.[9] Some enterprising spectators discovered that the left gallery had a crack in the floor, directly over the jury room. The spies began issuing reports that the first vote was 10–2 for acquittal. But then the bailiff locked the door that led to the gallery.

All over town, the only thing on people's lips was speculation about the verdict. And Emporia was not alone in this. The *Boston Daily Globe* declared in its November 16 edition, "There has been as much interest taken in her trial as was ever manifested in a presidential election."

More rumors surfaced that the 10–2 vote was inaccurate, and that it was actually 6–6. In the afternoon, the vote supposedly changed to 7–5 for acquittal. William Jay was, once again, flitting about nervously. Cruel pranksters would tell him that the jury was coming back with a guilty verdict, upon which poor Jay was sent into a veritable frenzy. They succeeded in this three times. While the jury was still out, someone estimated the cost of the trial to Lyon County to that point, and came up with $4,000 (over $92,000 today).

Minnie was asked about her post-trial plans, should she be acquitted, and she disingenuously claimed that she had not even thought about it. "It's time enough to think about that when the verdict is read," added her mother. When the reporter told her the current rumor was 9–3 in her favor, Minnie pouted, "I think there were two or three of those jurors who slept yesterday until after Mr. Feighan had got started to talking, and then just waking up in time to hear him make me out a perfect fiend, and they must be the ones who are holding out."

Even if Minnie wasn't making any plans for herself, plenty of men wanted to make some for her. One hundred of them in Cottonwood Falls said they would post her bond for her in any amount if she had to have a new trial. "Cinnamon Pete," a nearly illiterate cowboy in Dodge City (the supposed scene of some of James Walkup's sprees with Nat Morton), communicated the admiration he and his colleagues felt for Minnie:

> Deare Madam,
>   All ov the boyes is betting on you coming off cleer. Your a pritty little darlen with more sand [guts] than that snoozer ov a law sharp [presumably Sterry]. Doant you giv in and if you want help let us know.
>   Cinnamon Pete [amazingly, he could spell "cinnamon," but not "of," so perhaps this was a hoax][10]

At last, fifty-two hours later, it was announced that the jury had reached a verdict. And so, at 3:50 P.M. on Friday, November 6, the judge, the lawyers, the jury, the spectators, and Minnie trooped back to their places in the Lyon County courthouse.

Verdict

Citizens in 1885 obviously did not consider the jury deliberation process as sacrosanct as we do today.[11] Leakages of voting results in a modern-day case would be grounds for a mistrial. But people in the Gilded Age seemed to think of it as a game of Capture the Flag between themselves and the bailiff in charge of the jury. Hence, when Sheriff Jefferson Wilhite went to collect Minnie for the announcing of the verdict, a full ten minutes before it was read in court, he told her it was "not guilty." "My God! Is that so?" she responded, and her eyes filled with tears. But those tears never fell, and Elizabeth Wallace seemed much more overcome than her daughter.

When Minnie came into the courtroom, she already knew what the verdict was, and she was smiling and happy. At the official announcement of "not guilty," a loud shout erupted from the crowd, most of whom had thought perhaps it would be a hung jury, necessitating another trial. Out on the street, special edition newspapers were snatched up quickly. Bill Greer spoke with Kansas senator Preston B. Plumb, just in from Washington, who said that, in his travels, most of the people he encountered believed that Minnie would be acquitted, so the verdict would not be a big surprise to the rest of the country.

In the courtroom, Minnie shook hands with the judge and all the jurors, but it was Mrs. Wallace who was delirious with joy. She hugged and kissed Mr. Jay, thanked the jurors, then threw herself down on her knees before Judge Graves: "God bless you, Judge, God bless you! You have saved my child!"

Feighan, a good sport, thanked the jurors and told them they had done a good job even though he didn't agree with their verdict. William Scott declared that he would go home and get some well-deserved sleep.

The jurors revealed some inside information about the deliberations, who voted for what and when. When they first began, two of them nearly ended up in a fistfight because one of them said that "Jesus Christ could not make him believe that Mrs. Walkup was not twenty-five years old." Another juror declared, "It ain't so bad, after all. We got $2 a day and board, a good place to sleep, and plenty to eat and drink." And a third revealed, "If I had voted for that little girl's conviction, her face would haunt me to my dying day."

What was it that convinced the jury of Minnie's innocence? As it turned out, they weren't really all that sure she *was* innocent. But they were angry at the prosecution's depiction of William Jay, one of their most important citizens, as either crazy or a liar. They didn't really believe all those out-of-town witnesses, specifically Dr. Scott and Nat Morton, because they didn't know them. But they did know Jay, and they even took a separate vote as to his arsenic-on-the-knife story: It was evenly divided, 6–6.

In the end, the jurors thought that Walkup had probably ingested arsenic somewhere at some time, but they seem to have used that as an excuse to find Minnie not guilty ("I won't say that we believed the girl innocent, but there was room for doubt"). Their real reasoning appears to have been their reluctance to submit her to the death penalty and wanting to spare the county the expense of another trial or a lengthy appeals process.

Summing Up

Before we leave the trial completely, it might be beneficial to wrap up what is known and what can be reasonably assumed about the death of James Reeves Walkup:

1. *Walkup was not an arsenic eater.*
   a. No arsenic was found in the home.
   b. Not even an arsenic eater would have taken such a large dose (twenty grains).
   c. He would have told Dr. Jacobs he had taken arsenic so he could be saved.
   d. He would have given some to Minnie for her pimples (assuming she had any).
   e. No one could be found who had sold arsenic to him in any form.
   f. There were none of the signs of chronic arsenic use in his organs.
2. *Even if Walkup were an arsenic eater, Minnie did not know it.*
   a. She would have brought this up immediately when arsenic poisoning was suspected.
   b. She would have used this as her "reason for purchase" in the poison register. ("My husband sent me to buy it for him.")
   c. She would have told the investigators this was her purpose in getting arsenic, even if it were not true.
   d. She would have asked him for some if she really had those pimples.ʻ
   e. She never brought up the issue of Walkup's arsenic eating until after the September 5 newspaper article containing the interview with Dr. Scott in Kansas City.
3. *Minnie poisoned James Walkup.*
   a. She bought strychnine on Thursday when her husband was in Topeka, and the very same day he returned home he got strychnine poisoning.

b. There was no other strychnine in the Walkup house except for the empty bottle from the Bates drugstore, where she had purchased the poison.

c. Not even an arsenic eater would take strychnine for any purpose.

d. She bought arsenic on Sunday, and he got arsenic poisoning on Tuesday.

e. She did not poison him on Sunday or Monday, because Reverend Snodgrass was coming on Monday to hear the fake suicide story.

f. She bought arsenic on Thursday, and he got arsenic poisoning that night.

g. Nobody else gave him his food or medicine during this time except Minnie.

h. By Friday noon, when she was kept out of the sickroom, Walkup was already beyond the point of being saved, so nobody else could have been responsible for poisoning him after that time.

i. Nobody else in the household had made any purchases of poison.

4. *Elizabeth Wallace was not involved in a conspiracy to murder James Walkup.*

a. Her shock was so great at his death that she became sick from it.

b. At first, she doubted that the story was true.

c. She wanted her daughter to marry Walkup to avoid the clutches of the lustful and controlling Judge Houston. Murdering James Walkup would not promote this.

d. Her grief over her daughter's situation was so profound that she could not possibly have faked it.

5. *Walkup did not have syphilis.*

a. He had no mercury in his body, which was traditionally used to treat syphilis in the nineteenth century.

b. At autopsy, there were no signs of any of the stages of syphilis.

c. None of the medicines belonging to him were for the cure of syphilis.

6. *Walkup liked sex and alcohol.*

a. Eben Baldwin, a reliable witness, testified to both.

b. Two doctors, probably reliable, testified to both.

c. His affair with Lina Burnett seems to have been common knowledge.

d. It is probable that he did have gonorrhea.

Minnie probably had several motives in poisoning her husband. If she had married him for his money, she would have—in the ordinary course of things—been content to spend that money in the years to come. What could have happened in the space of a month that made her want to end that marriage immediately? Quite possibly she was somewhat overwhelmed by his enormous sexual appetite. Also, if it is true that Walkup had gonorrhea as late as May 1885, two months before their marriage, she might have discovered this and would not have wanted to subject herself to venereal disease.

Also, Minnie may have found that, once they were married, James Walkup was not quite so pliable and eager to please her as he had been in his New Orleans visits. And then her "consolation prize," the unlimited shopping trips, had been cut off and in a most humiliating way. This might have been a lifestyle she was not ready to take on for the duration. This was not what she had signed up for.

Minnie probably made the decision to get rid of her husband around the time of the Newman's incident, when he refused to allow the box to be sent to St. Louis. However, there are two indications that she may have preplanned this: the alleged purchase of strychnine in Cincinnati (where she was actually given quinine) and her buying of extra items at Newman's when she found out they would not appear on her husband's bill until September—if she knew he would not be alive to see that month.

Mr. Jay Gives a Party

William Jay had intended to give Minnie a "blowout," as he called it, replete with brass band, music, and dancing.[12] Instead, he had to content himself with a quickly cobbled get-together that began almost immediately after the verdict was given and Minnie was released from custody. His intentions were good, but the party was ill-advised. Just as the jurors resented prosecution attorneys calling Jay a crazy liar, so, too, did the citizenry resent what they saw as "dancing on Walkup's grave." It was unseemly on the part of William Jay, but even more so on that of the Widow Walkup.

Minnie provided the entertainment at the party, hobnobbing with the guests and playing the piano. Mary Jay teased her about having kissed attorney William Scott and two of the jurors (the latter were elderly men who pleaded for a kiss), and Minnie demurely acknowledged that she had but said, "I didn't do it in the courtroom." Elizabeth Wallace, looking as if a great burden had been taken from her shoulders, proudly read the fifty congratulatory telegrams sent to her daughter. And Minnie insisted that

The photo that Minnie had taken after her acquittal (courtesy of the Lyon County, Kansas, Historical Society)

she would not seek a single penny of James Walkup's fortune, something she had initially said in the courtroom at her acquittal. When a newspaper reporter at the party commented that he probably wouldn't be seeing her again, Minnie was disappointed: "Oh, I hope the newspapers are not going to drop me so soon as all that."

The next day, Minnie and the Jays (father and daughter) drove downtown while Minnie, dressed up in a "blue serge dress with scarlet trimmings and a white veil over her small round hat" (no widow's weeds for her), called on some of the people who had remained loyal to her and had her portrait taken at Delia Rich's studio. She ordered two dozen for herself and told Delia she could make copies available for anyone who wanted them. When people stared at her, she stared right back.

None of this sat well with the people of Emporia or, for that matter, the state of Kansas. They had thought Minnie's retirement from public life, not this tasteless, brazen display, would be more proper. She was accused of being "on a picnic" since the trial, which no "modest, sensitive woman" would have done: "A great deal has been said about her nerve, but to anyone who has studied her character, another name suggests itself."

Minnie's post-trial behavior even led people to believe that she was, in fact, guilty of murdering her husband. An editorial in the *Kansas City Times* presented a lose-lose proposition: either she was "entirely deficient in moral perception and womanly delicacy" or she was guilty.

A particularly vicious (but not inaccurate) letter to the editor in the *Emporia Daily News* (signed only "Justitia") said that most people are good and assume others are likewise, so they are easily duped by those who are not. Minnie, declared the writer, hid "a vicious, relentless, and cruel disposition behind a pretty face, large lustrous eyes and a countenance always wearing a serene look and a pleasant smile." She never seemed to get angry but had a disposition of equanimity and a childlike purity on the surface. Underneath, however, she was vindictive. If Minnie had been an ugly old woman, people would not have been so quick to lionize her.

There were hints of a wrongful death civil suit (probably being pondered by Mattie Hood and Libbie Walkup), in which a jury would not have to consider the death penalty and the standard of proof was much lower than that in a criminal trial. But nothing ever came of this.

Within a few days of the verdict, one of the jurors, forty-three-year-old Michael Myers, was dining at the home of some relatives when he suddenly collapsed and died of a heart attack. He had voted for acquittal right from the start, and it was said that the stress of the trial ultimately killed him.[13]

All too soon, from William Jay's point of view, Minnie and her mother packed up their belongings and departed on the AT&SF train for Kansas City, from whence they would proceed to New Orleans. And so Emporia would eventually return to what Bill Greer called "its wonted state of stagnation after a two months' sensation that has eclipsed all others in the known world."

Chapter 10

Intermission

⌣⟶

Sin has many tools, but a lie is the handle which fits them all.
—Oliver Wendell Holmes (1858)

Goodbye, Emporia. Hello, New Orleans

Minnie's train had barely arrived in Kansas City when she declared that not only did she intend to get as much of her late husband's estate as she could, but William Jay was already processing the documents necessary for that. So, even as she was telling Emporians she wouldn't touch a penny of the Walkup fortune, she was taking steps to make sure she *would* get it.

While she was in Kansas City, the *Times,* never a big Minnie fan, kept tabs on her and criticized her craving for attention. Naturally, crowds gathered wherever she went, but instead of retiring modestly from their view, she did everything she could to make sure they would be able to see her. At the Union Depot Hotel, she dined in a large restaurant and did not hide her pleasure at the attention she was getting. She shopped in stores, rode on the cable cars, and when it was time to get on the train to New Orleans, she chose a seat next to an open window looking out on the staring masses.[1]

In the meantime, Minnie's brother-in-law, Edward Findlay, reached New Orleans, having left Emporia while Minnie and her mother were reveling at the Jays'. He had been her ardent supporter from the begin-

ning, hastening to Kansas right after Walkup died, even thou
was in the late stages of pregnancy, so it's hard to know how
information is true and how much is "puffing."

Findlay claimed that right after the trial the defense was suc
find a whole lot of druggists (all out of town) who had sold ars
Walkup. Moreover, he said that Judge Graves had been in sympathy with
Minnie and declared after the trial that there would have been no way to
convict her on the evidence the state had. Now, while it is probable (judg-
ing from his instructions to the jury) that Judge Graves was sympathetic
to Minnie, it is unlikely that he would have commented on the evidence
in this way, as it was actually quite strongly circumstantial.[2]

Harry Hood had supposedly assured William Jay early on that he would
not hire extra lawyers for the prosecution, but this doesn't ring true: Why
would Hood bring this up at all? Findlay said that when Hood got more
lawyers in spite of his promise, Jay was thoroughly vexed. He wrote to
Harry's father, Major Hood, and declared that he, Jay, had "unsheathed
his sword and thrown away the scabbard" and that this meant war. Now,
that *does* sound like Jay!

What probably really happened is that Jay immediately hired William Scott to defend Minnie. Clinton Sterry, Harry Hood's best friend,
was already on the scene and doing some investigation and had assured
Harry—even before he and Mattie returned to Emporia—that he would not
rest until the poisoner was convicted. So Jay might have assumed that this
meant Harry was going to hire extra help for County Attorney Feighan. Jay
then got Thomas Fenlon, Hood responded with Isaac Lambert, and Jay
evened it up with Dodds. (Minnie's father, James Wallace, hired Edward
Ward, through Mrs. Augustus Wilson, but Ward does not seem to have
had anything to do with the defense, as his name is never mentioned after
the hiring, nor does he appear in any of the testimony.)

When Minnie finally arrived in New Orleans, she gave an interview to a
Daily Picayune reporter that she obviously (and naïvely) never intended to
leave the state of Louisiana, as the article was filled with scenes of fantasy
that never existed outside her own mind.[3]

The reporter (not Bill Greer) thought she was "a person of a peculiar
type," beautiful, but "not an ideal beauty," seemingly voluptuous, yet not
that, and with "soft, dreamy eyes." She had large hands and long fingers,
a protruding lower lip, good teeth, and black hair. Here is his typically
Victorian description of her: "There is a tint of bronze richness in the sunny

airness of the face, deepening to crimson in the cheeks and darkening into a setting for large gray eyes covered with heavy eyelids and fringed with heavy lashes of jet black which make the eyes look darker than they are. The face is full and needs to be because all its features are large."

Minnie seems to have been a compulsive liar, even telling untruths that didn't really gain her anything. For example, she told the *Picayune* reporter that she first found out she was suspected of poisoning her husband when Mary Moss told her, two days before he died. But that would have been Thursday, and nobody suspected poison for sure until Friday, when Dwight Bill and the other men told her and forbade her to give Walkup his medicine. How would it benefit her to say the information came to her on Thursday from Mary Moss instead of on Friday from Dwight Bill? This is merely a gratuitous lie.

Further, Minnie said she went to her husband, told him of the suspicions against her, and he told her not to worry about it. Yet, from noon on Friday there was always someone else in Walkup's room when Minnie was there, and we know the conversations that occurred at that time. He never told her not to worry and, in fact, said the evidence against her was strong.

Minnie said the prosecution was bitter because their fees were contingent on a guilty verdict (which was highly doubtful, especially since Feighan received a regular salary and the others were paid by Harry Hood), so they started those false stories about her staying in Walkup's room with the body parts. (It was the neighbors and the reporters who had witnessed this.) In the biggest fantasy of all, Minnie claimed that one of the prosecuting attorneys could not bring himself to put her through a stiff cross-examination, so he passed the duty on to a colleague and advised him to get half-drunk to prepare for the ordeal! Presumably, that "half-drunk" individual would have been Sterry, who was not only perfectly sober but more than capable of attacking her on cross-examination.

After Dr. Jacobs testified for the prosecution, Minnie told the reporter, he changed his mind and believed her innocent. (In truth, Dr. Jacobs never stopped thinking her guilty.) He and his wife then supposedly sent a bouquet of flowers with a note in which he declared his belief (a note, by the way, she didn't share with the reporter). And, during deliberations, an elderly juror—who was so impassioned about Minnie's innocence that he actually wept when the prosecution attacked her at trial—cold-cocked a fellow juror who voted for conviction. Another was in debt to Major Hood and had been planted on the jury by the prosecution—yet even *he* voted to acquit. (She was attempting to make them think that her innocence triumphed even over a setup.)

Minnie said that George Dodds was very popular, especially with the women, but Judge Houston had not made a good impression. (This was her revenge for his abandoning her without providing any money for her defense.) In the opinion of her friends in Emporia, Houston was "too French and polished," whereas William Scott wanted a guy who could "get up and swear like a good fellow when it was needed." Judge Houston gave her sympathy, but Minnie's friends informed him that sympathy also meant he should put his hands in his pockets and part with some money. Houston said he had none to give, so he went back to his vacation at Long Branch, "to resume some pleasant acquaintances he had there," she concluded dismissively.

Also, Minnie showed the reporter some of the messages she had received from admirers around the country. There was one from "the ladies of the Southern Hotel" in St. Louis (which actually sounds as if they could have been prostitutes). She had received many offers to go on the stage and "Bob" (nobody ever referred to him as Bob) Ingersoll's manager wanted to represent her. Adam Forepaugh would make her the new "$10,000 Beauty," but all of this was supposedly not to her taste.[4] Minnie declared she would be lying low and staying in New Orleans with her family. (Years later, Minnie would tell a reporter in Chicago that James Walkup had sent her to get arsenic for him and instructed her to tell the druggist that it was for her complexion, but in November of 1885 she had not thought up that lie yet.)[5]

Naturally, this article wasted no time in making its way to Emporia, where the *Daily News* retaliated with great sarcasm because the whole affair made the city look bad. It asked which prosecution counsel had to get drunk to question her. As for the old juror who knocked the other one down, "Who was this Adonis? And where was the sheriff during this terrible fracas?" Possibly there was a connection between this incident and the death of the juror. As for Minnie's going on the stage: "Is there a chance of her being mixed up with the fat girl and the skeleton?"[6]

The *Barber County (Kansas) Union* printed a bitter denunciation of Minnie and couldn't resist a dig at William Jay: "We notice by the *New York Clipper* that Minnie Walkup contemplates doing the dime museums. As to what figure she will represent in that category of living wonders and freaks of nature we cannot say, unless it would be in the character of the Lightning Husband Exterminator; or the Handsome Face Catches the Jay."[7]

Emporians probably hoped they would never again hear of Minnie Wallace Walkup. But they couldn't have been more wrong.

William Pitt Kellogg

Shortly after Minnie's return to New Orleans, her sister, Dora, and the Findlay family moved to New Mexico and Minnie went to visit them. At the same time, she embarked on a tour of the Southwest with former Louisiana governor and then-current U.S. senator William Pitt Kellogg, a carpetbagger from the North. On trains and in hotels, they stayed in the same room or the same Pullman car. Sometimes Minnie registered herself as "Mrs. M. A. Wallace of Chicago" but her disguise was soon penetrated, and newspapers around the country began publishing accounts of their travels. One paper claimed they were passing themselves off as husband and wife.[8]

Minnie said that she and Kellogg were accompanied by his sister, but it was obvious to observers that he was acting like a "decidedly 'gone' lover." Nobody but Minnie ever mentioned the presence of a sister.

William Pitt Kellogg, like Judge Houston and James Walkup, was older than Minnie (by thirty-nine years) and very rich. He was also very married. Kellogg had served as governor of Louisiana from 1873 to 1877, but it was a

William Pitt Kellogg (photo courtesy of the Library of Congress, LC-DIG-cwpbh-03666)

turbulent tenure that included a challenge to his government's legitimacy and an attempt at impeachment for misappropriation of state funds.

Minnie and Kellogg went to Texas, New Mexico, Illinois, and the District of Columbia together. They may have gone to Europe as well. It was probably due to Kellogg's influence that Minnie later decided to settle in Chicago, as he had practiced law in Peoria and had commanded an Illinois cavalry brigade in the Civil War. He was also willing to finance her move there.

The Gutekunst-Wilhite Affair

In December 1885, as Minnie's application for James Walkup's estate was proceeding, two Emporia teenagers came forward with a scandalous tale. Because Minnie was still, four months after her marriage to Walkup, hinting that she might be "enceinte" to gain an extra portion of her late husband's estate, the two young men claimed that they had had sex with her while she was in jail. This would cast a cloud on the legitimacy of any heir. The teenagers were put under oath for a deposition and made fully aware of the dangers of perjury.[9]

Oscar Milton ("Mit") Wilhite, nineteen-year-old son of the sheriff, and Edward Gutekunst, a seventeen-year-old janitor (and former inmate) at the Emporia jail, testified that Minnie had invited them into her cell and seduced them. This had happened more than once for each boy. Gutekunst's story was that Minnie had asked him to carry some trunks to her cell and, on occasion, to do other errands for her. He once brought her a dress and put it on her bed while she was in a partial state of undress, as she was at other times when she invited him into her cell. Eventually, at her instigation, he had sex with her a few times.

Prior to Mit Wilhite's sexual encounters with Minnie, she had given him "some dirty talk" and suggestive behavior, such as exposing herself to him. The two times he had sex with her were Saturday and Sunday nights, October 3 and 4.

Minnie's response was that Ed Gutekunst had sent her a note, signed "Ed the Fool," and told her to send $250 for him to keep quiet about an unspecified event. She said she had no idea what it was about and gave it to William Jay, who went to the sheriff and demanded an explanation. The insurance company for the AOUW, with which James Walkup had a policy, was in the process of trying to determine which portion of the

Family of Emporia, Kansas's Sheriff Jefferson Wilhite (Oscar "Mit" Wilhite is standing upper right), taken about 1885 (photo courtesy of Robert Lostutter)

$2,000 belonged to each beneficiary (Minnie and the three Walkup children). And, although Minnie would now claim she had never said she was definitely pregnant, and still didn't know this for sure, she had apparently stated quite clearly to the insurance company that she was—hence, the legal confusion as to the portions of the payoff.

Needless to say, this whole saga caused a great deal of turmoil and anguish in Emporia, which now found itself once again in the limelight because of Minnie Walkup. Minnie said she was surprised that Mit Wilhite would be involved in such a lie, but Ed Gutekunst was an illiterate hoodlum who was beneath her notice. Were these allegations true? While it is tempting to want to believe every piece of negative press about Minnie Walkup, the charges do seem preposterous—not necessarily because she was above such behavior (Harry Hood found sources in New Orleans who labeled her a "public woman") but because sexual dalliance with two working-class teenagers would not fit her modus operandi. What would she have to gain? At the same time, she stood to lose quite a bit if these two decided to talk before or during her trial.

Did someone put the boys up to this? Minnie, not surprisingly, claimed that Libbie and the Hoods had done so. But it is more likely that Wilhite and Gutekunst were trying to get some money out of her, and she called their bluff, after which they invented the sexual encounters. Here's another clue that they were lying: In his deposition, Gutekunst, when asked whether he had had sex with Minnie, answered, "I believe I did." John Reid, the interrogation expert, calls this an "estimation phrase" because it gives an estimation rather than a definite answer. But when coupled with something that the subject should know for sure, it signals deception. Certainly, Gutekunst would know definitely whether or not he had sex with Minnie, so with "I believe," he was likely not being truthful.[10]

But, under the "fool me once/fool me twice" principle, Emporians would cut Minnie no slack this time. The *Daily Republican,* claiming the two boys had no reason to lie about the encounters, declared, "It leaves the widow and those who sympathized with her during the trial in an unenviable position." The title to a letter to the editor of the *Daily News* said it all: "Minnie Again." The writer, "Country Lass," bemoaned how so many of the ladies were taken in "by her childish face and her luminous eyes, her pouting lips and pearly teeth that made her the envy of her own sex." She felt sorry for "that poor old man, her guardian" and hoped he did not see this new filth.[11]

Eventually, Wilhite and Gutekunst recanted their testimony, never revealing their motivation for it.

Minnie, the World Traveler

By 1890, Minnie was back in New Orleans, living with her mother in the house at 222 Canal Street. In the fall of that year, she went down to the New Orleans Vital Statistics office and registered the births of her two nephews and her niece, which had not been done when they were born, for some unknown reason. Since this would normally have been the province of their father, Edward Findlay, he was either dead by that time (as he certainly was by 1900) or the family was still living in New Mexico. Why the children needed birth certificates in 1890 is unclear.[12]

Apparently, Minnie's time in New Orleans after the trial was filled with "many startling incidents," but not sufficiently outrageous to have made the newspapers.[13] Around 1891, Minnie took her mother to Europe. She had received $250,000 from the Walkup estate, plus her husband's monthly

Civil War pension. Despite her disparaging statements about the stage, she made some attempts to get bookings but was turned down each time.[14]

Minnie spent a lot of her money in New York City as "the center of a brilliant and wealthy, if somewhat profligate, crowd." She was a woman of leisure there and abroad, "if pursuing pleasure at a furious pace can thus be called."[15]

Minnie and Elizabeth Wallace eventually moved to Chicago, just in time for the 1893 World's Columbian Exposition. Dora, now a widow, moved to New York City with her remaining children, Edwin and Minnie Jay Findlay (Milton, who had gone to Emporia and Cincinnati that fateful July with his aunt and his grandmother, had died by then).[16] Willie Willis, Minnie's cousin, died at 222 Canal Street a year and a half after the end of the Walkup trial, on March 24, 1887, of an inflammatory bowel.[17]

A year after the trial, Libbie Walkup married John Martin, the son of a U.S. senator from Kansas and himself later mayor of Emporia. When reports of the engagement were published, the *Arkansas City Republican,* erroneously thinking that Martin was marrying Minnie, commented, "It is hard to beat a Kansas man for bravery and pure sand."[18] In what must be considered a blessing, in light of what was to become of his protégée hereafter, William Jay passed away in 1892.

And, exactly eight days short of the thirteenth anniversary of the death of James Walkup, a newly divorced woman committed suicide by poisoning herself in the very same bedroom in which Walkup had died.[19]

Part Three

Chicago, 1893–1902

Chapter 11

The Levee

⌒

What is the chief end of man?—to get rich. In what way?—dishonestly if we can, honestly if we must.

—Mark Twain (1871)

By 1893, with her pleasure-seeking lifestyle, Minnie had depleted the estate she received from James Walkup. It was time to find another source of money, and her longtime desire to relocate to Chicago was bolstered by a potentially profitable event: the 1893 World's Columbian Exposition. People would be coming from all over to view the architectural wonders, taste exotic foods, marvel at cultural delights, and ride that new sensation, the Ferris Wheel.

Unlike the New Orleans Cotton Exposition in 1884–85, with its relatively paltry attendance, 27.5 million fairgoers would take in the Columbian Exposition over its six-month stand. It was estimated that 25 percent of the American population in 1893 visited the fair, which ultimately netted a profit of $1 million for its investors, after all expenses were paid. Perhaps Minnie thought she could cash in on this in some way.[1]

Minnie and Elizabeth Wallace moved into a flat at 1401 Michigan Avenue, which was not, strictly speaking, within the bounds of the Levee area but was close enough for her to participate in its lifestyle.[2]

The Levee, bordered by Eighteenth Street on the north, Twenty-second Street on the south, State Street on the east, and Armour Avenue (now

Federal Street) on the west, was located on the South Side of Chicago and arose in direct anticipation of the baser needs of the men who would be attending the fair. Concentrated in this vice district were saloons, "sporting clubs," restaurants, and brothels. In the heart of it were "'dollar a girl' joints, where the women provided services on a volume basis." Sadly, many of these girls had been kidnapped or lured there by the false promises of con men whose job was to furnish the Levee establishments with women.[3]

In 1894, a British journalist named William Stead published an exposé of what was euphemistically (and also sarcastically) termed Chicago's "underground economy." *If Christ Came to Chicago* included a map that identified all the saloons and brothels in the Levee area, which—despite the book's religious bent—may have been largely responsible for its astronomic sales (70,000 copies on the day it was released).[4]

As the years went on, the Levee would be responsible for the rise of the Chicago mob and men like Al Capone and Johnny Torrio. In Minnie's day, it was under the political protection of two crooked aldermen, "Bath House John" Coughlin and Michael "Hinky Dink" Kenna, colorful figures in Chicago's political scene and the "Lords of the Levee." In 1910, a vice commission revealed that the Levee took in a staggering $60 million each year and housed "1,000 brothels, 1,800 pimps and madames, and at least 4,000 prostitutes."[5]

The most notorious establishment in the notorious Levee at the turn of the century was a restaurant/saloon/brothel, Frank Wing's, located at Twenty-second and State Streets. People went there to have a good time and also lose a lot of their money. One hapless business visitor ended up in Frank Wing's and never got to where he was supposed to go. He spent $150 to $200 a day (of his employer's money) buying drinks and meals for everyone, and when he tried to leave, the establishment's denizens wouldn't let him. One woman even tore off all his coat buttons to get him to stay. The businessman was there an entire week but, oddly, would leave at times, then listen to the blandishments of Wing's patrons who beseeched him to come back. He even left to hire a lawyer to file a writ of habeas corpus so he could be freed from the saloon and its customers![6]

Frank Wing's, which we will have occasion to encounter again later, served liquor all night long, even after a law was passed forbidding saloons to do so after midnight. Although he was arrested for it, Wing continued to defy the ordinance, thereby demonstrating how financially advantageous it was for him to do so.[7]

Josephine Moffitt, date unknown. She routinely shaved years off her age, but her hands give her away. (photo courtesy of the Library of Congress, LC-DIG-ggbain-00792)

At her new residence at 1401 Michigan Avenue (today the site of the famous Firehouse Restaurant), Minnie met two women: Josephine Moffitt and Gladys Forbes, both well-known courtesans.[8] Josephine lived in the same building, and it is probable that she and Minnie were already friends. Born in New Orleans on January 10, 1869, just four days before Minnie, she attended the same convent school, the Ursuline Academy, at the same time.

Moffitt was not Josephine's real name. She was the fourth of eight children born to Josephine Carrel Carleton, a Mississippi-born "mulatto," and Adrien Guillemet (pronounced Gil-MET), a native of Bordeaux, France, who came to the United States in 1860 and settled in New Orleans. It was a common-law union, and Adrien had another, legitimate family, although he continued to support Josephine Carleton and their children until his death. As the child of a "mulatto," Josephine also bore this as her official racial designation, although she routinely passed for white and, once she left New Orleans, never acknowledged that she was a person of color.[9]

Around the time of her father's 1884 death from smallpox, Josephine caught the eye of an older, married man, J. Westley Moffitt, who began buying her expensive clothes. Eventually, he abandoned his wife and took Josephine to live with him in Hot Springs, Arkansas. Mrs. Moffitt followed them, begging Josephine to leave her husband alone, to no avail.[10]

Eventually, Moffitt tired of Josephine as well and in 1893 left her to seek employment in some fair-related activity in Chicago. Josephine followed him there, hunting him down at the Maine Hotel and—as his wife had done years earlier—pleaded with him not to abandon her. She simply showed up in his room one day and whiled away the time as she waited for him to come home from work by drinking several bottles of beer and leaving them strewn around the room. But Moffitt was through with Josephine Guillemet and was unmoved by her pleas.

Around this time, Josephine began using the surname "Moffitt," possibly to remind her former lover of his obligations to her but more likely to give herself an air of respectability as "Mrs. Moffitt." Although J. Westley Moffitt was out of her life, to account for his absence she told everyone— even the census taker—that her "husband" was a traveling salesman.

On her own in Chicago, Josephine made the acquaintance of Gladys Forbes, who owned the Monroe Restaurant and was a procuress of women for upper-class gentlemen. They shared flats off and on over the next several years, Gladys sometimes managing to snag a rich husband and Josephine sometimes rooming with another courtesan. Their "business" could not really be called a brothel, as the women they provided did not live with them. Instead, it was more of a men's club run by women, a much higher-class operation than the usual Levee dives. Josephine and Gladys held parties with lots of music, dancing, food, liquor, and pornographic pictures and movies. Sometimes a gentleman would pair off with one of the invited ladies and take her to a bedroom.

Neighbors frequently complained about the noise at these establishments, which included the sound of fancy automobiles coming and going at all hours of the night. As tuxedoed, drunken rich men would spill out into the streets after a night of revelry, they were often raucous.[11]

One visitor, Homer Hitt, was a widower whose wife had left him $65,000 in trust for their infant son. He had moved into Chicago's Auditorium Hotel, leaving his son in the care of his deceased wife's parents in western Illinois. His wife was hardly cold in the ground before he began frequenting Levee establishments and encountered Gladys Forbes. Soon, he and Gladys were

Gladys Forbes (center) in 1915 (DN-0064440, *Chicago Daily News* negatives collection, Chicago Historical Society)

married and living the high life on the $65,000, floating between Chicago and New York City and going through $30,000 (over three-quarters of a million dollars today) before Hitt was removed as executor and trustee of his wife's estate. Gladys divorced him not long after that.[12]

This, then, was the lifestyle that Minnie soon shared. Throughout her stay in Chicago, she never lived more than a few blocks away from Josephine Moffitt or Gladys Forbes.[13] It is not clear, however, that she was also a procuress, as she seems to have preferred to have the gentlemen come to her home and make her the center of their attention, but she was definitely a member of the city's demimonde. Now twenty-four, she hid her Kansas past by changing her name to Mrs. Mabel (sometimes Minnie) Estelle Wallace. She never used the name Walkup.[14]

On November 12, 1895, Elizabeth Wallace died of pneumonia, which she had contracted three weeks previously. She was sixty-six. Minnie purchased two plots in Forest Home Cemetery, one for Mrs. Wallace and—presumably— one for herself. She erected no stone to mark the spot or memorialize her mother.[15]

William Pitt Kellogg continued to be an ardent admirer and visited Minnie frequently. Although he was no longer a senator, he still lived in Washington, D.C. After Mrs. Wallace died, Kellogg bought Minnie a home of her own, a large yellow brick house at 3421 Indiana Avenue, and furnished it with expensive items.[16] She hired a butler, a young man named Joe Keller, and a cleaning lady, Mrs. Sena Torrey, a cousin of her mother's.

But, notwithstanding the financial help from Kellogg, Minnie had money troubles. She had run up bills for dresses ($600 worth) and other items in New Orleans and Chicago and now was being pressed for payment. She consulted a young attorney, Dethlef C. Hansen, about the statute of limitations on these debts: How much time had to pass before she would no longer be obligated to repay them?[17] She had selected Hansen because he was something of a con artist whose specialty was representing young women trying to blackmail older (and usually married) men because of sexual indiscretions. And he was a friend of Josephine Moffitt and Gladys Forbes.

Dethlef C. Hansen was born in 1871, two years after Minnie, and graduated high in the Chicago College of Law's Class of 1890 (today the Chicago-

Dethlef C. Hansen (sketch from the *Chicago Tribune*)

Kent College of Law, part of the Illinois Institute of Technology).[18] He seems to have had a promising career as a legal orator, but chose instead to affiliate himself with blackmailers and confidence men. He lived in Tacoma, Washington, for a few years, then moved back to Chicago, all the while practicing law and doing everything he could to avoid stepping into a courtroom.[19]

Hansen must have had political aspirations in his earlier years. While in Tacoma, he joined a group called the Democracy of the State of Washington and in March 1891 wrote to Grover Cleveland (who was at that time between presidencies) to ask if he would join them to celebrate Thomas Jefferson's birthday that April. Cleveland wrote a gracious reply in which he regretfully declined and took the opportunity to talk about the relevance of Jefferson to the current day.[20]

Dethlef Hansen had a more than passing acquaintance with a famous English blackmailer and flimflam man named Robert Davey (calling himself "Dr." Davey or "Sir" Robert Davey), who was marginally connected with one of Chicago's most sensational crimes: the 1897 murder of a woman by her sausage-maker husband, Adolph Luetgert (there was a strong rumor going around that Luetgert had actually ground up his wife in the sausage machine, but this was just urban legend). Davey was not connected with the murder but had bilked the prosperous Luetgert in a scam. It is not outside the realm of possibility, given Hansen's later career, that he and Davey had joined forces at some point to take advantage of some rich sucker.[21]

Then, around 1895, and in the nick of time, from Minnie's vantage point, a man of considerable wealth got caught in her web: John Berdan Ketcham, scion of a Toledo, Ohio, banking family. Thereafter, his life would never be the same.

Chapter 12

The Death of a Club Man

Where there is beauty, one finds death.

—Charles Baudelaire (1857)

John Berdan Ketcham, born in 1846, was the second of the four children of Valentine Hicks Ketcham and Rachel Berdan, the wealthiest people in Toledo, Ohio. Valentine was the founder and first president of the First National Bank of Toledo, and Rachel's father had been the first mayor of Toledo. Their three sons eventually became bankers themselves, and their daughter married the man who succeeded her father as president of the First National Bank.[1]

When V. H. Ketcham died in 1887, he left each of his children the sum of $500,000. John invested his money wisely, in stocks, bonds, and real estate, and went on to start a private bank of his own, which later became the Ketcham National Bank. He bought land and real estate parcels throughout Toledo, Chicago, Indiana, and elsewhere.

When John Ketcham's first wife, Mary Granger, died, he married socialite Nettie Poe (the "Belle of Toledo") on October 22, 1885, just as the Walkup trial was beginning in Emporia, Kansas. Nettie, a cousin of the famous author Edgar Allan Poe, was also from a banking family: Her father, Isaac, was the director of the Toledo Savings and Trust.[2]

Nettie and John were "leaders of the gay social life" in Toledo, which meant they gave and attended a lot of parties. John loved horses, as did

John Berdan Ketcham
(sketch from the *Chicago
Daily Tribune*)

Nettie, and so they had several of them with all kinds of carriages, from tiny
dog carts to large broughams. And they drank, John especially. Although
he maintained his investments, at a relatively young age he retired from
the business world to travel, tend to his horses, and party.

In 1892, John and Nettie Ketcham moved to Chicago's luxurious Lexington Hotel. John was what was known as a "club man" and belonged
to several of them: the Calumet, the Chicago, and the Chicago Athletic.
These all-male clubs had their heyday in the Gilded Age and were refuges
for wealthy members to escape the confines and responsibilities of family
and business. There, a man could take his meals, meet with his fellow rich
men, and play chess or backgammon. Some clubs could even accommodate
an overnight stay. The club man

was a social man, known and knowing in a totally socialized world.
. . . [H]e entered a zone of belongingness scarcely imaginable by the
hustling anonyms in the mean streets outside. Wherever he chose to
go—to the Member's Table to eat, to the paneled bar for a drink or
a game of backgammon, to the library for a snooze, or to the sweet-
smelling rest room for relief—the Club Man moved along paths of
affiliation and affinity so sure, so deeply traced, he might have been

a member of an ancient tribe following the song-lines of a collective destiny. To be social as the Club Man was social was to be cradled in a nexus of shared memories, comfortable expectations and instant, familiar (but not too familiar) recognitions.[3]

In Chicago, John's drinking increased. He began squiring around various young women, ignoring his wife, hanging out at race tracks, and—maybe the most egregious act of all—depleting his once considerable estate.[4] Leaving Nettie at the Lexington Hotel, John moved into the Auditorium Annex, where he acquired a new friend and drinking pal, Robert "Pony Bob" Haslam, whose once proud accomplishments were now reduced to his lowly position as greeter or doorman.[5]

"Pony Bob" had been a rider with the Pony Express, whose prominence in our national lore belies the fact that it only existed for eighteen months in 1860 and 1861. Haslam could change horses in twenty seconds and was a fearless rider. During the Paiute Indian uprising in Nevada, his replacement refused to carry the mail onward because of his fear of Indians, so Pony Bob did it for him. At another station, he found that the Paiutes had killed the stationmaster and everyone else had run off. There was no one else to continue the mail run except Haslam. By the time he got back to his original station, he had ridden 380 miles, the longest round trip in Pony Express history. He had also ridden himself into Wild West legend.[6]

From then on, Pony Bob was a true western hero and his tale of derring-do was recounted as an example of courage, loyalty, and responsibility. It was the stuff of dime novels, yet it was real. After that, he did some scouting for the army and appeared in Buffalo Bill's Wild West Show. Now in his fifties, however, Bob Haslam had become an impoverished drinker for whom someone, out of respect for his storied past, had arranged to get the job at the Auditorium.

In 1895, Minnie was trolling for wealthy men in the Auditorium Hotel when she hooked exactly the fish she was looking for. What made John Ketcham perfect, besides his wealth (which went without saying), was his vulnerability because of his drinking and his weakness when it came to female beauty. A drunken man could always be manipulated, and even Ketcham's friends noticed that this astute businessman was losing his ability to manage his finances.[7]

Ketcham began accompanying Minnie to the race track, to restaurants, and to the theater. And she reciprocated by having him come to her home on Indiana Avenue. By then, Nettie Poe Ketcham had had enough of her husband's errant ways and decided to divorce him. But first, in that era before the no-fault divorce, she would need proof.

Nettie hired the Thiel Detective Agency to follow her husband around. He led them to the Washington Park Race Track, to Chapin & Gore's wholesale liquor outlet, and—of course—to Minnie's home. Two of the operatives were a male-female team who showed up at Ketcham's office in the Monadnock Building every day at the same time, which irked him. He hired William Clarke to stand outside his office door every day to intercept them and try to find out who they were and what they wanted. Clarke was unsuccessful in discovering their names or purpose, but his presence discouraged their return visits. For this service, Ketcham promised Clarke $100 and a new suit.

But Nettie eventually got the proof that she needed of his dissipation and adultery, but she was a clever woman. Instead of instituting divorce proceedings, she asked the court to appoint a conservator over her husband's estate, as he was going through it at a substantial pace and was not competent to handle his financial affairs. If she had succeeded, he would no longer have control of his money, which would mean the end of the good times. As the price of Nettie's dropping the conservatorship, Ketcham had to agree not to contest the divorce. In addition, he had to give her some of the Toledo real estate (valued at $100,000) and Diamond Match stock (worth $50,000).

To establish the grounds for the divorce, Nettie's lawyers produced witnesses regarding her husband's drunkenness and debauchery. That day in court she was accompanied by her maid and her father, who had come all the way from Toledo to stand by his daughter. John didn't show up at all, in fulfillment of his part of the agreement.

In January 1897, John Ketcham—almost certainly at her insistence—moved into Minnie's home. He told nobody except Pony Bob Haslam where he was going and, in fact, continued to get his mail at the Auditorium, where he had also left his luggage. Nor did he ever give up his apartment there. These were all indications that he intended to get back there at some point.[8]

However, from the moment Ketcham entered the yellow brick house at 3421 Indiana Avenue, he was a virtual prisoner. Whenever anyone came to the door to ask for him, they were told—by Joe Keller or by Minnie herself—that he was not there. But he *was* there. Unbeknownst to Minnie, John

Minnie in 1897
(sketch from the *Chicago Daily Tribune*)

Ketcham's mother and siblings back in Toledo, alarmed at his disappearance from public life (he wasn't going to his clubs, he wasn't contacting his friends, he wasn't attending to his affairs), had taken up where Nettie left off and had private detectives watching the house. John might occasionally go out riding in a carriage, always accompanied by Minnie, but he rarely went elsewhere.[9]

In August, Minnie went to Dethlef Hansen and asked him how she could get Ketcham's bonds out of his safety deposit box at the bank. Hansen told her she would have to get him to sign an order to that effect and give her the password. Around that same time, Minnie asked Hansen if he could find out how rich he was, so she could see if it would be worth her while to marry him. The "old fool" was sick, and she didn't know how long he would live, but she obviously didn't want to commit herself to a long-term marriage without sufficient remuneration, particularly if he was going to be an invalid.[10]

August 1897 was a busy month for Minnie. She rented a flat down the street at 2238 Indiana Avenue, close to where Josephine Moffitt was living, for $16 a month, telling the landlord it was for her sister, a Mrs. Kellard or Kelly from Minneapolis. She brought some of the furniture from 3421 to the little flat, and the other residents watched the proceedings unabashedly, as the elegance of the new tenant was something entirely unfamiliar. Thirteen-year-old Arthur Reutlinger, who also lived in the building, was so overwhelmed by Minnie's beauty and her pretty dresses that he was sure she was French.[11]

Minnie spent many evenings at 2238, but to the disappointment of the other tenants, the curtains on her windows were always drawn. Her neighbors did notice, however, that she never had any female visitors, but only male ones. Unlike Josephine's and Gladys's visitors, Minnie's were quiet and well-mannered.

What went on at these get-togethers? There may have been pornographic pictures and films. We know there was liquor because Minnie later reneged on the bill (see chapter 13, pages 53–54). And we know there was food because Joe Keller was charged with bringing sandwiches. If there were no women visitors, then Minnie was not providing sexual partners for her guests, nor was it likely that she was taking part in orgies as the only female. Given Minnie's personality and incredible vanity, her "at-homes" were probably more in the nature of salons where she would hold court and accept the adoration of her worshipful subjects.

As Minnie got settled into her new life, John Ketcham was becoming more and more an invalid. For the first few months at 3421, he could not stand on his own and had to be wheeled around the house. From about September, however, he was bedridden. Although, certainly, Ketcham was suffering from cirrhosis of the liver, his infirmity nonetheless came on suddenly: One month he was running about town with his lady friends, drinking with Pony Bob, eating at one of his clubs, and spending part of every day in his Monadnock Building office, and the next he was in a wheelchair, his health on a downward slide.

What was Minnie's part in this? For one thing, she was keeping Ketcham—or allowing him to be—in an almost constant state of intoxication. He was going through a case of claret every ten days, plus other liquor as well.[12] Her wine cellar was stocked with champagne. She even declared later that it was necessary to give him alcohol just to keep him alive, and Sena Torrey frequently saw him with small bottles of liquor squirreled away in his pockets.[13] It is also possible that Minnie was drugging him.

On September 15, Minnie went back to Dethlef Hansen. She didn't think Ketcham would live much longer, and she wanted to hurry up and marry him, but she was afraid that a Chicago wedding would cause the newspapers to dig up the Emporia case. Hansen told her to go to a Milwaukee hotel under a false name, then find a preacher there. Well, this is what Hansen *said* he told her, but the odds are great that he meant not just any old preacher, but specifically "the marrying preacher."

Wesley A. Hunsberger was known as "the marrying parson of Milwaukee."[14] If there had been a *Guinness Book of World Records* then, he would have won the "Most Couples Married" category, hands down. Couples swarmed to him because he had his system so mechanized that he would have been the envy of any modern Las Vegas Chapel o' Love, and the wait in Chicago for a marriage license was very long. In August 1895 Hunsberger married eighty-seven couples, and in 1897, the number was a thousand—most of whom were from Chicago. The "suggested contribution" from the groom was anywhere from $5 to $50, with most people selecting the former (still a lot in the 1890s—equivalent to $134 today).

The *Chicago Daily Tribune* had run a lengthy article on Reverend Hunsberger in 1895, when it sent two undercover reporters, a man and a woman, to pretend they were waiting for friends to show up and get married. (They took their bicycles with them on the ferry so they could beat the crowd to the parsonage.) The reporters got a look at the operation, and Hunsberger—not knowing they were from the *Tribune*—gladly answered their questions. Dethlef Hansen probably remembered this article and thought that for sheer anonymity Minnie couldn't beat the marrying parson, who was processing so many couples he would never remember this particular one. But he reckoned without Minnie's overbearing personality.

Wedding in Milwaukee

On Thursday, September 23, 1897, Minnie and John, accompanied by Joe Keller, took a hack to the train station and went to Milwaukee. Ketcham was so ill and so weak he could not stand on his own. At the Plankinton Hotel, Minnie signed them in as "A. B. Young, wife, and servant, Boston." The next morning at 6:30, they headed off for the Hunsberger parsonage—or, rather, Minnie headed off with John Ketcham in tow. Keller stayed behind in the hotel. Everyone who encountered them that day noticed that she was in charge and making all the decisions. The groom seemed to be doped up and seriously ill. Many wondered why a beautiful, vibrant young woman would want to ally herself with a dying old man.[15]

Minnie's butler and "go-fer,"
Joe Keller (sketch from the
Chicago Daily Tribune)

At the Hunsbergers', Minnie exited the cab and rang the doorbell, leaving Ketcham behind with the driver. When Mrs. Hunsberger answered the door, Minnie informed her that they wished to marry but that Mr. Ketcham was very ill. Would it be possible to have the ceremony performed in the carriage? "We wish to be married as soon as possible," Minnie told the minister's wife. "Mr. Ketcham has been ill and we want to return to Chicago at once." Mrs. Hunsberger said that Ketcham would have to be brought into the house; there would be no ceremony in the cab. Minnie then walked into the house, leaving Mrs. Hunsberger and the cabbie to bring Ketcham up the stairs by themselves.

The marrying parson was out of town at a conference, but the minister across the street, Reverend I. P. Roberts, was available. John Ketcham was all wrapped up in blankets and robes and had a muffler around his head, but he was able to answer the questions in a clear, albeit weak, voice. Minnie asked if he could be seated during the ceremony, and this was granted.

The official record shows that Minnie gave her name as Minnie Walkup, which must have been a legal requirement, or she would never have revealed it.[16] The list of married couples was routinely sent to the Chicago papers because of the large number of people who had come from there, and Minnie went to Milwaukee solely to avoid publicity. But she would not want to do anything, such as using the wrong name, that would later invalidate the marriage. However, the list was delayed until the following Tuesday, and apparently nobody ever picked up on it.

But, to Minnie's eventual chagrin, she had not gone unnoticed among the unending stream of couples entering the Hunsberger parsonage. It was not just her imperious, take-charge attitude but the incredible discrepancy in age, health, and vitality between her and the groom that caused all the people there that day—the cab driver, Reverend Roberts, Mrs. Hunsberger, and the two witnesses, Miss Annie Miersch (an assistant) and Miss Mae Daugherty (the stenographer)—to carry a vivid memory of the Walkup-Ketcham wedding.

Once more back in Chicago, Minnie locked the marriage certificate in her husband's safety deposit box (she must have finally gotten the password from him). She told nobody that they were married. Joe Keller knew (he said) because Ketcham had told him. Minnie said she was angry at her husband for that, as she did not want *anyone* to know it, but this alleged statement might have been invented to prove that John Ketcham was compos mentis at the time of his marriage.

On October 1, Minnie went back to Dethlef Hansen's office and told him she had married "the old man." She wanted Hansen to draft a will but expressed doubt that she could get her husband to sign it—which indicates that, for all the seeming loss of his faculties, perhaps there was a remnant still left of Ketcham's business acumen. And, in some dim recess of his mind, he may have understood what was happening to him.

Hansen drew up two handwritten copies of the will, bequeathing everything to "my dearly beloved wife," and sent them on to Minnie. Once again, Ketcham exhibited signs of suspicion, as manifested in this note from Minnie to Hansen: "My Dear: A new idea has entered his head. He wants to know just what you want for having written those papers [the two copies of the will]. I told him I would send for you and let him talk with you, but he says he has no desire to meet you. Of course, I repeat our conversation because I know you care nothing about what he says. However, it will be as well for you to write a formal letter which I can show to him. As ever, M."

On October 15, George Ketcham finally managed to break through the barriers at 3421 and visit his brother, now a bedridden invalid. Minnie had hired a stenographer from a detective agency to hide under the bed and take notes on the conversation. George Ketcham was appalled at John's condition. His brother had been asleep when he first entered, and so he was hazy and confused when he first awakened, but even after that he seemed to be mentally adrift. He could not remember the location of certain pieces of property he owned, and often he would just gaze off into space. He seemed incapable of answering many of the questions put to him. (Regardless, in a gross error of judgment, George had a couple of drinks with his alcoholic brother!) Neither Minnie nor John told George that they were married, and it is distinctly possible that John was unaware of it himself.[17] After this meeting, George went to the Central Police Station to see if there were any way to extricate his brother from 3421 Indiana Avenue. But the police told him that if John were of sound mind and wanted to stay there, there was nothing they could do.[18]

In late October, Minnie took all the furniture out of the "party house" down the street. After that, a bill collector came looking for her a few times, but was never able to find her. On occasion, Minnie had Dr. Stephen DeVeny (who had also attended her mother) come in to see John Ketcham, but other than that—as she had done with James Walkup—she insisted on being the only one in the house to nurse him and give him his medicine.[19]

The Will

On November 1, 1897, according to Sena Torrey and Joe Keller, John Ketcham came to them (even though he was bedridden) and asked them to be witnesses to his will. Joe claimed that Ketcham read them the will before everybody signed, and in this little slipup the real circumstances are undoubtedly revealed. It is not necessary for the witnesses to know the contents of the will before signing: What they are witnesses to is not the will itself but the testator's *declaration* that it is his will, as well as his signing of it and their signing it also, all in the presence of each other on the stated date.

But Joe (or Minnie, if she instructed him to say this) might have thought the witnessing was invalid without a reading of the will. By November 1, however, Ketcham was so weak and so mentally gone that he could never have read it aloud.

A close examination of John Ketcham's will reveals a signature that is spidery and tenuous, uses his first and middle initials only (despite the importance of the document), and bears no relationship to his signature when he was healthy. And, although the document itself states that it is being signed by everyone on November 1, Dethlef Hansen drew up the

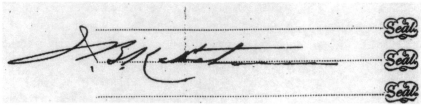

John B. Ketcham's normal signature

Ketcham's alleged signature on his will

will in early October and incorporated the November 1 date into the text at that time.

Now, it is entirely possible that John Ketcham signed this document himself. But it is even more likely that Minnie signed his name, probably after he died (she had told Dethlef Hansen that she doubted she could get John to sign a will), then bribed the witnesses to say they signed it on November 1. She would have wanted to truncate the signature so as to minimize the chances of someone's spotting the forgery and therefore would have used "J. B. Ketcham" instead of his full name. At any rate, when Ketcham signed his will—if he did so—he also signed his death warrant.

The Inquest

Twelve days after John Ketcham supposedly signed his will—November 13, 1897—he was dead, just ten months after moving into Minnie's house on Indiana Avenue. Minnie wisely called in Dr. DeVeny to sign a death certificate. He did so, indicating acute alcoholism as the cause.

uid will, wherefore your petitioner prays that said will may be admitted to pro-

stamentary thereon may be issued to *your petitioner Minnie Wallace*

tcham after proper hearing and proof, and that the hearing on said petition

28 day of *December* A. D. 1897 at 10 o'clock a.m.,

: as the matter can be heard, and that all other orders necessary may be made.

Minnie Wallace Walkup Ketcham

Minnie H. W. Ketcham (SEAL)

Two examples of Minnie's signatures on official documents

However, it didn't take long for authorities to discover that the woman claiming to be Mrs. Ketcham was the notorious Minnie Wallace Walkup, acquitted of poisoning her first husband in 1885, in a controversial verdict. In light of that discovery (with information furnished by the Ketchams in Toledo), an inquest was ordered, to determine whether the deceased's organs contained lethal amounts of poison.

For anyone who had been in Emporia, Kansas, in August 1885 and was now in Chicago in 1897, it must have seemed like déjà vu. Once again, Minnie's calm demeanor and lack of emotion were startling. She gave interviews in the luxuriously appointed rooms of the house where her husband's body was undergoing an autopsy, telling reporters it was John who wanted their marriage kept a secret (even though he had supposedly blurted it out to Joe Keller). But she did learn something from all that negative publicity in Emporia, and when she knew the neighbors were watching the house, she went upstairs and sat in a window overlooking the street, striking poses of anguish for their benefit.[20]

John's family was stunned to learn not only of his death but that he had been married for almost two months. They had no intention of letting what remained of his wealth pass to this woman who was obviously a gold digger. They would challenge both the will and the wedding: John could not have been in his right mind for either of those events. And they wanted their son and brother's body for burial in the family plot in Toledo. But they knew not with whom they reckoned, notwithstanding her young age, as Minnie gave every indication of fighting them on all fronts, including burial rights. She told reporters about the plot in Forest Home, conveniently omitting the fact that her mother already occupied one of the two sites: "John will be buried in my lot in [Forest Home] cemetery, where I expect to lie beside him when my time comes."[21]

There were challenges from others, as well. John Ketcham had dated quite a few women and it was rumored that some of these would come forward to claim rights as common-law wives. Indeed, two of them showed up on Minnie's doorstep hoping to scare her into settling with them, but she did not scare easily and they were sent away.[22]

In Illinois in 1897, as in some other states at the time, legislation regarding common-law marriages was an open invitation to fraud and blackmail. No third party was necessary to witness the promise the couple made to each other in a private exchange of vows, as long as there was some kind of evidence that the two people intended to ally themselves. What started out as a well-intentioned law often ended up with unscrupulous people coming forward to claim this relationship when a wealthy person died, as was the case with John Ketcham.[23]

Minnie was well aware of the law and wisely foresaw that she would have a better claim if she could actually get a marriage license rather than stand in line with all of John's other "spouses." She may have moved John to her house not only to control him but to establish just such a relationship, especially since she waited so long to marry him. However, the insistence of George Ketcham and friends of John to be allowed to see him must have alerted Minnie to the likelihood of a stiff challenge to a common-law marriage—hence, the trip to Milwaukee.

When the suspicions against Minnie hit the newspapers, Gladys Forbes and Josephine Moffitt came to assure her that they knew lawyers who could see to it that nothing would happen to her. Dethlef Hansen, who was probably more astute about public opinion than Minnie and also did not want to lose "his" case to another attorney, took her aside and told her that if people saw these courtesans calling on her, it would not look good. Besides, a story about the "party house" where Minnie spent her evenings with other men as her husband lay dying had already been published. It was important to avoid any new scandal.[24]

So when she testified at the inquest, Minnie showed no grief but told her story in a straightforward, unemotional way. However, when the coroner wanted to postpone the proceeding to examine the organs for poison and research the drugstores in the neighborhood of 3421 Indiana Avenue, Minnie lashed out. The coroner told her he would issue her a certificate of burial, but she refused to accept it: "No, I want more than that. I must have more than that. I demand it. I demand it. You can't imagine, gentlemen, how I have suffered. You say that you are delayed by the analysis. Can it not be hastened? Please, gentlemen." On this last, her tone changed from one of imperiousness to one of "great sweetness." They agreed to hurry.[25]

Minnie held her husband's body hostage until she got George Ketcham to agree not to open his head to examine his brain; she was afraid they would find some lesion or other indication that John was mentally incapable of making a will or consenting to a marriage, which would interfere with her chances of inheriting the estate. When George consented, Minnie turned the body over to him for burial in Toledo. However, she would not be accompanying her late husband to that city, because she didn't want to cause an uproar and was afraid the Ketchams wouldn't treat her right—the same reasons she used to absent herself from James Walkup's funeral. Although she said she would visit John's grave "in a few days," she never did so.[26]

At last the chemical analyses were completed, and the cause of death was determined to be "acute alcoholism," although Minnie got them to change it to the more euphemistic "cirrhosis of the liver." There were trace amounts of strychnine in Ketcham's organs, but nothing more than could be accounted for in the medicine prescribed for him by Dr. DeVeny, and certainly nothing close to a lethal dosage.

Did Minnie kill John Ketcham? It is a certainty that she was responsible for his death in some way, although she would have been afraid—because of her past, sure to be discovered—to give him arsenic or strychnine. In fact, she probably didn't think she would need to kill him at all, as he was already ill with cirrhosis and it would take its natural course. But it is doubtful whether the disease would, under normal circumstances, have acted as fast as it did, given his condition before he moved into Minnie's house and his precipitous deterioration within a very short time after that.

John's family had hired detectives to watch the house, and evidently part of their mission was to make every attempt to enter it. That's how they knew visitors were being told the story about John's being away when they were very well aware that he was still in the house. Minnie must have felt some of this pressure and therefore consented to let George see his brother on October 15, but she must have realized that she was losing control of the situation. The Ketchams could get a court order to remove

John, and, even though she was his wife, the fight might have been a long and costly one. Minnie would not want to risk having John removed from her home; he would have to die first. The timing is interesting: Two weeks after George's visit (and his subsequent inquiry at the police station about getting John out of Minnie's house), the will was signed, and twelve days after that John Ketcham died.

How did Minnie kill John Ketcham? Not with any of the classic poisons, as she would have been leery of those, in case her true identity were to be discovered. But there are a few other things she might have done with equal success. First, she was allowing him access to alcohol, and even actively providing him with it, which was exacerbating his condition. Second, she may have been using drugs to keep him sedated; the organ analysis seems to have been focused on poisons and may not have tested for drugs. If it were not for Minnie's past, there would have been no analysis at all, and probably not even an autopsy. Since Minnie's history was the primary reason for the analysis, it is more than likely they were just testing for the poisons she was accused of using in 1885: arsenic and strychnine, with maybe a test for cyanide thrown in for good measure. A drug overdose might have been overlooked completely. Once the poison tests showed up negative and the cirrhosis was discovered, there would be no need to look further, especially with Minnie's clamoring for closure.

But the most probable method Minnie used to kill John Ketcham was a tried and true one, at least before today's forensic detection methods, and that is a pillow over his face. She simply smothered him, and he was too weak to resist, as he was in a drunken stupor or drugged (or both) and debilitated by cirrhosis. The telltale petechial hemorrhaging in the eyes, indicating suffocation, might have been discounted or overlooked, as would pillow fibers in his mouth or lacerations on the tongue or the inside of the mouth, caused as the victim struggled for air.

The Challenge

Not long after John Ketcham's death, a startling accusation was made: It was not John Ketcham who had been the bridegroom at the Milwaukee wedding but the butler, Joe Keller, disguised as Ketcham! The groom had had his head wrapped up in a muffler, but the Reverend Roberts, who had performed the ceremony, could see a mustache poking through. John Ketcham did not have a mustache; however, Joe Keller did. And people also noticed that the groom was much shorter than the bride, whereas John Ketcham was taller than Minnie (and Joe Keller was shorter). Tom Riley, the hackman who drove them to the Hunsbergers', said the groom was a "little sawed-off man." Reverend Roberts, shown pictures of both men, said that Joe Keller looked like the bridegroom he saw.[27]

Minnie avoided all questioning reporters by claiming to be bedridden with "nervous prostration" because all the events since her husband's death were "too much for her strength." This new attack on the marriage was probably the result of investigation by the Ketcham family, which was determined to show it as invalid.

Joe Keller was taken to the police station for questioning—actually, to several stations. They couldn't arrest him then because they didn't have enough evidence, but they were convinced he knew something, and they wanted to get it out of him before Minnie's lawyer could spring him. Keller was reported as having disappeared, since he never went back to 3421 Indiana that night. This added to everyone's suspicions that he had guilty knowledge, and this theory was magnified by Minnie's becoming unnerved at his absence. Was she worried he might say something that would incriminate her?

As a result of this, Dethlef Hansen moved into Minnie's house, supposedly to be on call should she be arrested. When Joe didn't come back, Hansen took over his duties as butler, turning reporters away because of Minnie's "nervous prostration." When Minnie became more and more hysterical at Joe's absence, Hansen left Sena Torrey to look after her while he tried to find out from the police where Joe Keller was. He had an idea that Keller was still in custody somewhere, and he was right: The police had shuttled him from the station at Thirty-fifth Street to that at Hyde Park, then on to Woodlawn, and finally to Halsted Street, all to avoid Hansen. Eventually, the lawyer got a writ of habeas corpus and Keller was released.

It all turned out to be a tempest in a teapot, though, as, one by one, those who said the groom was Keller and not Ketcham tempered their statements. Reverend Roberts ultimately stated that he believed it was Ketcham after all, and Tom Riley said it was obvious the man was really ill and not shamming. Even the Ketchams' attorney admitted that they knew John had gone to Milwaukee (probably followed by those detectives), so the Case of the Spurious Bridegroom quietly disappeared from the newspapers. But which was the truth? And what made the witnesses change their stories?

Even if they couldn't invalidate John Ketcham's marriage, his family had no intention of letting the will go unchallenged. They were convinced that Minnie had used undue influence and that John was mentally incompetent when he signed the will. George Ketcham violated his agreement with Minnie and had his brother's body exhumed and the brain examined for signs of incapacity, but nothing was found.[28]

Minnie, Joe Keller, and Sena Torrey appeared in court to testify as to the circumstances surrounding the signing of the will. When first informed that the Ketchams would try to break it, Minnie was furious: "Let them try it," she snapped. "I will make someone smart for the insult of the coroner's inquest." James Purnell, the Ketcham family's lawyer, had already gone to the Illinois Trust and Savings Bank to prevent Minnie from gaining access to John's safety deposit box, but—even if he were successful—he was probably too late, as she already seems to have had access to it, keeping the marriage certificate and the will there.[29]

On her day in court, Minnie "fluttered" in, perfectly aware that the unusually large crowd present that day was there to see her. When she heard their dismay at only seeing her back as she faced the court, Minnie obliged by turning to them "so that her beauty might have the effect on the spectators that it was calculated to have on the attorneys and witnesses."[30]

At some point, the Ketchams realized that they would not be able to break the will and either bowed out or settled with Minnie. She was then duly appointed executrix and went about settling the estate, which proved to be a protracted chore spanning the next few years—possibly because she disputed some of the claims presented by John Ketcham's creditors. For example, in early 1897, Ketcham had boarded a horse with a veterinarian, Dr. John Hamilton, because the animal had leg problems. After that, of course, Ketcham was not allowed to leave 3421 Indiana, so the horse was neither picked up nor paid for. After Ketcham died, Dr. Hamilton told Minnie he wanted her to take the horse and reimburse him for the animal's care, but Minnie claimed she knew nothing about it and that her husband had never owned that horse. Hamilton was forced to apply to the probate court, saying that the horse was "eating his head off every day." In the end, he was allowed to sell the animal, apply the proceeds to the bill, and submit a creditor's claim against the estate for the balance due.[31]

Another creditor was the noted architect Thomas Wing, designer of one of the 1893 World's Exposition buildings, who had drawn up plans for a building John Ketcham wanted to erect on Dearborn Street between

Twenty-second and Twenty-third Streets (close to the building eventually chosen by the Everleigh sisters for their famous brothel in 1900).[32]

During the estate process, Dethlef Hansen, who had no courtroom experience (and didn't seem to want to acquire any), brought in the Trude brothers, George and Alfred, to assist him. The Trudes were infinitely more accomplished and established as attorneys than Hansen was or ever would be, so they must have decided to play second and third chairs to him on the basis of wanting to be connected in some way with this famous probate case. (In 1893 Alfred Trude had successfully prosecuted Patrick Prendergast, a mentally unbalanced and disgruntled office-seeker who had assassinated Carter Harrison I, the mayor of Chicago.)[33]

The Ketcham estate was not finally settled until the middle of 1900. Long before that, however, Minnie had a falling out with Dethlef Hansen, the result of two con artists trying to cheat each other. She had refused to pay his bill after all the work he had done, especially in the beginning when it looked as if she might be arrested for murder or fraud. And he had grossly inflated his bill, padding it with items such as responding to newspaper articles that brought up negative items about Minnie (when it is very likely that he himself had spread the rumors that spawned the articles!).

Despite John Ketcham's profligacy in his later years, his estate brought his widow $250,000, the same amount she had received from her first husband, James Walkup. On a visit to New Orleans, Minnie declared that most of the Ketcham fortune would be allocated to the building and maintenance of a home in Chicago for "enfeebled and deformed" children and that she would live on the grounds and help out with the project. Needless to say, none of this ever happened.[34]

Chapter 13

Hansen versus Ketcham

There is no honor among thieves.

Minnie Wallace Walkup Ketcham and Dethlef Hansen had tried to cheat each other. Now they would see which of them was the more successful scam artist. Their original alliance had come about as a desire to get John Ketcham's wealth by any means possible.[1]

Hansen knew Minnie was vulnerable to blackmail because of her past and her somewhat incriminating letters to him and also because she was not only affiliated with courtesans but was little better than one herself. On top of that, she was a source of easy money for him if she succeeded in getting John Ketcham's still-substantial wealth. He decided to bide his time.

When John Ketcham died, Minnie summoned Hansen to her home, as she was almost immediately under suspicion and could be arrested at any minute. The attorney saw right away that his best approach was to feed her fears, and his first move was to ensconce himself at 3421 Indiana—ostensibly to be on hand to provide bail if she should be arrested but in reality to be on top of the situation and see what items he could use to help out his own cause. When he found a collection of letters from various individuals, including Minnie's mother, he took control of them and all her papers—even scrapbooks—"so the police wouldn't get them."

Dethlef Hansen's goal was to get Minnie to split the estate with him, and she may have even encouraged this idea herself by telling him that if he could prevent her from being arrested and could get her the estate, she would give him half the Ketcham fortune and he would never have to practice law again. But when he asked her to sign a written agreement to that effect, she put him off.

Hansen's response was to turn up the heat on Minnie's fears: He told her that James Purnell, the Ketchams' attorney, had entered into a conspiracy with a deputy coroner to plant poison in John's organs to implicate Minnie. To lend credence to this alleged plot, Hansen had gone to Jacob Kern, a former state's attorney, to get him to join forces. Kern was to validate the Ketcham-coroner plot and encourage Minnie to sign the agreement about splitting the fortune so he and Hansen could prevent her from losing the entire estate and going to jail. Kern, however, refused to go along with it and later told Minnie what Hansen had done.

There was, of course, no conspiracy on the part of the Ketchams. They did, however, suspect that John had died as the result of some kind of foul play, and it was at their insistence that the inquest was held. As John had been previously ill and under the care of a reputable physician who had signed a death certificate, this normally would not have been required.

Dethlef Hansen spent a lot of his time putting out fires in the form of rumors that had sprung up in the press about Minnie. But how did these rumors start? Minnie later claimed (probably correctly) that Hansen himself had spread them so he could add to her bill (and her fears) by refuting them through newspaper interviews. He had even paid one reporter $100 to write up these stories.

Hansen eventually realized that he was not going to get one-half interest in the Ketcham estate, which he was convinced was his due, and Minnie simultaneously concluded that he had been lying to her. They had a falling-out around Christmastime in 1897 (they may have even been lovers, as Hansen was a very handsome and charming young man), and she ordered him out of her home on New Year's Day 1898. He promptly presented her with his bill for $20,000: $10,415 for his advice and his services vis-à-vis the coroner, and $9,585 for his services in the probate court. Minnie refused to pay it.

After he was kicked out of Minnie's house and Alfred Trude had taken over the Ketcham probate case, the young lawyer continually harassed her for his fee. In February 1898, the estate still not settled, he put a lien on the proceeds of one of John Ketcham's insurance policies for the amount of his fee, and he advised a brewery to do the same when Minnie failed to pay her

$250 bill with them (probably incurred at the "party house" and her reason for precipitously vacating the premises there). Minnie's response was to have Trude file contempt charges against Hansen in probate court, as his lien prevented her from discharging her duties as executrix of the estate.

Trude presented evidence that the services Hansen performed in probate court, for which he was charging Minnie $9,585, consisted entirely of filling in a form that the court clerks had to help him with and saying "All right" when Judge Kohlsaat angrily told him to remove his silk hat from in front of the judge's face ("Take that thing away, sir"). But the lien was allowed to remain.

Nothing more was heard of Hansen until 1901, although he was no doubt dunning Minnie in the two years intervening. In June of that year, frustrated at not getting his attorney's fees, he filed suit in Cook County Superior Court. (Minnie was reluctant to pay any of her creditors; she had only given him $385 while he was still working for her. He should have seen the handwriting on the wall.)

On the first day of the trial of *Hansen v. Ketcham,* Minnie—who had moved to New York City over the previous year and was staying at the posh Grand Hotel in Chicago—was accompanied by her cousin Sena Torrey (one of the witnesses to the Ketcham will) and a new wealthy admirer: fifty-year-old DeLancey Horton Louderback, a partner of robber baron Charles Tyson Yerkes in establishing Chicago's railway system.

Each day, the jurors—who had been told not to read anything about the case—sat in the box before trial and read the newspaper. But those newspapers quickly disappeared once the action began.

The opening statement of Minnie's lawyer, Alfred Trude (who had been Dethlef Hansen's colleague for the Ketcham probate case and had actually praised him for his work with it), was a sarcastic piece of theater meant to ridicule Hansen and, at the same time, divert the jury from the fact that the defense could not refute his testimony. Trude told how Hansen had returned to the house at 3421 Indiana Avenue after Minnie had kicked him out (it was never stated why he had returned), got drunk, then went down to the cellar for more champagne. When he came back upstairs, he had something red smeared all over his face, and the "terrified occupants" thought he was either wounded or had killed someone down there. But no. He had broken into a can of Minnie's homemade red plum jelly, and Trude presented this little drama in mock epic style: "Yes, gentlemen of the jury, the services for which this complaint demands $20,000 compensation consisted mainly in making away with the dead husband's champagne and the widow's plum jam," at which the crowded courtroom laughed and even the judge had to hide a smile.

Before Trude's dramatic statement, however, Hugo Pam (he would go on to serve as a judge for many years) was much more subdued and straightforward in his opening for the plaintiff. Not only did he outline the work Dethlef Hansen had done for Minnie (for example, trying for three weeks to get witnesses who would testify that Ketcham was sane), he also brought out the elements of their relationship that would show her to be out for Ketcham's money: her constantly seeking him out for advice as to "the old fool's" wealth, her attempt at accessing the safety deposit box, and Hansen's drawing up of the will that left everything to Minnie.

During his direct examination, Hansen produced a letter from Minnie, in which she addressed him as "my dear" and she asked about evading her debts in Illinois and Louisiana. It was on her stationery and in her handwriting, yet Trude characterized it as a forgery. His cross-examination of Hansen resumed the tone of sarcastic melodrama he had adopted for his opening statement, leading the *Chicago Daily Tribune* to characterize it as "opera bouffe." There was so much raucous enjoyment of this in the courtroom that Judge Tuthill had to admonish everyone: "This is not a town meeting nor a vaudeville show, and disturbances will not be permitted." This had absolutely no effect on Trude's approach to the witness, however.

Trude seemed to focus on the fact that Hansen had never actually presented a case in a courtroom, insinuating that he was not a real lawyer because of this. Once, while Hansen was living in Minnie's house, he took it upon himself to fire Joe Keller: "Remember, I am the lawyer in this case," he reminded him. Keller, however, did not consider Hansen to be his boss and retorted, "Well, if you're the lawyer in this case, why don't you practice law in the courtroom or your office?" Apparently, Hansen's constant presence and his bossy attitude did not sit well with the household.

Turning serious for a brief moment, Trude thundered, "I invoke the lightning of God's wrath if his Honor's clerk can tell of a single case Hansen ever tried in this atmosphere. I pause for a reply." When none came, other than the clerk merely shaking his head, Trude picked up the tone of ridicule again: "Why, Hansen wouldn't know a legal proposition if he saw it coming down Clark Street with a placard on it and a red lantern on each side." All this sarcasm served to hide the fact that Trude could not refute Hansen's claims about the meretricious scheming of the designing woman who was his client.

Hugo Pam had presented a witness who was invited to dinner at Minnie's house, when Minnie told the guest that Hansen was "slaving night and day" for her case and was working so hard that he had to live there. In his cross-examination, Trude continued to belittle Hansen:

Trude: You didn't see any of Hansen's legal services about, did you?

Witness: Nothing but the dinner service.

Trude: Well, did you see anything of the plum jelly which later came to a mysterious end at Hansen's hands?

Pam: I object to this, your Honor.

Trude: All right, I withdraw the jelly. Mr. Clerk, strike out the jam.

Pam [shaking his finger at Trude]: Oh, you'll bear watching. You know the tricks, you old bird.

Trude: I object to his calling me a bird, your Honor.

When Hansen revealed all of Minnie's schemes to get Ketcham's money, Trude had no rebuttal but chose instead to chastise the plaintiff for violating attorney-client confidences and "playing into the hands of her enemies." He never alleged that the testimony was untrue.

Trude even mocked Hansen for his practice of taking people out on Lake Michigan in an excursion steamer named the *Chief Justice Waite,* then treating them to champagne from cases he had stored on board. This certainly had no bearing on the issues in the trial, but Trude was leaving no stone unturned in his effort to paint Dethlef Hansen as a corrupt and inept attorney, one who did very little actual practice of law. Perhaps he meant to imply that he was using the excursions to bribe rich or influential people.

(Hansen's Lake Michigan trips may have paid off by getting him at least one case, however, if the wealthy Arlington Heights merchant Frederick Seeberg had ever been a guest on the *Chief Justice Waite.* In August 1898, Seeberg experienced a problem that would be a nightmare for any parent: His seventeen-year-old son, Fred, was accused of raping an eleven-year-old girl in Desplaines in broad daylight. All the witnesses, who were eleven and twelve years old, identified young Seeberg and his bicycle, although he claimed he was somewhere else at the time. Hansen got him a stay, got his bond reduced, and must have made the problem go away completely, as nothing about it ever appeared in the newspapers again.)[2]

On the third day of trial, Hansen was still on the stand undergoing Trude's snide cross-examination. When Minnie's attorney accused him of stealing her letters and other papers, Hansen cried out, "I did not! I did not!" and Trude shouted right back at him, "Yes, you did—you stole them!"

At noon, Hansen finally broke down. Trude had been trying to show that he had taken advantage of Minnie by sponging off her and inviting people to eat at her home:

Trude: Why did you not have Judge Shope dine with you and Mrs. Ketcham down-town when you wanted him to enter the case, instead of taking him to the Ketcham house?

Hansen [sobbing uncontrollably]: Because I did not want to parade her in a public hotel. Crowds followed her everywhere and I wanted to save her the notoriety.

Hansen was unable to regain his composure, so the judge took pity on him and ended the session for that day. But Trude, an astute lawyer, decided to take advantage of it in a way that would save face for his client. He could see that, notwithstanding the entertaining sarcasm and drama, Minnie would have to take the stand and refute Hansen's claims, and he knew she could not do so without perjuring herself and exposing herself to Hugo Pam's cross-examination. He went for one last jab at the down-and-out plaintiff: "Look at this man in tears. Why, this Niobe in 'pants' breaks me all up. Even my client's hatred of him is turned to sympathy at the sight of his weeping. I am going to offer Hansen the opportunity of settling for what it has cost him to try the case, and if he doesn't accept it, why God help him." But Hugo Pam was not fooled by Trude's theatrics: "I guess you're a little bit anxious to settle anyway, aren't you? You're beginning to have chills when you think of the cross-examination we will give Mrs. Ketcham."

Trude convinced Minnie to settle the case before she had to take the stand and told the court he did so to spare Dethlef Hansen any further breakdowns. Minnie must have been reluctant, because Trude ended up throwing in $500 of his own money. The settlement was for $3,000, to cover his expenses in attaching the life insurance proceeds, although Hugo Pam said it was *in addition to* his expenses in that matter.

And so Minnie's long-running feud with her former coconspirator Dethlef Hansen ended. Hansen found out, to his dismay, who was the abler con artist. He had tried to scam Minnie and ended up being scammed himself. He had probably portrayed his own role in the fleecing of John Berdan Ketcham in a more benign light than was actually the case; however, he wasn't lying about Minnie's part. Not only did he have the letters to prove it, but Minnie was also very tellingly silent on this issue and she agreed to a settlement to avoid taking the stand.

Dethlef Hansen must have felt stung by the betrayal of one he had once considered a friend and humiliated by her turning the tables on him. But he had one more card he had not played, and he would soon get his revenge in a very public way.

Chapter 14

Billy, Baby Jo, and the Prince

Nothing succeeds like excess.

—Oscar Wilde (1893)

William Hale Thompson wanted to give a bachelor party for his brother Gale, who was about to get married. Thompson would later be known as "Big Bill," mayor of Chicago and one of its most corrupt politicians, but in February 1898, he was just the twenty-nine-year-old big brother of the groom. He set up what he thought would be the perfect celebration for the boys in the bridal party: drinks at the Chicago Athletic Club, followed by dinner at Gladys Forbes's Monroe Restaurant (where they would see a little vaudeville entertainment), and then maybe end the night at Frank Wing's—a boozy, bawdy sendoff for Gale.[1]

One of the invitees to Thompson's shindig was William Wallace "Billy" Pike, twenty-six, a bachelor who still lived with his parents, Mr. and Mrs. Eugene S. Pike, at 2101 Prairie Avenue. Eugene Pike was an extremely successful and influential capitalist involved in real estate and banking, and his address included him among the city's wealthiest people. Across the street, at 2100, was John B. Sherman, general manager of the Union Stock Yards, whose home had been designed by his son-in-law, the famous architect Daniel Burnham, who also resided there. Down the street, at 2115, was Phillip Armour of the meat-packing company. Department store

William Hale "Big Bill" Thompson
(photo courtesy of the Library of Congress, LC-ggbain-19321)

magnate Marshall Field lived a couple of blocks away at 1905, and George Pullman, of railroad car fame, was at 1729.[2]

To have a Prairie Avenue address was to have arrived among the movers and shakers of the Chicago—and, indeed, even the national—scene. But by 1898, residents were becoming more than a little nervous at the increasing encroachment of the nearby Levee district. There could have been no greater disparity than that between elite Prairie Avenue and the venal Levee, and by the end of the first decade of the twentieth century, many of the mansion dwellers would move to Lake Forest and other locales, far away from the vice center.

On that Saturday night in early February, the men of the bridal party had several before-dinner drinks at the Chicago Athletic Club, then at 10:00 P.M. headed out for the Monroe Restaurant—where they had even more drinks with dinner. Around midnight, a parade of prostitutes showed up. They had been tipped off—probably by Gladys Forbes—about the presence of the rich boys and, under pretense of "wanting to see the vaudeville show," swarmed in at short intervals. There were at least ten of them and maybe as many as fifteen. Among them were Minnie Ketcham's old pal Josephine Moffitt and Josephine's current roommate, Alice Morris, another courtesan.

Billy Pike at the time of the trial
(from the *Chicago Daily Tribune*)

The arrival of "these females, as you call them," as William Hale Thompson would later say, broke up the party, especially since the prospective bridegroom wanted no part of their company. Everyone left the Monroe Restaurant, and Thompson hailed a cab for himself, his twenty-one-year-old brother Percy, and Billy Pike. Outside the restaurant, Josephine Moffitt and Alice Morris bemoaned the fact that they had no way to get back to their flat at 3000 Indiana Avenue (although no one seems to have thought to ask how they got to the Monroe from there). "Come on, get in, girls," William Thompson told them. "We'll take you home."

There wasn't enough room for everyone inside the landau, so Billy sat outside with the driver. (The roof of a landau covered only the back part of the carriage.) A chubby young man with an easygoing, ingratiating manner and a slight lisp, Billy was often shy around women. He was the youngest of the three Pike sons, with Charles Burrall "Charley" Pike two years older and Eugene Rockwell "Gene" Pike the eldest by five years. All three boys were intensely devoted to their parents and to one another.

Billy had a "proneness to conviviality" in general and a fondness for alcohol in particular. Like John Berdan Ketcham, he was a club man, and his opportunities for socializing were enhanced by his memberships in the University, Saddle and Cycle, Chicago Athletic, Chicago Golf, and Tolleston Clubs.

After a while, Billy began to get cold and also thought he was missing out on the opportunity of being in close contact with the two women. He climbed down and got inside, snuggling up next to Josephine, who was by herself on a short seat. Alice was sitting between the two Thompson brothers.

Somewhere along the line, the party decided to proceed to Frank Wing's, but by then William Hale Thompson had begun to have second thoughts. At that time, he probably entertained political ambitions and realized that a public trip to Frank Wing's in the company of two "women of easy virtue" would do him no good. Besides, he was disgusted with the behavior of Josephine Moffitt, who—within five minutes of Billy's getting inside the cab—had begun making out with him and asking him to come home with her that night. Outside Wing's, Thompson announced that he was calling it a night and told his brother Percy to make sure Billy got home all right, as he was drunk and in the hands of "bad company." Unfortunately, Percy seems to have had a different idea of what "seeing that Billy gets home all right" entailed.

Percy, Billy, Josephine, and Alice went into Wing's and spent about an hour there drinking a quart of champagne, after which they all went back to 3000 Indiana, where the boys spent the night. The next morning, Sunday, while William Hale Thompson was having breakfast at the Metropole, Charley and Gene Pike came to him to find out what had happened to Billy, as he had not returned home the night before. Mrs. Pike was literally sick with worry, and her sons asked Thompson to write a note to Billy and tell him that he was to return home immediately. Thompson, who knew exactly where Billy was, wrote the note and sent it by messenger to 3000 Indiana.

Billy does not seem to have been very experienced with women, as he was absolutely enthralled with Josephine, whom he called, variously, "Baby Jo," "Dearie," "My Little Jo," and "Sugar Heart" in the many letters he sent her over the years they were involved. At first, he thought she was single, but she eventually told him she was "Mrs. Moffitt," separated from her husband because of his addiction to drinking and betting on horses.

Early on in the relationship, Josephine sought advice from Minnie Walkup Ketcham as to how to get the most money out of Billy Pike. Minnie advised her to get him drunk (not a difficult task where Billy was concerned) and have him sign some kind of paper saying they were married. Hence, she could establish a common-law relationship and easily get money out of the young man or his family to avoid a scandal. Josephine had no intention of marrying him but wanted some leverage in case they ever split up.

Josephine Moffitt at the trial (from the *Chicago Daily Tribune*)

In the meantime, Josephine had a good thing going, and she intended to keep it as long as she could. She wanted to find a new flat that she could share with Billy. He intended to continue living at home, mostly to please his mother, but two months after meeting Josephine at the Monroe Restaurant, he signed a lease for a flat at 2342 Calumet Avenue (next door to where she had formerly roomed with Gladys Forbes). He gave her $300 for new furniture (she would later use this furniture as collateral for a $370 loan), paid the rent each month, bought all the groceries, and even paid the wages for a maid.

An example of how taken Billy was with Josephine Moffitt, but also of the strength of his devotion to his mother and his social obligations, can be seen in this undated letter:

Dearie: I tried to get up and see you this afternoon, as I wanted to see you, if just to talk to you a second, but I promised Percy [Thompson] I would go to the theater with him, and my mother got me to come home right after the theater, and I just happened in and said good night, and as it is not 12 o'clock, you see I have kept my word. Last evening I didn't get away from the supper until after 11, and I would have gone to see you then, but, Jo, it is hard to stay out when I know my mother is fretting about me, so I came right home. O, Jo, I wish I could see you now. I feel so blue, and I know you would cheer me up. Just think, Jo, I have told you all my secrets, so I must think a great deal of you.

In May 1898, just after Billy had signed the lease for the flat for Josephine, his brother Charley was married to Frances Aura Alger, the daughter of President William McKinley's secretary of war. The wedding took place in Washington, D.C., and Billy was the best man. The president and his wife attended the wedding, and there were many other notables present, which should have been a big thrill for Billy, but he was consumed instead with thoughts of his "Baby Jo." Here is the letter he wrote to her from there:

My Little Jo: Will drop you a line before going to luncheon. Am having a pretty fair time here, but feel awfully tired, as I have been on the go so much—dinner party last night and then a breakfast this morning at 10:30, and now have to go again at 2 to a luncheon, and to another dinner again tonight.

Have met most of the high life down here. They seem too stuck up, which seems unnatural to me, being the same old rough rider. I had a few moments to myself this morning, so took a cab and went down to the postoffice and was much disappointed not to get a letter from you. I miss you so much and have thought of you a hundred times and the many pleasant times we have spent together. I have not drunk anything to speak of, as it worries the family, and then there is nothing in it.

The bridesmaids seem like nice girls, but seem too stuck up, which gives me a pain. This evening am going over to [the] White [H]ouse with the bunch and give [President] Bill McK. the glad hand. I wish I was out of this place and back in our flat. I know I would feel more at home and would get a glad welcome. . . . Well, I must go, as the [others] are waiting for me. Yours, affectionately, with much love, Billy.

As Billy was certainly raised with wealth and privilege, his finding everyone—including the undoubtedly attractive bridesmaids—"stuck up" was probably just meant to reassure Josephine that he did not esteem her less because of her lower station in life. The reference to his not drinking "anything to speak of" lets us see that Billy was on his way to developing a problem that even his family noticed. For whatever motivation she might have had for it—maybe to exert her control over him, as this was toward the end of their relationship—Josephine once had Billy sign a pledge that "he will not drink one drop of intoxicating liquor until January 20, 1902, and that he will treat his little Jo better and will not go any place that is not proper for a gentleman."

But Josephine was no stranger to the excessive use of alcohol and was quite the party girl herself. She frequently had guests at the flat—at Billy's expense. One get-together got quite noisy, and other tenants in the building complained. Billy had invited some of his friends for dinner, and Josephine brought in "ladies" with names like Freckled Sal and Sheeny Cora.

Josephine's prime failing was that she was too "over the top," too obviously a courtesan, a style that could only work with someone as inexperienced as Billy Pike. She was common, cheap, and tawdry, whereas her friend Minnie Ketcham was much more subtle. Josephine would have done well to have learned more from her.

Sometimes Billy would get daring and take Josephine to 2101 Prairie Avenue, but never when the family was home. On one occasion, he had forgotten his keys and Michael Toomey, the elderly neighborhood watchman, let them in through the door to the furnace room. Toomey could see at a glance what kind of woman Josephine was, and he cautioned Billy: "You will see some young lady some day you will want to marry and this woman will make trouble for you." But Billy paid no attention.

At times, whether through family or business obligations, or maybe through shame, Billy would stay away from Josephine. When that happened, she would show up on his street, wearing gaudy, conspicuous clothing that fairly shouted out what she was, and ask Toomey if he'd seen Billy. Toomey always said he hadn't, even if he had, and then she would stand in the street and watch the Pike house, often two or three times a week, waiting for Billy to appear.

Surely, Josephine knew better than to show up on Prairie Avenue dressed like a prostitute, and if she had any hopes of marrying Billy, she would have attired herself more in keeping with the women in his society.

However, her motive was not marriage but blackmail. By standing outside his house, she was saying, "See how much trouble I can cause for you if you don't do what I want?"

Josephine thought nothing of attacking Billy physically, sometimes raising deep scratches on his face. Nonetheless, when the lease on the Calumet Avenue flat expired in May 1899, they set out to find another (why they could not continue in the old one was never stated). Billy was about to sign a lease on another flat when the landlord backed off because he "didn't like the looks of [Josephine Moffitt]." Instead, they found lodging at 2803 Indiana Avenue, and once again Billy paid the rent there.

But Josephine was very possessive of Billy and attempted to keep tabs on him at all times. She would sometimes call one of his clubs to see if he was there, and once she called his brother Gene at the Athletic Club and told him that Billy was out with some man, drunk, and she couldn't find him. The drinking friend's name was William F. Berman, whom Billy had met around 1900.

Berman did not meet with Josephine's approval as a companion for Billy, probably because he could see right away what she was up to. When the couple was having difficulties getting along, Josephine called Berman and screamed at him: "Keep your hands off of this matter, you miserable scoundrel, you! You are a drunkard. You are taking my Billy away from me; you are taking him to other women."

Dethlef Hansen's Revenge

Dethlef Hansen's humiliating public breakdown during the trial of his lawsuit against Minnie Ketcham rankled him deeply. He had asked Josephine Moffitt to be a witness for him against Minnie (probably to corroborate her meretricious motives in marrying John Ketcham), but she was friends with Minnie and had refused. So now Hansen sought revenge against both of them. And, of course, he knew about Josephine's scamming of Billy Pike and Minnie's part in it. He would have also learned, either from Josephine herself or from Minnie, who had known her in New Orleans, that Josephine was not white, but a person of color.

The *Hansen v. Ketcham* trial ended in mid-June 1901. Approximately a month later, Billy's father received a note (signed only "Lawyer") that warned him his son was in danger because he was "infatuated with the daughter of a New Orleans negress." Eugene Pike wasted no time confronting his son and told him in no uncertain terms to end the affair. Although Billy might have put up some resistance earlier in the relationship, by July 1901, he seems to have been glad to be able to get out of it. At any rate, his family's wishes would always come first.

On the evening of July 31, Billy, Josephine, and William Berman dined and drank at a beer garden at Cottage Grove Avenue and Twenty-third Street. Cowardly Billy had decided this would be his last date with Josephine, but he would leave it to Berman to tell her this; he had already tried to break up with her, unsuccessfully, in April 1900.

After the trio left the beer garden, Billy and Berman walked far enough ahead of Josie that she could not hear what they were saying. It was uncharacteristically ungentlemanly of Billy, and Josephine called out, "You must be in a hurry." "I am," Billy replied. "Are you ashamed of me?" she asked. "I am," he told her. She wanted him to go home with her, but he refused, saying he was going to his parents' home on Prairie Avenue. A terrific argument ensued. "I'll give you money," Billy concluded feebly. "You better give me a whole lot," Josephine retorted angrily.

Billy gave Berman the note his father had received from "Lawyer" and told him to show it to Josephine. It would serve as an explanation for their breakup, and he could avoid further confrontations with her. So the next day, Berman went to her flat and told her she must have enemies. "Why do you say that?" she asked. When he showed her the letter, she scoffed at it. "How ridiculous it is. I never had any idea of marrying Billy Pike." Berman told her she would probably be paid a visit by Billy's father, and she said, "If he does come down here, I don't know anything about Billy Pike and I will tell him so. How ridiculous it is to call me a nigger." Then she began to cry.

But that was the last Josephine saw of Billy Pike for over a year. She tried her old trick of standing on his street, but he never appeared. Under advice from Minnie Ketcham as to how to extort money from his family, she began a letter-writing campaign, sending missives to Billy's parents separately—primarily targeting his mother—and telling them she had a common-law marriage with their son. She hinted that some money could make her go away; otherwise, an embarrassing public lawsuit would follow. They didn't cave in.

Josephine bided her time as long as she could, and when her letters yielded no results, she went lawyer shopping. First she tried Hugo Pam,

Dethlef Hansen's attorney from *Hansen v. Ketcham* (she had rightly deduced that Hansen had been the author of the letter that was her undoing, so she could not hire him). Then she went to the Mayer brothers, Levy and Isaac, and after that to George Trude. She told each attorney she had a wedding ring and a signed statement of their marriage from Billy. But when she was told to bring those in before they could proceed, she had to give up. "You know I can't go back to see [George Trude] because I have not got that little paper," she told Gladys Forbes. She had been hoping that Trude or one of the other lawyers could succeed in getting a settlement without the papers.

Somehow, Josephine managed to convince Elmer Bishop to take her case, possibly with the idea that once a lawyer was in the picture, the Pikes would be more amenable to settlement. The suit was filed in April 1902, but no settlement was forthcoming. She had no choice but to go to trial, which was set for November, on the matter of "separate maintenance," the term for alimony to be given to a "divorced" spouse in a common-law marriage. Josephine would have to prove that there was, indeed, a marriage, that Billy had abandoned her, and that he thus owed her a monthly allowance.

"The Child of the Ketcham Case"

Billy was represented by none other than Alfred S. Trude, who had defended Minnie Ketcham when Dethlef Hansen sued her, and also by the distinguished John Barton Payne, who would go on to serve as the U.S. secretary of the interior under President Woodrow Wilson. Trude and Payne had shrewdly waived a jury trial and elected instead to let Judge Clifford decide the case. This is always the prerogative of a defendant, with the court's concurrence, and Billy's lawyers didn't want to take a chance on Josephine's tears swaying a jury in her favor.

From start to finish, eight days in all, the case of *Moffitt v. Pike* (Josephine would have to establish her right to the use of the name Pike) was an enormous source of entertainment for the crowds who attended it daily and the newspapers that covered it. The distinction of the defendant and some of his witnesses, the flamboyance of the plaintiff, her lifestyle, and her claims—all provided viewers and readers with an almost vaudeville-like environment. For some of the testimony, the court crowd had such a good time that Judge Clifford banged his gavel constantly.

MRS. JOSEPHINE MOFFITT.

WILLIAM WALLACE PIKE.

Scenes from the trial of *Moffitt v. Pike* (from the *Chicago Daily Tribune*)

Unlike the trend with prominent murder cases, where women showed up in droves, the Moffitt-Pike separate maintenance trial was attended predominantly by men—possibly hoping to find out how to avoid ending up in the same situation with women they were dating but had no intention of marrying.

Bishop's opening statement presented Josephine Moffitt as succumbing to the wiles of the defendant, then being betrayed by him after he got her to consent to a "marriage" during their meal at a restaurant. Trude's statement painted a different picture, one of a "designing woman" who had found out how wealthy Billy's family was and wanted to hold on to him by threat of exposing the affair to his parents. When he talked about Josephine's "haunting of the Pike neighborhood dressed in gorgeous raiment to make herself conspicuous for the purpose of annoying his family," Josephine had such a fit of hysteria that she had to be taken out of the courtroom. Trude was unmoved: "We were told that at a certain stage of the trial this woman was to weep and become hysterical, but I did not expect it to come so soon." (Trude would give Josephine no quarter, as he had to a sobbing Dethlef Hansen in his lawsuit against Minnie.)

And, in fact, Josephine's entire direct examination was punctuated with frequent jags of hysterical crying, a problem she did not have during Trude's cross-examination. She described her relationship with Billy in great detail and told of the "wedding vows" exchanged between the courses at the DeJonghe Restaurant, located in the Masonic Temple building. She had not known Billy for more than a couple of weeks when he proposed, she said, and she replied that she would be proud to be his wife.

There were problems, however, because Billy's parents would object and would disinherit him, so he wanted it kept secret. At first, he thought they should go to Milwaukee (Josephine was no doubt remembering Minnie's wedding trip to the "marrying parson," Reverend Hunsberger), then changed his mind, took out a pencil, and wrote: "This is to certify that Josie is my own little wife and whatever happens I shall never leave her." They held hands and exchanged private vows.

Now, although Josephine had approximately fifty letters Billy had sent her over the years, she did not have this all-important "marriage certificate." Someone had stolen it, she said. Billy had also given her a ring in the carriage after the meal at the DeJonghe, but she had lost that. So she had no written document and no wedding ring. Trude wanted to know why Billy had waited until the carriage ride to give her the ring. Wasn't the usual thing to do it at the exchange of vows? Shouldn't he have done this in the restaurant? Josephine had no answer.

During her direct examination, Josephine was waxing long on the endearments the two lovers shared and how much Billy cared for her. Finally, Trude had had enough. "There is a lot of slush going on here, and we haven't objected to it because we don't want to appear to be captious."

Naturally, Josephine lied about everything that made her look bad. She denied introducing Mrs. Margaret White, an older prostitute, to Billy as "Mamma." She denied calling Gene at the Athletic Club and also denied telling Berman to stop interfering with her relationship with Billy. She claimed she didn't know beforehand that Alice Morris was a prostitute, and that discovery was one of the reasons she wanted to get out of the flat she shared with her and get a new one with Billy. She shaved five years off her age, claiming she was twenty-eight when she was really thirty-three, although nobody knew that at the time. (By 1921, she was taking twenty years from her actual age, and in 1930 a whopping twenty-five—which would have made her just four years old when she first met Billy Pike!)

The most sensational witness of the trial appeared on the second day: William Hale Thompson, who since that 1898 bachelor party had gone on to serve as alderman in Chicago's Second Ward and had just before the trial been elected as county commissioner. So many men showed up to watch that they could not all see the "stage," so they stood anywhere they could find a bare spot: the radiators, the chairs, the tables, and even the window ledges. Thompson's testimony caused so much laughter that Judge Clifford was constantly threatening to clear the courtroom—though he never followed through.

Thompson was mortified by having to give this testimony because it revealed that he and his pals had frequented Levee places. Consequently, he tended to give his answers in a stiff, quick voice. Of all Billy's friends

"Big Bill" Thompson testifying at the trial (from the *Chicago Daily Tribune*)

at the bachelor party that night in 1898, Thompson was the only one to testify. The others had left town so they wouldn't have to reveal their own peccadilloes on the stand. (Percy Thompson, who knew a good deal more about the evening than his brother, was supposedly laid up because of an appendectomy.)

William Hale Thompson claimed not to know anything about the prostitutes' being at the Monroe Restaurant, that "someone had played a trick on him by bringing [them] in." As he described the scene of the women entering the restaurant, with the spectators enjoying it more than they should have in a staid court of law, the judge was forced to stop the proceedings: "I wish this audience would understand this is not a vaudeville show and if they don't keep order the sheriff will clear the room." But they didn't keep order and the sheriff didn't clear the room.

During cross-examination by Elmer Bishop, Thompson revealed his political persona when Bishop was trying to get him to admit that everyone, particularly Billy, was drunk. The witness refused to commit himself either way: He wouldn't say they were drunk, but would not say they were sober, either. Billy was not drunk, but "possibly he may not have been entirely sober." (After Thompson's testimony, he was so embarrassed that he left Chicago for a full two months because he could not face his fellow county commissioners. But when he came back, they welcomed him with open arms and didn't seem to have even remembered his humiliation.)

Trude and Payne focused their defense on presenting witnesses who would testify that Josephine Moffitt had never moved about in the world as other than a woman named Moffitt—sometimes "Miss," but more often "Mrs." She never used the name Pike or told anyone she was married to Billy. In fact, she sometimes told people that her "husband" Moffitt was a traveling salesman. And when she took out a loan with a man named Mogg, using as collateral the furniture Billy provided, she declared on the documentation that she was a single woman.

Another sensational witness appeared for the defense: Josephine Moffitt's former friend Gladys Forbes. It was she who revealed the plan hatched between Josephine and Minnie Ketcham to milk Billy Pike for his fortune and also the fact that the former intended to have a hysterical fit at some point during the trial. The reason for their breakup was never explained, but if Gladys knew about Josephine's plan to sham hysteria, it must have happened between the filing of the lawsuit in April and the beginning of the trial in November.

By then Gladys Forbes was living with Thomas P. Shannon, who had at one time been a Chicago supervisor. Although she sometimes referred to herself as Mrs. Shannon, they were never married. A somewhat sinister incident had occurred a couple of months before Josephine Moffitt filed her lawsuit. In 1896, Gladys's mother, Mrs. Ann Foley of Milwaukee, somehow got a four-year-old orphan girl from a Catholic foundling hospital in New York City, then gave the child to Gladys and Tom Shannon for "adoption."

Gladys and Tom took no legal steps to adopt the little girl, whose name was Margaret Thorpe, but raised her and provided her with nice clothes and toys. When Margaret was ten, the nuns at the orphanage came to the conclusion that Gladys was "not a fit guardian" and wanted the girl back. Since Gladys and Tom had never done anything about adoption, the judge decreed that the hospital still had jurisdiction over Margaret Thorpe and ruled that she would have to go back to New York City; the issue of Gladys's parental fitness was not addressed.

Margaret, obviously having picked up some of Gladys's devious ways, asked if she could go back to their flat at 2001 Michigan Avenue, to "say goodbye to Mother." She was allowed to do so, and while she was there, excused herself to go to the bathroom . . . and never returned. While the orphanage employees were out looking for Margaret, Gladys Forbes and Tom Shannon cleaned out their flat—including the carpets—and vanished with the girl.[3] (Given Gladys Forbes's lifestyle, she hardly seems the type to want to raise a child, so the question must be asked: To what purpose did she acquire this little girl?)

On the stand in *Moffitt v. Pike,* Gladys presented a scene that may give a clue as to the eventual falling out of the two friends. Supposedly, when Tom Shannon realized that Josephine intended to blackmail Billy Pike over their relationship, Shannon picked up the phone to call Billy's brother Gene and warn him. Josephine flew into a rage, took a pair of scissors, and cut the telephone wire. Now, as Gladys and Tom were con artists themselves, it seems unlikely that either would suddenly succumb to a spasm of moral rectitude regarding Josephine's blackmail plan. It may be that the two were angry at being left out of the scheme (after all, it was at Gladys's restaurant that Josephine and Billy met) or perhaps Josephine had just revealed that she intended to cut them out of it.

Josephine claimed that she could not have cut the phone wire because she had locked herself in her room after Tom Shannon threatened to hit her (although she did not say why he wanted to do that). Gladys's response to this on cross-examination was "Mrs. Moffitt is capable of taking care of herself. She has scratched men's faces that I know of." Between Gladys's version and Josephine's, we may be seeing hints of greed on both parts as to whether Gladys would get a share or how big that share would be. That might be why Tom would threaten to hit Josephine, if he did in fact do so, and why he would call (or pretend to call) Gene Pike to reveal the scam.

When Billy Pike finally took the stand for himself, the vaudeville show reached a new level. Billy was red with embarrassment and extremely uncomfortable at the testimony he had to give, Josephine spent much of the time sobbing while he was testifying, and the audience was highly amused by it all. Pike had to admit that he had been to Frank Wing's more than just that one time on the night he met Josephine, that he had made out with her in the landau, that he had spent that first night with her and later shared flats with her, and that he had given her a lot of money over the years.

But the highlight for the crowd was when Billy had to answer questions regarding the "guest list" for the dinner party to which he invited his friends and Josephine invited some "young ladies": There was Fanny (last name unknown), Myrtle Goodrich, Freckled Sal, and a mother-daughter pair of prostitutes named Woodward. And how about Sheeny Cora? Billy thought she hadn't been invited and so probably wasn't there. These were all known prostitutes, and Judge Clifford's gavel hardly ever got a rest during the description of the party.

(Another entertaining moment for the courtroom audience came with the testimony of Gus Dreyfus, a cigar dealer, who had roomed at 2340 Calumet Avenue when Josephine lived there. He had complained of the noise coming from her flat, but then admitted that one time the noise might have been coming from his own—because of a little supper he and his roommate had given for another male friend, two young ladies, and an old woman who acted as a chaperone. Apparently, one of the women—possibly a little the worse for wine—had a fit of hysteria. When Trude asked Dreyfus who the guests were, the flustered witness caused much amusement when he admitted, "I really can't think of their names now to save my life.")

In his closing argument for Josephine Moffitt, Elmer Bishop argued, "She is just as worthy as he is, a little better morally, and just as good physically, I think, and all she lacks is the money and the social position, both of which ought to be supplied by her husband."

Trude took a more worldly look at the whole thing, particularly the bachelor party, where he said that probably not all the young men there were entirely shocked at the presence of the prostitutes: "I believe that at least one-third of them were engaged at the time in the agricultural pursuit of sowing their wild oats." But, he stated, most of them had settled down since that time, "for when the crop is gathered reason usually returns once more."

However, Trude must have been uncomfortable at his position because of the role his former client Minnie Ketcham had played in scamming Billy Pike, so he had his cocounsel, John Barton Payne, handle it. Payne called *Moffitt v. Pike* "the child of the Ketcham case": "How Mrs. Ketcham won, by what means I don't know, and Mrs. Ketcham advised this woman to do what she did. I think the Pikes deserve credit for resisting the attempts to blackmail them."

Judge Clifford took the matter under advisement and issued his ruling about ten days later. He found that Billy and Josephine were not married but that "if her testimony is to be believed as to what happened at the Masonic temple and afterward, there is no doubt they were husband and wife," which illustrates the nature of Illinois law at the time and how easy it was to establish—or claim to have established—a common-law marriage.

Clifford found it telling that Josephine had lost "the most important [paper] Pike had ever entrusted her with," as well as the wedding ring, yet had kept all those letters from him over a three-year span. Regarding her letting Billy and Percy spend the night with her and Alice the very first time she met them, Clifford was critical: "If a girl thinks lightly of her reputation, she cannot expect others to have a high opinion of her."

Finally, the judge pointed out all the evidence that showed Josephine Moffitt acting as one unattached and using the surname Moffitt, never Pike. He concluded that the relationship was "meretricious in its inception and never has been changed, and that no common law marriage ever took place between them."

Josephine appealed Judge Clifford's verdict, and in 1904 the appellate court upheld that decision in an opinion that seemed to be directing the legislature to get rid of this dangerous law, that it should not be legally permissible to have such marriages with no third person present. In the meantime, such common-law claims should be "closely scrutinized and never sustained unless clearly proven by credible and satisfactory evidence."

A year later, the Illinois legislature took the appellate court's advice and repealed the legislation regarding common-law marriages because of its susceptibility to schemes like the one perpetrated by Josephine Moffitt.[4]

Lessons Not Learned

After the failure of her lawsuit, Josephine went to New York City and worked as a chorus girl, claiming to be twenty years old, although she was close to forty by then. It didn't take long for her to glom onto a man she probably perceived as wealthy: Prince Victor of Thurn and Taxis, a title given his family by the King of Prussia for their handling of the Royal Mail. But Victor wasn't wealthy; he just seemed so. And, like Josephine, he was a con artist. He had borrowed $120,000 from a woman in Paris so he could go to America and try to entice an heiress to marry him.[5]

But Josephine, to her dismay, discovered that Prince Victor wasn't rich at all. Not only that, he had a serious gambling habit and would frequently pawn expensive items for less than half their value, then lose that money at the track. When he ran away from her and escaped to Europe, she thought she could get money from his family by pulling the common-law marriage trick again. She wrote to his brother, Prince Maximilian, and told him she and Victor had exchanged vows in a restaurant and therefore were legally married under U.S. law, that they had to get married that way until Prince Victor could get permission from the Emperor of Austria.

Josephine hinted to Max that money would make her forget all about her claims against his brother, but not how much it would take. He ignored her, so she declared—in the press—that she would go to Europe and find her "husband." If necessary, she would appeal to the Emperor of Austria. She now began calling herself "Princess Josephine of Thurn and Taxis."

In the meantime, the woman who had loaned Prince Victor the "bait" money got nervous at not having received any of it back, especially as she had borrowed it from various sources. She got a court order in Paris and had the prince's belongings confiscated from his hotel room, but he had next to nothing there. Probably as a result of not paying his debts, which was something no gentleman ever did, Prince Victor was kicked out of all his clubs and also had his commission in the Austrian Army revoked.

To protect himself against Josephine Moffitt, Prince Victor filed an injunction in London to prevent her from claiming they were married and also from calling herself Princess of Thurn and Taxis. Besides, he said, Josephine was already married . . . to Billy Pike! As he had expected, Victor was denied his injunction. He had merely wanted to let Josephine know that he would not capitulate to her demands.

And so Josephine Moffitt disappears from our story for now, but—like a bad penny—will eventually return. While she was pursuing her latest scheme, her friend Minnie Wallace Walkup Ketcham had embarked on her own next adventure.

Part Four

Chicago, 1902–1915

Chapter 15

The Robber Baron's Partner

*The secret of success in my business is to buy old junk, fix it up a
little, and unload it upon other fellows.*
—Charles Tyson Yerkes (circa 1897)

Two interesting news items concerning Minnie Wallace Walkup Ketcham
surfaced after John Ketcham's death. The first was the discovery that a
woman who lived in the vicinity of Indiana Avenue was the niece of Minnie's first husband, James Walkup. Mrs. Titus, the niece, had been fifteen
years old at the time of Walkup's death, but remembered the incident—and
the subsequent hoopla—quite clearly. But she had no idea that her neighbor
Mrs. Ketcham, aka Mrs. Wallace, was the famous Minnie Walkup until after
the death of John Ketcham, when her real identity was discovered.[1]

The second item, never proved or disproved, was from 1901, just before
the trial in *Hansen v. Ketcham*. Minnie was living in New York City, and
the rumor had reached Emporia from Chicago that she was about to marry
a rich New Yorker "who loves her madly" and was going to move her into
a Fifth Avenue home. Her lawyer, George Trude, said he knew nothing
about it and viewed it as untrue. The reason for the marriage, of course,
according to the article, was that her money was nearly gone.[2]

Whether Minnie was out of cash or not, by 1900 she had latched onto
another rich man, one who was still married: DeLancey Horton Louderback, twenty years her senior, who accompanied her to her trial in Chicago

DeLancey Horton Louderback
(from the *Chicago Daily Tribune*)

every day. By then he had been married for thirty-three years to Virginia Mixsell Louderback, born the same month and year as her husband (August 1849). DeLancey Louderback's main claim to fame was his partnership with robber baron Charles Tyson Yerkes.

Louderback, the son of an Episcopal minister, was born in Iowa in the house that had been built by the owner of the famous slave Dred Scott.[3] The very prolific Reverend Alfred Louderback had thirteen children: nine with his first wife, Susan, and four with his second, Sarah, whom he married after Susan died. By 1860, the family had moved to Alfred's native state of Pennsylvania, settling in Philadelphia, with a brief stint in upstate New York.

DeLancey was a boy who was small for his age (and he would be small as a man as well), but very ambitious. He saved all the money he got from running errands until he had the princely sum of $5, at which point—at the age of fourteen—he left home to make his living on his first love, the railroad. Whether it was the large number of children in his home or an intolerable situation there that precipitated his leaving is unknown, but his older brother David had done the same thing at an early age, finally disappearing completely in 1889. Nobody ever found out what had become of David.[4]

When fourteen-year-old DeLancey approached the superintendent of the New York Central Railroad in Batavia, New York, and asked for a job as a telegraph operator, the older man scoffed. "Young boy," he told him, "you should be at home with your mother." "But I want to get out into the world and be a man," DeLancey replied. His dedicated persistence finally wore the superintendent down, and he gave the boy the job. "But remember," the older man warned, "you must not sleep on duty; if you do, two trains will surely crash together and you will be hung."

DeLancey was a quick learner and a dedicated telegraph operator. He used his $30 monthly wages to buy books that taught him the principles of electricity and spent his nights studying when he had no railroad chores. Eventually, his proficiency netted him the job of train dispatcher in Buffalo, and from there he became a player in the growing field of telegraph companies. In 1876 Louderback was in charge of Western Electric's sales department, and after that he was placed at the head of Western Union's New York enterprise.

Through his connection with Western Electric and Western Union, Louderback came in contact with Cornelius Vanderbilt's son-in-law, Hamilton M. Twombly, who was in charge of Western Union and whose telephone company was engaged in a bitter competition with Boston's Bell Company. Louderback's intervention caused a peace settlement between the two warring factions, and he was rewarded with telephone stock and franchises.

When Louderback was twenty-seven, a hunting companion accidentally shot him, completely blowing out his left eye and leaving shotgun pellets embedded in his brain and skull.[5] However, this had no effect on his business acumen, and he eventually came to the attention of Charles Tyson Yerkes, a ruthless financier who had his sights set on improving and gaining a monopoly of Chicago's streetcar system, particularly the elevated, or "L," lines. Yerkes's method of gaining control through franchises was to bribe Chicago's aldermen, which was fairly common in the Windy City at that time. If an alderman balked at bribery, Yerkes would hire a courtesan to seduce him, then blackmail the hapless politician.[6]

Yerkes placed Louderback in charge of the Lake Street Elevated, which was to be a crucial aspect of the proposed Loop system, a difficult enterprise from both a political and an engineering point of view. But Yerkes solved both problems—the former through shenanigans that earned him the everlasting scorn of the public—and today the Chicago Loop is a mainstay of the business district.[7]

One day, during the construction of the Loop, a watchman was fired for being drunk while on duty. The employee was so irate that he stalked off to Louderback's office, claiming he intended to kill him. The ex-watchman was a large man and Louderback was a small one, yet the latter was able to calm him down by hearing him out, again demonstrating his considerable diplomatic skills.[8]

In 1897, Yerkes, Louderback, and another investor, doing business as the Philadelphia Trust Company (both Yerkes and Louderback were Philadelphia residents), signed a contract to buy four hundred acres of a farm for $1,500 per acre. In the meantime, the heirs of the landowner, realizing that the land was worth $1,000 more per acre than the contract price, petitioned the court to get out of the deal. In Illinois at that time, an alien (non-Illinois entity) could not take or hold title as trustee, so the Chancery Court granted the heirs their petition to re-sell the property.

A year later, the land was still unsold and the heirs finally allowed the Yerkes-Louderback syndicate to purchase it for the 1897 contract price of $600,000. (It can only be imagined what machinations were involved that prevented the heirs from selling the land to someone else and causing them to capitulate on the price.) The syndicate then subdivided the property and sold it off at a profit.[9]

DeLancey Louderback also engaged in various silver mining enterprises in Colorado with his brother-in-law, Philip Mixsell, and had lumber interests in Louisiana and the Pacific Northwest. When he and his cousin James registered at a hotel in Tacoma in 1890, they gave their occupation as "capitalist," the favored designation of men of that era who had accumulated riches through land, lumber, and livestock. It was a term of distinction and had none of the pejorative connotations it would later acquire.[10]

In July 1900, Louderback resigned his positions as president of the Northwestern Electrical Railway Company and of the Lake Street Elevated Road to go to London and take charge of Yerkes's next project, the Charing Cross Underground Railway (known today as the Tube). But by the end of that year, supposedly because of his wife's ill health, Louderback sent a cable to Yerkes telling him that he had to resign and return to America. There were rumors of a rift between Yerkes and Louderback, which Louderback denied, but it was entirely possible that this falling out was the primary reason for his severance from Yerkes and his projects.[11]

In May 1901 Louderback was in New York City, where Minnie was then living, and staying with his wife at the Waldorf-Astoria Hotel. In June the Louderbacks were back in Chicago, where DeLancey was spending his days with Minnie at the *Hansen v. Ketcham* trial. In June 1902 Louderback went back to Europe, sailing with his wife on the ship *La Lorraine,* to visit Switzerland and Paris. In December of that year, he told a reporter that he and his wife were on their way to the Riviera to spend the winter at the Winter Palace Hotel in Mentone, a move suggested by Virginia's doctor as a tonic for her ongoing ill health. Along with them on the ship and in Europe was Minnie Ketcham, whom DeLancey was introducing to society as their daughter.[12]

As Minnie was on the same ship, Virginia Louderback probably knew of her presence. But did she know that her husband was escorting Minnie around Europe as their daughter as she lay sick in their hotel room? Instead of "wintering in Mentone," the Louderbacks, with Minnie still in tow, boarded the SS *St. Paul* in Southampton, England, on January 24, 1903, and arrived in New York City on February 2.[13]

Virginia Louderback had been in ill health fairly continuously since 1896. On June 7, 1911, she died of colon cancer at the family's home in Chicago and was buried back in Philadelphia. Four months after his wife died, DeLancey Louderback purchased an entire block in Chicago, in the fancy Ravenswood neighborhood, and proceeded to build a unique home, known as "The Crystal House" or "The Glass House," at 4918 North Bernard Street. It was a house within a house, with an exterior shell of iron and glass surrounding a three-story home of 7,500 square feet. Twenty-five feet of space separated the two buildings, with verandas furnished extravagantly in an Oriental theme connecting the two structures at each floor.[14]

Enter Agnes Sowka

DeLancey Louderback had a weakness for young women, a weakness that twenty-one-year-old Agnes Sowka thought could be used to her advantage. She worked as a stenographer in the office of Alonzo H. Hill, a Chicago real estate magnate, across the way from Louderback's real estate offices.[15]

In the spring of 1912, Agnes became romantically involved with Hill's twenty-nine-year-old son Harvey, a ne'er-do-well whose forte was pass-ing bad checks, which his mother would then cover for him to keep him out of trouble—against Alonzo's wishes. (Harvey was not the Hills' only troubled child. In 1908, their youngest, twenty-year-old Elmer, depressed over a failed love affair, had gone up to a room over his father's office and committed suicide by shooting himself in the head.)[16]

Harvey was on his second marriage, and his wife was expecting their child in September, yet he and Agnes began seeing each other regularly, frequently hanging out in Levee dives such as Frank Wing's. Agnes and Harvey would spend the night together in various Chicago area hotels, registering as husband and wife, then take a taxi back to the city. On one occasion, Harvey asked Agnes for money to pay the cab fare, and she en-tertained the downtown crowd by pulling up her dress and removing the money from her stocking.

Their little outings ended up costing Harvey Hill about $5,000, and when his father heard about them—some having taken place while Harvey's wife was in the hospital giving birth—he cut him off entirely. Harvey and Agnes would need to come up with something to finance their entertainment.

Over the course of the spring and summer, Agnes had been working on DeLancey Louderback. She found excuses to go to his office and often sat on a bench with him, chatting, and eventually agreed to have dinner with him on Saturday, August 31.

After dinner, Louderback asked Agnes if she'd like to go somewhere they "could be more comfortable," surely a code she understood. She replied, "Anything that suits you," and he took her to a suite he kept on the third floor of a north side apartment building. There, he made advances, which were probably reciprocated to some extent. It is unlikely that they had full-blown sex, however, as she would have wanted to lead him on a little more.

Whether Agnes planned to blackmail DeLancey Louderback from the start or only hoped to keep him on a string for future financial favors is not known, but when Harvey Hill's father disowned him, he and Agnes concocted a scheme to extort some money from Louderback. On October 26, undoubtedly after unsuccessful attempts at getting money from her victim by threats of exposure, Agnes Sowka filed suit against him for $25,000 (the equivalent of over half a million dollars today) for attempt-ing to attack her in the apartment building. She said she only agreed to have dinner with him because she thought of him as a "kindly, lonely old man" but that he then lured her up to the apartment on a ruse.

DeLancey Louderback's response was that Agnes was "an adventuress and blackmailer," the partner in a conspiracy with Harvey Hill. The girl could have yelled for help out the apartment windows, he pointed out, which were wide open in August and overlooking a busy street. Moreover, he claimed he had made no advances "not countenanced by her," which tells us that *something* happened between them.

Louderback hired detectives to investigate the matter, and they discovered the entire scope of Agnes and Harvey's wild courtship. His countermove was to seek criminal indictments against them for conspiracy and attempted blackmail, upon which Agnes immediately withdrew her suit. But, when Louderback's lawyer tried to file the dismissal with the court, the entire file was discovered to be missing. This could have been a clerical error or a ploy by Louderback's attorney to keep the case open indefinitely, always hanging over Agnes Sowka's head because of the depositions in it that revealed actions by her that were considered very shocking. Or it might have been taken by someone connected with Agnes's side to prevent the suit from being dismissed.

By the end of the Sowka-Hill saga, DeLancey Louderback was sixty-four years old and feeling his age. At that point he was suffering from Bright's disease (a liver problem, possibly indicative of alcohol abuse), dropsy (edema of the brain), arteriosclerosis, and acute gastritis. He began to think about retiring from the business world.[17]

Chapter 16

Death from Afar

We do not count a man's years unless he has nothing else to count.
—Ralph Waldo Emerson (1870)

DeLancey Louderback may have left home at an early age, but he kept in close contact with his siblings. When the youngest member of the clan, Sarah Eckert Louderback—eighteen years younger than her half-brother— lost her husband to a stroke, DeLancey had a solution. Sallie (as she was known) had married Chicago attorney Henry App Ritter in 1891, and when he died suddenly in February 1913 at the age of fifty-five, she had no means of support. Their twenty-one-year-old son, Henry Jr., was in college, and their younger son, DeLancey Louderback Ritter, had died a year or so earlier.[1]

At the time of Henry Sr.'s death, the Ritter family was living next door to Louderback at 4920 North Kimball on the block he owned, quite possibly in a home he had built for them. Henry Ritter had been a successful attorney, but income ceased at his death and Sallie would soon be alone, when her son went out on his own.[2]

Sallie's big brother proposed something that would benefit both of them: Sallie and Henry Jr. would move into the "Crystal House" at 4918 North Bernard Street, where she would supervise all the household affairs and pay DeLancey $75 per month toward expenses. Louderback would pay everything over $75. (It sounds like a terrific deal for Sallie and young Henry, until you realize that $75 in 1913 is the equivalent of $1,682.) Ever the businessman, Louderback had his sister sign a written contract that would expire in September 1914, unless Sallie wanted to terminate it earlier.

As an example of what it took to run this household of three in 1914, here are a typical month's expenses with today's equivalents in parentheses:

groceries, $70 ($1,555)
wages for Tony, the butler/chauffeur/handyman, $70 ($1,555)
laundry sent out, $3 ($67)
telephone, $8 ($178)
ice, $7 ($156)
dairy products, $13 ($289)
electric lights, $16 ($356)
gas, $4 ($98)

Although some of these figures would fluctuate from month to month, on average the household expenses came to $200 (around $4,444), of which Sallie would be responsible for $75 ($1,666) and DeLancey the remainder. Ordinarily, Louderback would have had to pay a housekeeper/cook for the services Sallie performed, and that would have added another $70 ($1,555) or more to his budget, but without the benefit of Sallie's $75 offset.

In July 1913, Louderback had contracted with architect Charles Bostrom to design plans for a residence at the corner of Kimball and Ainsley, on the opposite end of the block from the "Crystal House" at North Bernard and Ainsley. (If this was the site of the Ritter residence—and it seems to have been—perhaps the plans were for renovations rather than an entirely new house.) Who was going to live there? Another relative? Or perhaps Minnie Ketcham? If this house *had* been built or renovated, it was sold before April 1914.

In January 1914, Louderback had Bostrom draw up more plans, this time for a combination store and apartment building at Western and Sunnyside Avenues. A much more ambitious project, these plans cost twice as much as those for the house, but this building never materialized. However, both events illustrate that, as of January, anyway, Louderback was looking to the future.

In February 1914, several things happened in DeLancey Louderback's life. He made plans to retire with an eye to spending the rest of his days in Europe, and on the seventh drew up a new will, which he had not done since his wife's death in 1911. In it, he left a life interest in one-quarter of his estate to "my friend, Mrs. Minnie Wallace Ketcham." Then he sold off all his real estate and railway stock holdings in the amount of three and a half million dollars.

Around this time, Minnie was on her way back to Europe, and Louderback undoubtedly was making plans to join her there when his affairs were wrapped up in the States. This is a logical assumption, as her address in London was in care of a business owned by Louderback's brother-in-law Charles Braun, widower of his sister Claribel. In fact, as the proceeds from the real estate and stock sales were never found, it may be that he entrusted Minnie with them, or sent them to her, to hold for him or invest with Braun until he arrived in Europe.

According to a news item whose contents were possibly apocryphal, Minnie gave DeLancey Louderback a special sleeping potion before she left for Europe. She said it would prevent him from lying awake at night, sleepless from missing her.[3] In that critical month of February, then, Louderback began taking various sleeping powders to cure his insomnia, whether due to his missing Minnie or from some other cause. He also developed severe headaches, sometimes so bad that he bandaged up his head in a futile effort to dispel them. His friend William Stuart, chief clerk of the election board in Chicago, visited him one day that month and noticed eight to ten bottles on Louderback's dresser. DeLancey told him they were to help him sleep. Louderback's headaches and general ill health got so bad that he went to California to try to cure himself (many people in that era were great believers in going to another climate to regain health), but it didn't work. He returned to Chicago.

In March, with his plans firmly set to leave for Europe in April, Louderback's friends gave him a big send-off dinner at the Blackstone Hotel. By the end of that month, he was suffering from a severe cold along with the headaches.

At the beginning of April, Louderback closed up the separate apartment he had kept on Wilson Avenue just off Broadway—the one he had taken Agnes Sowka to in 1912. His current love interest, spied on by the neighbors as much as they could get away with, was a tall, beautiful young woman whose taste in dress suggested that she was a secretary or stenographer. She was described as "strikingly handsome" rather than pretty, somewhere between a blonde and a brunette in coloring. This was probably *not* Minnie Ketcham, as her hair was decidedly black and she would have been forty-five years old then—hardly considered young. Moreover, the mystery woman's wardrobe seems more subdued than Minnie's characteristic glamor. Also, Minnie was in Europe in April 1914.

The security surrounding this apartment was enormous. Clearly, Louderback wanted to prevent the very thing the neighbors wanted to do most: determine the identity of DeLancey Louderback's frequent female visitor. The door of the hallway leading to the apartment had six locks on it and the windows of the apartment itself had double blinds. Still, despite all the secrecy, the two were frequently seen riding together on the "L" and shopping for candy in the local confectioner's shop.

Louderback himself supervised the removal of the furnishings on April 5. There were ornate mirrors, exotic Oriental rugs, and expensive furniture. Coincidentally, Louderback's secretary, thirty-three-year-old Bertha Schneider, whose home was farther down Wilson Avenue, received a shipment of furniture that same day. In the will that Louderback had drawn up just two months before, he left $5,000 to Miss Schneider, and there were rumors that he had proposed to her. However, this seems unlikely, as his plans to spend the rest of his life in Europe did not include Bertha Schneider.

From the beginning of April, Louderback's health seemed to get worse. On the first and the fourth, he had Sallie Ritter send Minnie cablegrams in London (contents unknown), and somewhere in there he had an associate send her a package (likewise unknown). Despite his illness, he was still able to get up and take his meals at the table, but after breakfast on Thursday, April 9, his condition grew severe, and a doctor, Paul Kelly, was sent for. By the time he arrived, Louderback was in a coma. Among the bottles on the patient's dresser was one labeled "cyanamide," which undoubtedly caused Dr. Kelly's next action: He pumped Louderback's stomach.

Cyanamide had only recently been developed, around 1896, as a pesticide and a fertilizer. It came in crystal form and had no known medicinal function because it was so deadly. However, the *Online Medical Dictionary* says that "cyanamide often occurs as calcium salt" and that calcium salt, to which citric acid has been added ("citrated"), is used to treat alcoholism.[4] Was this known in 1914? If so, would Louderback have taken it with that in mind? It seems strange that he would have deliberately taken crystals from a bottle clearly labeled "cyanamide" to help with his insomnia. However, Louderback's symptoms—the headaches, the severe cold—are those associated with the inhalation or ingestion of small amounts of cyanamide.

Dr. Kelly's stomach pumping was too late to help DeLancey Louderback, who died at 9:40 A.M. that same day. His body was sent to a funeral home for embalming in preparation for shipment to Philadelphia, where he would be buried next to his wife, Virginia. But after the embalming, someone became concerned enough about the circumstances of Louderback's death to call in the coroner, who promptly ordered an inquest.

Rumors immediately began to circulate that Louderback had committed suicide because Chicago residents had just that Tuesday voted down a subway bond pertaining to a route along which Louderback had extensive real estate holdings. However, he had sold all those in February, so that wouldn't have affected his economic status.

The coroner expressed his opinion that Louderback had *not* died of cyanamide, but this was before the autopsy (which was made difficult because of the stomach pumping and the embalming, which would have removed much of whatever poison remained in the body). The dead man's addiction to sleeping potions now became public knowledge, and people indulged in rumors regarding his supposed proposal to Bertha Schneider and the identity of the mystery woman in the Wilson Avenue apartment.

In Chicago in 1914, people were highly critical of Dr. Paul Kelly for having pumped out Louderback's stomach and for sending the body in for embalming so quickly after his death. Louderback's business partner, Michael J. Faherty, who was also a witness to the will, defended Kelly's actions and his refusal to talk to reporters about his decisions. Faherty made a strange statement, indicating that possibly he, too, thought his partner had committed suicide: Louderback, he told reporters, was now dead and left behind no widow or children, so just leave him alone and Paul Kelly, too.

Despite the coroner's assurance that the cyanamide found in Louderback's room did not cause his death, the autopsy proved otherwise. The cause of death was ruled to be "an overdose of cyanamide, taken medicinally"—this, despite the earlier statement that there *was* no medicinal value to cyanamide.

By this time, the contents of Louderback's will had been made public, and there was a great buzz about Minnie's inheriting a quarter of the estate, especially as most of DeLancey's colleagues had no idea that the two were friends. Besides the generous gift to Bertha Schneider, there was a $500 bequest to the nurse who had attended Virginia Louderback throughout her illness, with the rest of the estate being divided among DeLancey's living siblings or the sons and daughters of deceased siblings (with the notable—and unexplained—omission of a living son of his dead sister Claribel). And, while other siblings or their children got outright bequests, Sallie alone of all Louderback's relatives received exactly the same inheritance as Minnie Ketcham: a one-quarter life interest. After Sallie's and Minnie's deaths, their shares were to be vested in Louderback's other siblings and their heirs. This meant that Sallie's son Henry would not get any share of the estate. Maybe Louderback did not trust him, or possibly he felt that he had done enough for the Ritter family.

As Sallie Ritter was testifying at the inquest, a young man entered the courtroom and claimed that he was a distant relative named Albert Louderback Jr. and that he was upset at having been left out of the will. His request to ask Sallie a question was granted by the judge and it concerned another mystery woman: "Did a Mrs. Hopkins visit the Louderback home at any time during the past two months?" "No," Sallie answered, "I never heard of such a woman."

The young man, a waiter at the prestigious Union League Club, said that he had heard from his brother that the traction magnate had often escorted "Mrs. Hopkins" to dinner at the Grand Pacific Hotel. Michael Faherty then stepped forward and spoke sternly to "Albert Louderback": "You don't belong here. You get out." The young man replied, "Yes, sir," and left the courthouse. ("Waiter meekness heard the voice of command" was the *Chicago Times*'s comment.)

At least one reporter was sure that "Mrs. Hopkins" was really Minnie, and possibly he was right. When she was living in New York City and traveling around, she used the Grand Pacific as her home base while in Chicago. Minnie was not averse to making up names for herself (Mabel Estelle Wallace in 1895, not the last time she used a pseudonym) when she wanted to avoid publicity. But Minnie was probably already in Europe the two months before Louderback's death.

Although the bottle in Louderback's room was labeled "cyanamide" and this term was also used by most newspaper articles, the official terminology used by the inquest jury and on the death certificate was "Acute Pulmonary and Cerebral Oedema, caused by Potassium Cyanide poisoning." And the most startling part of the jury's decision was that the cyanide was "self-administered *unintentionally* [emphasis added] in excessive quantities on April 9, 1914."[5]

It's hard to believe a verdict of accidental overdose. The jury was probably influenced by the lack of any obvious motive, the reputation of the deceased, and all the testimony regarding his addiction to sleeping potions. Because, unless he were deluded as to the true nature of cyanamide, Louderback would not have taken it unless he wanted to kill himself. There could be no "unintentional" overdose if, in fact, it had come from the bottle labeled "cyanamide." Other than suicide, then, the only possibility is murder.

Reporters, digging up everything they could on DeLancey Louderback, discovered that the title to the "Crystal House" was not held by the dead man, but by his secretary, Bertha Schneider. This was revealed to them by people who said they were relatives of Louderback—possibly Sallie or Henry, as they were the only ones living in the Chicago area. When a reporter telephoned Bertha about it, she refused to talk to him. "I don't care to say anything about the matter at all," she told him, then hung up abruptly when he tried to get her to say what the quid pro quo was in exchange for the house, obviously intimating that it was sexual favors.

The so-called relatives who had first alerted the reporters as to this arrangement also voiced their concern about Bertha Schneider and the large monetary bequest she was given. They wanted to contest the will, but Louderback—anticipating exactly that—had put in a clause awarding only one dollar and no more to anyone who did so.

Bertha Schneider would have been better off squelching all this talk by telling reporters what was really going on, that the title was put in her name to disguise the house's true owners from the public. The Ravens-wood house and property didn't belong to Louderback after all, or even to Bertha Schneider, but to his Northwest Land Association, of which he was president. Bertha had to sign a separate contract stating that she would transfer the property to the NWLA whenever they asked for it. Given Louderback's past dealings, this whole contrivance must have been con-cocted to achieve some tax or other economic advantage. But the bottom line was that Louderback did not own the house personally, so his heirs didn't, either. And, in fact, it is not even listed in the probate files. (There was even a later rumor, one that never materialized, that Minnie would come back from London and live in the famous house.)

As for Minnie, despite her bequest, in March 1915 she hired a stateside law firm to represent her in her suit against the Louderback estate for the amount of $2,550, which she said she had deposited with DeLancey over a four-month period in 1904. Then, on March 20, having applied for her new passport in December of 1914, she boarded the RMS *Lusitania* and arrived in New York City on Monday, March 26, 1915—just six weeks before the fatal sinking of that ship by a German U-boat off the coast of Ireland on Tuesday, May 1. She gave her address in Chicago as 156 West Washington Street and shaved a year off her age.[6]

Eventually, Minnie would drop her lawsuit against Louderback's estate, possibly feeling it would prolong the time before she could get her life interest. For some reason, the Louderback attorney, John Cummings, dragged his feet on presenting the final accounting and even had to be threatened by the probate court in December 1917 to take care of it or be fined. It was finally settled in 1918, and the entire amount of the estate, consisting solely of personal property, was a mere $10,000. A newspaper from Emporia, a city periodically embarrassed about its connection with Minnie and her inability to stay out of the news, commented that the depletion of the millionaire's assets was "due to the expensiveness of Mrs. Ketcham's friendship."

As it turned out, Bertha Schneider probably profited the most from DeLancey Louderback's estate. His $5,000 bequest to her and the $500 gift to Virginia's nurse, as well as payment of his debts and funeral expenses, were to be taken care of before any other inheritances were disbursed. Minnie and the relatives got percentages of the remainder instead of actual dollar amounts.

Who Killed DeLancey Louderback?

Minnie Ketcham was overseas when DeLancey Louderback took his fatal dose of cyanide, but otherwise the circumstantial evidence is just too co-incidental to be dismissed in her favor. What are the odds that one woman would have three men intimately connected with her—all of whom left her substantial inheritances—die soon after making out their wills? Her first victim, James Walkup, was poisoned exactly a month after she married him. Her second, John Ketcham, died two months after she married him and two weeks after he made out his will. DeLancey Louderback, potentially her third known victim, died of poisoning two months after making out his will. In addition, it is safe to assume that he gave her or allowed her access to the proceeds of his $3.5 million real estate and stock sales, and this would have given her an even greater motive than the inheritance.

Louderback must have intended to connect with Minnie when he got to Europe, since he knew her mailing address, and he was wiring cablegrams to her there. And the day after his death, Sallie Ritter sent her two cable-grams, indicating that Minnie had a close connection with that household, not merely a casual one.

Minnie went to Europe around February, when Louderback began tak-ing—or increasing his intake of—sleeping powders. After that, he experi-enced severe headaches and cold symptoms, which could have come from cyanide. If the news item about Minnie's giving Louderback the sleeping potion is true, then that could have been the source of the cyanide that killed him—either the actual bottle labeled "cyanamide" or one that was unlabeled. Since both cyanide and cyanamide occur only in crystal or pow-der form, she could have mixed it in with other kinds of crystals or powders. Or she could have given him the cyanamide bottle, telling him it was a new, effective kind of sleeping potion, or a cure for alcoholism (which Louderback might have had at that point and assuming Minnie knew the poison was used for this).

Another possibility is that Louderback was slipped the fatal dosage by Sallie or Henry or both, either on their own or as part of a conspiracy with Minnie. It is interesting to note that although Minnie always allied herself to older men because of their wealth, in the case of each death, there was a young man living in the household: her cousin Willie Willis (Walkup), butler Joe Keller (Ketcham), and Henry Ritter (Louderback).

The Ritters, mostly Sallie, had the means, the motive, and the opportu-nity to kill DeLancey Louderback. He seems to have received a large dose around breakfast time on the day he died (with cyanide, any decent amount produces immediate results, usually fatal, so we can assume it was taken close to his collapse), a time he would ordinarily not be taking a sleeping potion. Sallie might have been afraid of what would happen to her when DeLancey left for Europe and her contract expired in September. Her son Henry was just getting out of college and about to go out into the world, so he would be unable to support his mother for a while. Surrounded by excess and privilege, as she was, it might have been an incredible temptation. If she is the relative quoted by the newspapers, her consternation over Bertha Schneider's supposed ownership of the "Crystal House" is evident.

Yet, nobody ever suggested that Louderback had been murdered, so nobody was ever looked at closely for it. What about suicide? This, too, is a distinct possibility. Louderback had pretty much taken care of his af-fairs in preparation for leaving for his retirement in England and France. Moreover, he was feeling so poorly by the time of his death that he must have wondered how much longer he actually had left. He would have preferred ending his life in familiar and comfortable surroundings. But this begs a very important question: *Why* was he feeling so sick? Because he was ingesting or inhaling small amounts of cyanamide, something he would not have done on his own if he wanted to commit suicide. Why torment himself in little bits when he could get it over with in one big dose? In an ironic ending, it may be that the cyanide given to him by Minnie—or Sallie—was causing him so much distress that he killed himself instead.

If we could only know what was in those cablegrams and the package that Louderback sent to Minnie just before he died, we might have important clues that would shed light on the mystery. As it is, readers will have to decide for themselves which is the most likely solution: murder by Minnie, murder by Sallie, murder by Henry, murder by two or three of them in a conspiracy, or suicide.

The verdict of the inquest jury (accidental overdose) was the only one that could *not* have been the cause of death. Louderback was either murdered or he committed suicide, and if Minnie had been anywhere near Chicago, she would have been an immediate suspect once that will was filed.

What Was Minnie's Relationship to DeLancey Louderback?

Although Louderback was probably infatuated with Minnie when he first met her and throughout their trip to Europe in 1902, he had plenty of opportunity to marry her after his wife's death in 1911. It's hard to see why *she* would not have consented to this, as she had said "yes" twice before to older wealthy men she was obviously not in love with, so it must have been his own choice. By the time of Virginia's death, Minnie would have been in her forties, a little older than DeLancey liked his women.

In the end, then, the designation in his will—"my friend"—was probably just that. Louderback seems to have been more a William Jay to her than a John Ketcham. And she may have even helped him out in the procuring of his young women, given her own associations with people like Gladys Forbes and Josephine Moffitt.

With the death of DeLancey Louderback, our story is nearly at an end. It only remains to be seen how some of our "characters" fared in their later lives and whether Minnie Wallace Walkup Ketcham, the consummate adventuress, had any more "adventures."

Part Five

Lagniappe

Chapter 17

Where Are They Now?

⌐⌐⌐

It is impossible to cheat life. There are no answers to the problems of life in the back of the book.

—Søren Kierkegaard (circa 1850)

Part 1: New Orleans

The Wallaces and the Findlays
Elizabeth Wallace had died in Chicago in 1895 while living there with Minnie. Her ex-husband, James, died on Christmas Eve in 1908 at the age of eighty in a New Orleans almshouse. Cause of death was chronic diarrhea and senility.[1]

Dora's husband, Edward Findlay, who had been so loyal and dedicated to his sister-in-law, Minnie Walkup, was dead by 1900, as was his son Milton. At the age of eighteen, his other son, Edwin, joined the U.S. Navy and was assigned to the USS *Iowa* in Bremerton, Washington, as a seaman apprentice first class. Dora and Minnie Findlay moved to Brooklyn, New York, where Dora declared herself a widow who had borne six children, only two of whom were still living.

In 1910, Dora and her two children (Edwin and Minnie) were living in Chicago, where Dora worked as a milliner in a hat shop and Edwin was a repairman for the telephone company, a job he would hold for the rest of his working life. Somewhere between 1900 and 1910, Dora married a man named Edward Smith and divorced him. Her daughter, Minnie, had married a man named Fisher, who was dead by 1910. In 1911, Minnie Findlay Fisher married a man from Indiana (on her aunt and namesake's birthday), with whom she raised several children. Edwin Findlay married a young woman who was boarding in their Chicago home and they had one child, a daughter. He died in 1951.

When Edwin and his wife established their new home, Dora moved in with them. She died in 1921 of chronic nephritis (kidney disease) and chronic myocarditis and was buried in her sister Minnie's second plot in Forest Home Cemetery, next to their mother, Elizabeth Wallace. Neither grave bears a stone.

Judge William T. Houston

Judge William T. Houston moved from New Orleans to New York City around 1890 and established a law practice there. In 1907, he represented a woman who claimed to be the daughter of "Silent" James Henry Smith, who had just died and left an estate of $25 million. Smith had once been considered New York's richest bachelor, after inheriting $30 million from an eccentric uncle. Shy and retiring (hence the nickname), he blossomed into a society man and, in September 1906—over fifty at the time—married the ex-wife of another rich man, Rhinelander Stewart. He died six months later, still on his around-the-world honeymoon.[2]

Judge Houston's client had a marriage certificate that showed her mother had married a James Henry Smith in 1866. Smith abandoned his wife and daughter and went to live in England. However, "Silent" James Henry Smith would have been only twelve years old at the time of the alleged marriage.

In 1910, Judge Houston was involved in another estate problem, this one concerning the will of his sister, who had left her entire estate to an adopted nephew. The Houston family claimed that the nephew had exerted "undue influence" over her, and they were trying to break the will. The nephew said he'd kill them if they contested it. No outcome of this case was ever reported.

Judge William T. Houston died in Washington, D.C., on August 8, 1918, at the age of eighty-four.

James D. Houston

J. D. Houston continued his violent ways after the *Mascot* shooting in 1885. In 1888, New Orleans police commissioner Patrick Mealey was assassinated by a man who had purchased the murder weapon with a note written by Houston asking the gun shop owner to sell it to him.[3]

In 1889, the last bare-knuckle prize fight in the United States was held in Richburg, Mississippi, across from New Orleans, a seventy-five-round affair between John L. Sullivan and Jake Kilrain (won by Sullivan). It was held in Mississippi because such fights were illegal in Louisiana. The famous fight was organized by James D. Houston and others, and before it began someone nominated Houston as referee. However, the honor went to another man.

In 1891, Houston was one of the leaders of a "vigilance committee," which was responsible for what has been called the "largest mass lynching in American history." An estimated 6,000–8,000 people showed up to watch or participate in the lynching of eleven Italians who were suspected of having assassinated New Orleans police chief David Hennessy.

James D. Houston died of leukemia in New Orleans on January 29, 1894. He was forty-five years old.

William Pitt Kellogg

William Pitt Kellogg, the former governor of Louisiana who scandalized America by traveling around the country with Minnie Walkup after her trial and who bought the house for her in Chicago, died in Washington, D.C., on August 10, 1918. He left an estate of $1.2 million but made no bequest to Minnie.[4]

Part 2: Emporia

The Walkup Family

Elizabeth (Libbie) Walkup married John Elmore Martin, son of a former governor of Kansas, on October 10, 1886, a little over a year after the death of her father. They had two children, both sons. John was elected mayor of Emporia in 1892 and, like his father-in-law, James Walkup, belonged to many fraternal organizations, including the Ancient Order of United Workmen.[5]

Martha (Mattie) Walkup Hood and her husband, Harry, never had children. They lived in Emporia for the rest of their lives. Mattie Hood's father-in-law, the redoubtable Major Calvin Hood, died in Emporia on February 4, 1910, at the age of seventy-eight, just thirteen months after the death of his wife.

Eben Baldwin

After James Walkup's death in 1885, Baldwin took over his job of figuring out the road taxes for the Atchison, Topeka, & Santa Fe Railway Company. His great-grandson's widow reports that the beautiful stone barn that Eben Baldwin had built in 1879 is still standing off Highway 70 near Lawrence, Kansas. He died on August 4, 1917, in Lawrence.[6]

Dr. Luther Jacobs

Dr. Jacobs continued practicing medicine in Emporia. In 1904, he contracted blood poisoning and went to Chicago to find a cure. He died there, just short of his sixty-second birthday, on April 28 of that year.[7]

Luther Severy

In 1898, at the age of seventy, James Walkup's old neighbor and witness to Minnie's spilling the box of arsenic, decided to run for mayor. He lost the election, and the young, callow new owner of the *Emporia Gazette*, William Allen White—who would eventually become that city's most well-known citizen—wrote an unkind article about Severy. "I had no grudge against him," White said later. "I was just a young smart aleck, and he was a man of seventy."[8]

The next day, having completely forgotten the article, White saw the defeated candidate on the street and greeted him. Before White even knew what was happening, Severy, who hadn't forgotten, had taken his walking stick and broken it over the younger man's head. White good-naturedly figured he had it coming to him, so he went back to his newspaper and wrote a humorous article about the encounter. The day after that, he saw Severy again: "I saw his hand fluttering and quickly reached out to grab it. There we stood, he with tears in his eyes, and I tried to say quickly that I was sorry, then he said it, so we both said it—and it was all over. It was a case of temper with him and idle meanness with me, put into rather cutting and unjustified rhetoric. I think it taught me a lesson."

Oscar Wilhite

Oscar Milton "Mit" Wilhite, teenage son of the sheriff at the time of the Walkup trial, had sworn under oath that he and a companion, Ed Gutekunst, had had sex with Minnie while she was in jail, then later recanted. Around 1909, Mit went into the hotel business with some financial help from Major Hood, who also took Wilhite into his confidence concerning a memorial the major wished to leave the city when he died. Mit's hotel-restaurant combination in Emporia was called the Mit-Way.[9]

Mit Wilhite married a woman named Emma and had two daughters. In 1933, at the age of sixty-seven, he committed suicide. Mit's father, Sheriff Jefferson Wilhite, died in 1904.

Mary Jay

Mary Jay, the daughter of William Jay, who sat by Minnie every day during her trial, never married. She lived for the remainder of her life with another single woman, named Mary Richards, whom she designated as her "partner" in the 1910 census. As neither had any occupation or owned a business, but were independently wealthy, the appellation is puzzling. It probably did not signify the sort of relationship that it does today, but it's possible that to Mary Jay, it did. And maybe she, like her father, had a crush on the captivating Minnie Walkup back in 1885. Mary Jay died near Kansas City, Missouri, on August 30, 1926, at the age of seventy-five.[10]

The Lawyers

Chief prosecutor Colonel John W. Feighan moved to the Pacific Northwest after the Walkup trial and became city attorney in Spokane, Washington. In 1890, he applied to the government to receive an invalid pension for his Civil War service and was dead by 1898, when his widow filed for her pension.[11]

Clinton N. Sterry, hired by Harry Hood to assist in the prosecution of Minnie Walkup, later became a judge and, like his colleague Colonel Feighan, moved to the West—in his case, to New Mexico and then Arizona, where he was general attorney for the Santa Fe Pacific Railroad Company. In 1900, he and his family were living in Los Angeles, California, where he died before 1910.

Minnie's defense attorney Thomas P. Fenlon died suddenly in the Ryan Building in Leavenworth, Kansas, while he was there on business. He was sixty-five, still practicing law.

George S. Dodds of Hazlehurst, Mississippi, the young heartthrob of the Emporia ladies, had a successful career as an attorney, and in 1904 he argued a case before the U.S. Supreme Court (he lost).

Dr. S. Emory Lanphear

S. Emory Lanphear was the defense witness whose answers on cross-examination caused so much disruptive laughter in the courtroom, much to the chagrin of Judge Graves. At the time of the Walkup trial, Lanphear was only twenty-six and had earlier run into some legal trouble for selling alcohol out of a drugstore.[12]

Dr. Lanphear's specialty was gynecology. In 1908 he wrote to the chief of police of Newark, Ohio, for information on that city's "red light" district for an article he was writing. Eventually, he moved with his family to Campbell, California (near San Jose), but in 1914, his wife divorced him on the grounds of desertion. He had been gone for some time before that, as in 1910 he was living in St. Louis with a twenty-nine-year-old female "lodger" who was a ceramic artist.

In 1915, Dr. Lanphear was arrested in St. Louis because two women there accused him of having fathered their children. At the same time, he was being investigated for violation of the Mann Act (taking a woman across a state line for immoral purposes). Possibly he was still researching for his "red light" article. Lanphear died in Tampa, Florida, in 1920, at the age of sixty-one.

Part 3: Chicago, 1893–1902

Dethlef C. Hansen

A month after the *Hansen v. Ketcham* trial, Minnie's former partner in crime accused two young women of robbing him of $50 in a restaurant. He had them arrested but then never showed up at the trial to testify against them. It would be interesting to know the details: Were they prostitutes? Prospective clients? And how, exactly, did they rob him?[13]

By 1904, Hansen had moved to New York City, where he then represented a young woman named Violette Watson (a "casino girl"), who was suing an elderly, wealthy Colorado mine owner named Thomas F. Walsh for breach of promise to marry her. She claimed that she had been on vacation in Europe with her family and encountered Walsh, who then convinced her to leave her family and accompany him to New York City as his ward. She was sixteen at the time and he was in his fifties (shades of Minnie and James Walkup!). He had promised to marry her, Miss Watson said, and in the meantime was to give her $15,000 a year to live on. He had already showered her with many expensive pieces of jewelry and other gifts when he was enticing her to come to the United States with him.

However, no marriage was forthcoming and, in fact, Walsh was already married. In the summer of 1905, he and his family were renting Grace Vanderbilt's Newport estate, Beaulieu, for $100,000.

Violette Watson went to Dethlef Hansen (he was never more than very vague as to how she found him; to be more specific would reveal his reputation as a "blackmail" lawyer) to file three separate suits against Walsh:

1. $250,000 for assault (presumably sexual)
2. $100,000 for breach of promise to marry
3. $40,000 for failure to keep his promise to support her with the $15,000 annual maintenance

Watson and Hansen agreed that the lawyer would receive 40 percent of whatever he could get in a settlement from Walsh. It was obvious that these two never intended the case to get to trial, nor did they even desire that. But she double-crossed him, settled with Walsh on her own for $55,000, then refused to pay Hansen. She told him to file a dismissal of the suits, but he didn't want to let go of his fee, so he refused. In addition, he let on to the court that the cases were still alive when, in fact, they had been settled. For his trouble, he was suspended from practice for a year for "unprofessional conduct" and for not dismissing the suits when his client instructed him to.

Although he was suspended from practicing law, Hansen was still entitled to represent himself. The desperate attorney went back and forth between Walsh and Watson, trying to get his money from either of them. Naturally, it was Walsh who had the deep pockets, so Hansen filed suit against him. But Walsh was shrewd and had the money to hire shrewd lawyers, so for Dethlef, it was like coming up against a brick wall.

In late June 1907, he got an order to depose Violette Watson on the grounds that she was about to leave New York City and he needed her testimony for his case. But Walsh got the order vacated by showing that Watson had no plans to leave the city, and the judge who granted it also stated that, since she was a minor at the time she signed the 40 percent agreement with Dethlef Hansen, it couldn't be enforced. Walsh's attorney asserted (probably correctly) that the deposition of Violette Watson was merely for the purpose of forcing a settlement from Walsh because of the facts likely to come out during it and the resultant scandalous publicity.

Nothing came of Hansen's lawsuit against Walsh for his fees, but we know from the *Hansen v. Ketcham* affair how tenacious he could be when it came to money he felt was owed him. In 1910 he sued Thomas Walsh for libel and conspiracy in a District of Columbia court for statements attributed to the latter in a July 1905 Denver newspaper, in which he called Hansen a "blackmailer and perjurer." Hansen added the conspiracy allegation because he said Walsh tried to ruin his reputation when he was practicing law in New York. As nothing more was ever reported about this case, it must be assumed that it came to nothing.

In 1919, now back in Chicago, Dethlef Hansen represented a stenographer accused of stealing $10,000 in bonds from the brokerage company she worked for. When the police found the bonds in his client's room, Hansen claimed she had purchased them by scrimping and saving. A few weeks before this woman's arrest for bond theft, she had been arrested and fined $10 for throwing a book at a woman, and two weeks before the book-throwing incident, she had been in a mental hospital. Hansen didn't have very much good luck with his clients over the years.

Dethlef Hansen never married. He was still practicing law when he died in Chicago's Alexian Brothers Hospital on May 3, 1932, at the age of sixty-one. At the time, his sister was head of the Department of Applied Arts at Iowa State University, obviously much more successful than Dethlef, who never lived up to the talents he exhibited in law school.

Billy Pike

Billy Pike was so relieved at escaping the clutches of Josephine Moffitt that, shortly after the trial, he married a German girl. A few years later they had a daughter, then moved to Germany, where he died in Munich on April 20, 1932, at the age of sixty. He left a million-dollar estate, much of which was in trust for his daughter.[14]

Gladys Forbes

Gladys Forbes continued her "career" of catering to rich men by throwing nightly parties at her home, to which prostitutes were invited. In 1915, a man at the Blackstone Hotel (site of DeLancey Louderback's farewell dinner the year before) was handing out Gladys's cards to men who were staying there, so there was quite a parade in and out of 3132 Calumet Avenue.[15]

Women who lived in the vicinity of Gladys Forbes's home, fed up with the constant late-night noise, traffic, and "ragtime music at all hours," as well as the "uncensored living pictures glimpsed through open windows," decided to do something about it. They armed themselves with flashlights and cameras to see license plate numbers of cars that stopped there and take pictures of the patrons. One of these irate women was Mrs. William Hale Thompson, whose husband was then mayor of Chicago.

Shortly after the town meeting at which this moral outrage was expressed, Margaret Forbes (formerly Margaret Thorpe, the young girl who tricked the foundling hospital and got to stay with Gladys and Tom Shannon) beat a female neighbor with a horsewhip for the comments she had made about her foster mother. Margaret was charged with assault.

Inspired by the women of the neighborhood, and maybe shamed by them, too, the city prosecutor decided to do a little sleuthing of his own. He hid out all night across the street from Gladys's place, hoping to get enough evidence to apply for a warrant and raid the place, but nobody came! It turned out that someone with inside information about the raid, who was also no doubt a patron of the Forbes establishment, tipped Gladys off.

Josephine Moffitt

When last we saw "Baby Jo," she was on her way to Europe to find Prince Victor of Thurn and Taxis, who she claimed was her common-law husband. In July 1914, she was in London, as was Minnie Ketcham, and still calling herself Princess Josephine of Thurn and Taxis. But Prince Victor had gotten married in 1911, and the real Princess of Thurn and Taxis was a force to be reckoned with. Calling Josephine "an adventuress and an impostor," she sued her for the misrepresentation and won a judgment of $500 (although was probably unable to collect it).[16]

The real princess was an ambitious, wealthy socialite from Pennsylvania named Lida Nicolls, by all reports a loud, profane, and difficult woman. She was one of those rich Americans who wanted to marry a titled European, and she had done so with her first husband, Lord Gerald Purcell Fitzgerald, an admiral in the Royal Navy and nephew of Edward Fitzgerald, translator of *The Rubaiyat* by Omar Khayyam. Lida had three sons with him, then divorced him in 1906.

In 1920, Princess Lida was sued by a Count Bernard Francis Gregory, who had been part of the Newport and Long Island horse and society set since around 1915, for damaging his reputation with high society by calling him a "thief and a swindler" as well as a dishonorable impostor. Gregory was asking for $50,000 for the slander. In response, Lida claimed he had tried to get her involved in a swindle for $10,000.

And it turned out Princess Lida was right. "Count Gregory" of Great Britain was really Bernard Greenbaum of Brooklyn and St. Louis, and he had a rap sheet that went back to 1896 for grand larceny, passing bad checks, and obtaining money under false pretenses. In September 1915, he had taken an emerald pin from a Newport jeweler, saying he was going to take it home and decide if he wanted to buy it. As the count presented himself as a dapper, rich gentleman (complete with British accent and monocle), the jeweler let him. But then Gregory never came back to pay the jeweler for the pin and in the meantime was trying to get an associate to fence it for him.

In jail, Gregory kept up his charade. He fainted in his cell, claimed he couldn't sleep on the iron cot because he couldn't have his pillows, and every morning would ask, "Is my bath ready?"

In 1921, the "count" got in trouble again, this time for giving an art store a $150 bad check for a painting. When he was arrested on the street, he was dressed to the nines in a derby, a frock coat, striped trousers, spats, patent leather shoes, and carrying a cane. "Unhand me, sirs! You are making a terrible mistake in arresting me," he protested to the police, who were richly amused at the swindler.

Josephine Moffitt, calling herself Josephine Moffitt-Thurn, was arrested in London in May 1915 for running a gambling operation in her apartment. The police, tipped off by an informant, found Josephine, eight other women, and five men in her apartment while a card game was going on. One of the men gallantly insisted that Josephine knew nothing about the cards and had let him use her "gorgeously appointed apartment" for a party. Right after she returned from an errand (so his story went), the police showed up and arrested everyone. "The idea of my being accused of running a gambling house is simply terrible," Josephine commented in her typical histrionic style.

Ironically, when Josephine was living in London and passing herself off as the Princess of Thurn and Taxis, she was herself the recipient of blackmail letters that threatened to expose unspecified incidents if she didn't pay up. Obviously, her high-profile lifestyle there led the letter-writers (there were two men involved) to think she not only had money but would be an easy touch. They were wrong on both counts.

Josephine returned to the United States in 1922, now going back to her birth name of Guillemet, and settled in New York City. In 1926, shortly after her fifty-seventh birthday, she auctioned off her expensive furniture, silverware, rugs, and other items through a New York gallery. The 1930 census, the last known record of her, shows her still living in New York City. She does not show up in the Death Index for New York, California, Illinois, or Louisiana.

And so ends the entertaining saga of Josephine Moffitt. She spent her entire life trying to make herself younger and richer by lying and scheming, with only a modicum of success. Yet she never resorted to murder, as did her friend Minnie Ketcham.

William Hale Thompson

"Big Bill" Thompson served as Chicago's mayor from 1915 to 1923 and again from 1927 to 1931. One of his aides was Billy Pike's brother Gene. Thompson was one of the most colorful of Chicago's politicians, "the Huey Long of his time and locale." His administration was marked by great accomplishments, but also great corruption, as he was an ally of Al Capone, who contributed heavily to his campaigns. Thompson died on March 18, 1944 (see also this chapter, page 214).[17]

The Lawyers

Dethlef Hansen's lawyer, Hugo Pam, went on to serve on Chicago's Superior Court bench as a judge for nineteen years. He died of a heart attack at the Drake Hotel in New York City on May 30, 1930.[18]

Minnie's lawyer (and later Billy Pike's), Alfred S. Trude, had the dubious distinction of having a fly fishing lure named after him. Trude owned a ranch in Big Springs, Idaho, and in 1906, Carter Harrison II (who had served as mayor of Chicago, like his father, and would be elected for another term in 1911) was visiting. As a joke, Harrison wound together some carpet wool and dog hair on a hook, named it the "Trude," and presented it to his host. But the fly looked good and it worked well, so a new western lure was born and today there are many variations on the original Trude, most containing some type of animal hair. Alfred S. Trude died in Chicago on December 12, 1933, at the age of eighty-seven.

Pony Bob Haslam

Robert "Pony Bob" Haslam was discovered by "Buffalo Bill" Cody in a run-down Chicago apartment in 1911, crippled from a stroke. Cody launched a fund-raising campaign to help out his old friend and contributed to it quite generously. But it was no use: Haslam died—an alcoholic, impoverished, and paralyzed—in 1912. He is buried in Chicago's Mount Greenwood Cemetery with a marker paid for by Buffalo Bill that reads: "Famed Pony Express Rider, Robert H. Haslam, 'Pony Bob' 1840–1912."[19]

Part 4: Chicago, 1902–1915

Sallie Ritter and Henry Jr.

Sallie remained in Chicago, dying there on February 16, 1923. Her son Henry moved to Passaic, New Jersey, shortly after the Louderback case and worked for a rubber company as a clerk in the auditing department. When he filed his mandatory registration for the World War I draft in June 1917, he indicated that he had served with the Illinois National Guard in the artillery branch for a year and a half.[20]

On September 8, 1917, Henry married Mary Turnbull Hall of Glencoe, Illinois, and they had one child, a son. By 1930, Mary was dead and Henry was a sales manager for the Manhattan Rubber Company and living in Radnor, Pennsylvania. Some time after that, Henry married Helen Krick, the daughter of a man who had made his fortune in railroads. He died suddenly on October 12, 1936, at the age of forty-four.

Agnes Sowka and Harvey Hill

Agnes Sowka obviously came to her senses after having sowed her wild oats with the incorrigible Harvey Hill. She settled down in 1914, marrying a salesman and bearing him two sons.[21]

Harvey Hill kept on passing bad checks. In September 1916, his father, Alonzo, then sixty-one, married eighteen-year-old Elizabeth McMillan. A month later, Harvey was arrested after a night of partying with a woman named Ella Goodchild and having a fight with a cab driver. His father had had enough and refused to post his bond. Harvey couldn't believe it: "I don't see why any man should let his son remain in a place like this," he complained to a reporter. When the reporter went to Alonzo, now president of his own bank (the A. H. Hill State Bank), to plead Harvey's case, the older man said: "Well, I am through with Harvey; I have no further interest in him. I am clean as a whip and nobody has anything on me. . . . He must extricate himself from his present difficulty without my aid. . . . Harvey needs the lesson. Let him clear himself from that disorderly conduct charge and those two cases of passing bogus checks and make a man of himself, and then, perhaps, I'll help him again." Two weeks after the disorderly conduct arrest, Harvey was picked up again, this time for passing a $28 bad check. At the same time, the Milwaukee police had a warrant for his arrest on a similar charge. Once again, Alonzo refused to intervene.

In February 1920, Harvey was arrested in Muskogee, Oklahoma, on a charge of bigamy filed by a woman who claimed to be his common-law wife. When reporters went to the Alonzo Hill home to interview Harvey's father about this new charge, Elizabeth Hill told reporters that they had not seen Harvey for three years.

However, it looks as if Harvey might have straightened himself up and reconciled with his family. In 1930, he was married and living in Chicago, still a real estate salesman. When his father died, on December 18, 1937, his obituary said he was the "fond father" of Harvey and two other children (one born to him and his young wife, who was still married to him at his death).

Bertha Schneider

Not long after the death of her employer DeLancey Louderback, stenographer Bertha Schneider married Everett Peacock, a successful entrepreneur who had started his own seed company as a young man in his twenties and was also the first president of the Milwaukee-Irving State Bank, which he had founded in 1919. The couple moved into the residence formerly occupied by Bertha and her parents on Wilson Avenue.[22]

But in 1921, the wunderkind ran into difficulties when his bank was found to be short the whopping sum of $468,000. The shortfall was traced to Peacock and two others, who were involved in a check-kiting and Ponzi scheme to the tune of one million dollars and involving other banks besides his own. The three were indicted, and the Illinois State's Attorney's office questioned Bertha for several hours. They knew from the start that she had guilty knowledge, and after interrogating her they realized that Peacock still had most of the proceeds. (The bank had already made up the shortage on its own.)

Peacock's bank was across the street from his seed company, and soon after the former was established, Peacock went to work on his check-kiting scheme. He would buy cashier's checks, either in his name or that of his seed company, at other banks, then deposit the cashier's checks in his own bank. After that, he "borrowed" the money from the Milwaukee-Irving bank, some of which he put into his seed company.

When he was being investigated, Peacock was unrepentant: "I do not deny that I borrowed the money," he said. "I borrowed a lot of money. What I object to is being made the goat. I borrowed the money with the knowledge of the bank officials and some of the Directors. . . . They are as much to blame as I am." He was fired as president of his own bank in January 1921.

The case did not come to trial until 1924. The prosecution introduced ninety-two checks that were used in the scheme, the last of which were just before the defendants were to be investigated. The prosecution thought this showed they knew they were about to be discovered and wanted to steal as much money as possible.

The jury in the Peacock case spent twenty-five hours in deliberation, and from the start the vote was 11–1 for conviction. The holdout juror could not be convinced to change his mind, so there was no choice but to declare a hung jury. Then it was discovered that the holdout juror had actually done the same thing in another trial, that of sixteen-year-old thief Willie Dalton (he had stolen three-quarters of a million dollars in Liberty bonds from his employer, the Northern Trust Company). However, he had a legitimate reason for holding out—or at least one that could not be contravened—and the decision stood. The state's attorney does not seem to have refiled the case, probably because the bank had already replaced the stolen money.

In 1924 a printing company sued William Hale Thompson, Eugene R. Pike, and two others for $150,000 for unpaid campaign literature. The defendants won the first trial, but an appellate court ordered a new one. At the new trial, a verdict of $151,000 was granted against one of the defendants (not Thompson or Pike), but then it was discovered that some jurors had been bribed, so yet another trial was granted.

In 1928, the printing company filed a conspiracy suit against Everett Peacock and others for trying to prevent them from pursuing their suit against Thompson. Peacock was the financial manager of the printing company (possibly not the wisest hiring choice for its managers to have made, under the circumstances) and was trying to force the owner to sell it to a magazine company. So once again, Bertha Schneider's husband found himself the subject of litigation and negative publicity.

In the late 1930s, Bertha, her husband, Everett, and their two children—Hubert and Bertha—moved to Kenosha, Wisconsin. On July 2, 1942, twenty-four-year-old Staff Sergeant Hubert Everett Peacock was killed in action in World War II. On October 19, 1949, Everett R. Peacock died in Kenosha, leaving behind his widow, Bertha, and his married daughter.

And Finally . . . Minnie

Minnie remains a mystery woman. After she returned from Europe in 1915, she settled again in Chicago. By the time of her sister, Dora's, death in 1921, her last name had changed to Keating—it isn't clear whether it was a pseudonym or she changed it because of marriage. (As the owner of the plot at Forest Home Cemetery, she informed the office there of the change when Dora was buried.) If there was a Mr. Keating, he was dead, by fair means or foul, by 1930, and Minnie was a widow again, living under the name of Estelle Keating in a large apartment building on North LaSalle Avenue.[23]

On May 10, 1957, Estelle (aka Estella) Minnie Keating (aka Ketchum [*sic*]) died of heart failure in San Diego, California, at the age of eighty-eight. She is buried in Mt. Hope Cemetery with no stone marker, sole occupier of her plot, which was purchased by "the Estate of Minnie Keating." None of the twenty names buried within a fifteen-foot radius of her grave have appeared in our story. Her great-grandnephew recalls going to her funeral as a young boy, but he never saw her when she was alive, even though his family also lived in Southern California.

According to her death certificate, Minnie had lived in San Diego for ten years, which means she had gone there in the late 1940s. What brought her there? And what is the significance of the "aka Ketchum" after the name Keating? If she had remarried, that name would supersede any others, which leads to the conclusion that "Keating" was most likely a pseudonym. Still, she doesn't seem to have been shy about letting people know that her real name was Ketcham. Maybe she spent her later years regaling people with tales of her two triumphs over the legal system.

In the end, then, Minnie outlived everyone—her parents, her sister, her nephew, her niece—and died alone in a remote western city. The information on her death certificate was not supplied by any relative or friend, as is the usual case, but by San Diego County records, which probably means she was under county care when she died.

Minnie not only outlived everyone but had probably alienated most of her acquaintances, and maybe her relatives, long before that. Now she lies, alone and anonymous, her secrets buried with her.

Notes

The names of these newspapers have been abbreviated:

Chicago Daily News = CDN
Chicago Daily Tribune = CDT
Emporia Daily News = EDN
Emporia Daily Republican = EDR
New Orleans Daily Picayune = NODP
New Orleans Mascot = NOM
New Orleans Times-Democrat = NOTD
New York Times = NYT

The names of all other newspapers are spelled out in full.

Money value equivalencies have been provided by Lawrence H. Officer and Samuel H. Williamson, "Purchasing Power of Money in the United States from 1774 to 2008," at MeasuringWorth.com (2009), http://www.measuringworth.com/ppowerus/. Money values denoted as "today" are those for 2008.

1. A Shootout and a World's Fair

1. Minnie's physical attributes were a constant fixture in all the newspapers, with the only variable being the color of her eyes: sometimes black, sometimes gray, sometimes green. They were probably hazel.

2. "The Walkup Case," *NOTD*, Oct. 30, 1885.

3. Al Rose, *Storyville, New Orleans: Being an Authentic, Illustrated Account of the Notorious Red-Light District* (Tuscaloosa: Univ. of Alabama Press, 1974), 125–26.

4. Articles on this event can be found in a special edition of the *NOM*, dedicated completely to the shooting, published on January 14, 1885. This was a weekly paper, and its normal publication would not be until that Saturday, January 17. The

January 17 issue has an elaborate diagram of the shooting scene. Less hysterical and more informative articles were published in the *NODP* ("Sharp Shooting," Jan. 13, 1885, and "The Mascot Case," Jan. 14, 1885).

5. What a pleasant surprise it was to encounter Jones, an "old friend" first met in the pages of Robert Manson Myers's epistolary work, *The Children of Pride: A True Story of Georgia and the Civil War* (New Haven: Yale Univ. Press, 1972). The collected letters of the Reverend Charles Colcock Jones family from before, during, and after the Civil War are a wonderful window into the past and an insight into how southerners felt about those issues.

6. "The Obituary Record," *NYT*, Jan. 30, 1894.

7. "Chivalrous Southrons," *NYT*, June 8, 1882; "Assassinated at the Polls," *NYT*, Dec. 15, 1883; "The New-Orleans Affray," *NYT*, Dec. 17, 1883; "The Wrong Man Indicted," *NYT*, Feb. 16, 1884.

8. "Political All Saints' Day, A.D. 1909; Or, Twenty-Five Years Hence," *NOM*, Nov. 1, 1884.

9. "Editorial," *NOM*, Jan. 14, 1885.

10. "Letters from the People," *NOM*, Jan. 17, 1885; "The Mascot's Mission," *NOM*, Jan. 24, 1885.

11. Information about the Wallaces comes from Vital Records, the testimony of Minnie, her mother, Willie Willis, and information provided to *NOM* by James Wallace (see "The Emporia Sensation," *NOM*, Aug. 29, 1885). The only reference to a possible murder in the Wallace boardinghouse comes in a letter from Mattie Walkup Hood to her father after he married Minnie (see chapter 3, page 22), but there was never any proof it had ever occurred. It is possible that Mrs. Hood confused the *Mascot* shooting with a murder in the boardinghouse.

12. "Minnie's History," *CDT*, Sept. 20, 1885.

13. Rose, *Storyville, New Orleans,* 100–102.

14. Given the subsequent experiences of her sister, Minnie, it would seem that Dora would also have set her sights on someone of loftier status than a somewhat impoverished portrait painter. However, if she found herself pregnant, she may have had to settle for Edward Findlay in order to get out of her predicament. This, of course, assumes that Findlay was not the father of this child.

15. Herbert S. Fairall, *The World's Industrial and Cotton Exposition, New Orleans, 1884–1885* (Iowa City: N.p., 1885), quoted in "New Orleans: Gateway to the Americas—Cotton Exposition, 1884," New Orleans Public Library Web site, http://nutrias.org/~nopl/exhibits/gateway/1884.htm.

16. Kenneth R. Speth, "The World's Industrial and Cotton Centennial Exposition," *Kenblog*, Nov. 17, 2008, http://expoguy2.blogspot.com/2008/11/new-orleans-exposition-of-1885.html.

2. The Visitor from Kansas

1. "The Walkup Case," *EDR*, Oct. 21, 28, 1885 (same title both days); Dr. Filkins of Emporia stated that he had never seen Walkup when he was not "more or less under the influence."

2. "The Walkup Case," *EDR*, Oct. 28, 29, 1885. There were other physicians who testified that Walkup had syphilis, but these were all from outside Emporia and it

was believed at the time that they had been bribed by the defense. The Emporia doctors seemed more legitimate, especially as they had not come forward on their own and only revealed their information reluctantly.

3. "Court Notes," *EDN*, Oct. 23, 1885; "Minnie Wallace Walkup," *NODP*, Oct. 27, 1885.

4. Biographical facts about J. R. Walkup are from "J. R. Walkup Dead," *EDR*, Aug. 23, 1885.

5. Elizabeth Wallace told a reporter in New Orleans that the talk in Emporia was that Walkup's second wife was very ill-used ("Minnie Wallace's Mother," *NODP*, Sept. 8, 1885). As she tended to exaggerate quite a bit, her statements are often suspect. However, Walkup's daughter Mattie said the same thing in her letter to him and stated that everyone in Emporia knew it to be true ("The Walkup Case," *EDR*, Oct. 31, 1885).

6. This is supposition on my part, based on what was revealed about Walkup's personality and habits, and on Eben Baldwin's testimony that Walkup was spending a lot of time in these brothels. Baldwin said he himself was at the fair every day, which suggests that Walkup was not.

7. Information about the trip to New Orleans is from Eben Baldwin's testimony: "Walkup's Wife," *EDR*, Sept. 1, 1885; "The Walkup Case," *EDR*, Oct. 21, 27, 1885. The defense would later contend that Walkup was both an arsenic eater and syphilitic and that the medicine purchased on the trip was some form of arsenic to cure the syphilis. As it turned out (see chapter 6, pages 69–70), it was not, although its true nature was never stated.

8. Anthony L. Komaroff, ed., *Harvard Medical School Family Health Guide* (New York: Simon & Schuster, 1999), 818–20.

9. Eben Baldwin testified as to the unsuitability of the lodging house. Information about Walkup's stay at the Wallaces' is from Baldwin's testimony (see note 7 and "Minnie Wallace Walkup," *NODP*, Oct. 27, 1885) and from that of Minnie and her mother ("The Walkup Case," *EDR*, Oct. 30, 31, 1885).

10. "The Walkup Case," *EDR*, Oct. 31, 1885 (emphasis in original).

11. "The Walkup Case," *EDR*, Nov. 3, 1885. Minnie later claimed that she had already consented to marry Walkup before going to Emporia because it made her seem less of a gold digger, but Walkup's letter to Edward Findlay put the lie to that.

3. The Mayor Takes a Wife

1. "The Emporia Sensation," *Mascot*, Aug. 29, 1885.

2. "Calvin Hood" [obituary], *Emporia Gazette*, Feb. 4, 1910.

3. "The Walkup Case," *EDR*, Oct. 31, 1885.

4. "Walkup's Marriage in Covington, Ky.," *EDR*, Aug. 27, 1885.

5. "The Walkup Case," *EDR*, Oct. 31, 1885.

6. "Not Guilty," *EDR*, Sept. 2, 1885.

7. "The Walkup Case," *EDR*, Oct. 21, 1885.

8. "The Walkup Case," *EDR*, Oct. 27, 1885.

9. "Accused of Murder," *NOTD*, Aug. 23, 1885, and "Minnie Wallace," *NOTD*, Aug. 25, 1885.

10. "Letters Written by Mr. Walkup," *EDN*, Oct. 29, 1885.

11. "Her Face Her Fortune," *EDN*, Nov. 10, 1885.

12. "The Walkup Case," *EDR*, Oct. 21, 1885.

13. Ibid.

14. Ibid. Libbie said that Mattie told her about the boxes being shipped out, but Mattie was in Colorado at the time, so I assume that the neighborhood women were the source of this information—especially since they spent a lot of time watching Minnie.

15. Ibid., also "Minnie Wallace Walkup," *NODP*, Oct. 21, 26, 1885.

4. Minnie Goes Downtown

1. "The Walkup Case," *EDR*, Oct. 29, 1885 (emphasis added).

2. Minnie's drugstore encounters were covered in the testimony of the druggists at the inquest ("J. R. Walkup Dead," *EDR*, Aug. 23, 1885) and at the trial ("The Walkup Case," *EDR*, Oct. 21, 22, 1885).

3. "The Walkup Case," *EDR*, Oct. 30, 1885.

4. Dr. Jacobs's care of James Walkup is covered in his testimony at the inquest ("The Walkup Case," *EDR*, Aug. 25, 1885, "Poisoned," *EDR*, Aug. 28, 1885) and at the trial ("The Walkup Case," *EDR*, Oct. 21, 23, 1885).

5. Dr. Jacobs's biographical information is from William G. Cutler's *History of the State of Kansas* (Chicago: A. T. Andreas, 1883).

6. The "butter" incident is from Mary Moss's testimony at the inquest ("The Inquest," *EDR*, Aug. 27, 1885) and at the trial ("The Walkup Case," Oct. 21, 1885). The contents of the note sent by Minnie to Moses Bates are in "Minnie Wallace Walkup," *NODP*, Oct. 21, 1885.

7. "The Walkup Case," *EDR*, Oct. 21, 22, 1885. Neighbors Julia Sommers and Sallie McKinney always seemed to be chatting together, sometimes joined by Carrie Roberts, who lived across the street from the Walkups. Carrie saw Minnie change quickly into her street clothes and back again to the Mother Hubbard, obviously watching her from her own window.

8. "The Walkup Case," *EDR*, Oct. 22, 1885.

9. "The Walkup Case," *EDR*, Oct. 24, 1885.

10. "Minnie Wallace," *NODP*, Aug. 25, 1885, and "Minnie Wallace Walkup," *NODP*, Oct. 14, 1885.

11. "The Walkup Case," *EDR*, Oct. 22, 1885.

12. Ibid.

13. The oysters and pop testimony is from Mary Moss ("The Inquest," *EDR*, Aug. 27, 1885, and "The Walkup Case," *EDR*, Oct. 21, 1885). Willie's comments are from "Points on Poison," *EDR*, Aug. 29, 1885.

14. Libbie's comment about the cloaks and also the story of the fire in her bedroom are from her testimony ("The Walkup Case," *EDR*, Oct. 21, 1885).

15. "J. R. Walkup Dead," *EDR*, Aug. 2, 3, 1885; "The Inquest," *EDR*, Aug. 27, 1885; "The Walkup Case," *EDR*, Oct. 21, 1885. Mary said that after Minnie and James returned from their wedding, while Libbie was home, she normally slept next door at the Sommers'; they had an African American maid she was very friendly with. However, this leaves open the question of where she slept before the marriage—possibly on the cot downstairs now occupied by Willie, possibly in

Libbie's bedroom (although she said she did not), or possibly those stories of her being James Walkup's mistress were true.

16. Testimony about the last day of James Walkup's life, Minnie's explanation about the poison purchases, and her spilling of the arsenic are from Dwight Bill, Libbie Walkup, Luther Severy, William Ireland, and Dr. Jacobs ("J. R. Walkup Dead," *EDR*, Aug. 23, 1885; "The Walkup Case," *EDR*, Aug. 25, Oct. 22, 1885; "Points on Poison," *EDR*, Aug. 29, 1885; "Walkup's Wife," *EDR*, Sept. 1, 1885).

17. "The Walkup Case," *EDR*, Nov. 4, 1885.

18. "The Walkup Case," *EDR*, Oct. 30, 31, 1885.

19. "Minnie Wallace Walkup," *NODP*, Oct. 22, 1885.

5. The Death of a Mayor

1. "Minnie Wallace Walkup," *NODP*, Oct. 26, 1885. This reporter had no byline or any identifying information. However, since his coverage of the case was so important and his personality so engaging, I felt he needed a name, so I have given him this one (my brother-in-law's). His nonstop energy and enthusiasm, plus his having to stay in Emporia for almost three months, made me think he was young and unmarried; his editor would probably not send an older family man so far away for such a prolonged stay.

2. "Minnie Wallace Walkup," *NODP*, Oct. 14, 1885.

3. "Her Face Her Fortune," *EDN*, Nov. 10, 1885.

4. "The Walkup Case," *NOTD*, Aug. 25, 1885; "The Walkup Case," *EDR*, Aug. 25, Oct. 30, 1885; "Mrs. Walkup," *NYT*, Sept. 13, 1885; "In Rebuttal," *EDN*, Oct. 31, 1885; "Minnie Wallace Walkup," *NODP*, Nov. 1, 1885; "The Walkup Case," *EDR*, Oct. 22, 1885.

5. "Minnie Wallace," *NODP*, Aug. 25, 1885.

6. "The Walkup Case," *NOTD*, Aug. 28, 1885; "Emporia," *NODP*, Sept. 8, 1885.

7. "Her Face Her Fortune," *EDN*, Nov. 10, 1885.

8. "J. R. Walkup Dead," *EDR*, Aug. 23, 1885.

9. "The Emporia Sensation," *NOM*, Aug. 29, 1885. Because of the scandalous and libelous nature of this article, the *EDR* and other newspapers refused to print it. See "Opinion," *EDR*, Sept. 1, 1885.

10. "The Walkup Case," *EDR*, Oct. 30, 1885, and also the same title in *NOTD*, Oct. 30, 1885.

11. "Accused of Murder," *NOTD*, Aug. 23, 1885.

12. "The Walkup Case," *EDR*, Aug. 25, 1885; "Minnie Wallace," *NODP*, Aug. 25, 1885.

13. "The Walkup Case," *NOTD*, Aug. 25, 1885; "The Funeral," *EDR*, Aug. 25, 1885.

14. "The Funeral," *EDR*, Aug. 25, 1885; "Emporia," *NODP*, Sept. 8, 1885.

15. "Taking Testimony," *EDR*, Aug. 26, 1885; "The Walkup Case," *NOTD*, Aug. 26, 1885.

16. The inquest testimony can be found in *EDR* and *EDN* from Aug. 23 to Sept. 1, 1885.

17. Squibb was a highly successful and respected manufacturer of pharmaceuticals. Today his accomplishment is reflected in the name of the Bristol-Myers

Squibb Company. Those interested in the bismuth-arsenic controversy from the New Orleans point of view can find it in "The Walkup Case," *NOTD,* Aug. 28, 1885; "Was It the Bismuth?" *NOTD,* Aug. 29, 1885; and "The Bismuth Theory," *NOTD,* Aug. 30, 1885.

18. "The Walkup Poisoning," *EDR,* Sept. 5, 1885; "The Walkup Case," *EDR,* Oct. 28, 1885.

19. William W. Scott's biography can be found in Cutler, *History of the State of Kansas.*

20. "What W. W. Scott Says," *EDN,* Sept. 7, 1885.

21. "The Walkup Case," *EDR,* Oct. 28, 1885; Philippa Martyr, "When Doctors Fail: Ludwig Bruck's List of Unregistered Practitioners: A Complete List of all the Medical Colleges of America That Are Not Recognized in the United States" (1886), *Electronic Journal of Australian and New Zealand History,* 1997, http://www. jcu.edu.au/aff/history/articles/bruck.htm.

22. "Emporia," *NODP,* Sept. 8, 1885.

23. "Walkup's Wife," *EDR,* Sept. 1, 1885; "Walkup Trial," *EDN,* Oct. 22, 1885; "Still in the Meshes," *EDN,* Oct. 23, 1885; "The Walkup Case," *EDR,* Oct. 23, 1885.

24. "Minnie Wallace," *NODP,* Sept. 20, 1885.

25. "Mrs. Walkup," *Winfield (Kans.) Courier,* Sept. 3, 1885.

26. "The Kansas City Theory," *EDN,* Sept. 5, 1885.

27. Cutler, *History of the State of Kansas;* "Minnie Wallace Walkup," *NODP,* Oct. 29, 1885.

28. "Fair Play," *EDN,* Oct. 20, 1885.

29. "Her Face Her Fortune," *EDN,* Nov. 10, 1885.

30. "The Walkup Case," *EDN,* Sept. 8, 1885.

31. "The Walkup Case," *NOTD,* Aug. 31, 1885; "Emporia," *NODP,* Sept. 1, 1885; "Not Guilty," *EDR,* Sept. 2, 1885; "Mrs. Walkup's Trial," *Boston Daily Globe,* Nov. 16, 1885.

32. "Not Guilty," *EDR,* Sept. 2, 1885.

33. "The Walkup Case," *NOTD,* Nov. 2, 1885.

34. "Minnie Wallace," *NODP,* Sept. 20, 1885. Information about the baby's middle name comes from her birth certificate (New Orleans Vital Statistics), which was, interestingly, not recorded until 1890 . . . and by Minnie Walkup. It is possible that Edward Findlay was dead by then (see chapter 10, page 123).

35. "Fair Play," *EDN,* Oct. 20, 1885, and "Walkup's Widow," *EDR,* Oct. 20, 1885. In the 1900 census, Minnie declared she had no children born to her. As there were never any children mentioned throughout her escapades, I assume she never had any, especially as motherhood and its responsibilities would not have suited her lifestyle.

36. "Minnie Wallace's Mother," *NODP,* Sept. 8, 1885. For the true Major Hood story, see "The Walkup Case," *NOTD,* Aug. 30, 1885.

37. "Minnie Wallace," *NODP,* Sept. 20, 1885.

38. "Minnie Wallace Walkup," *NODP,* Oct. 14, 1885.

39. "Minnie Wallace," *NODP,* Sept. 20, 1885.

6. A Sensation in Emporia

1. Unless otherwise indicated, facts herein come from "Court Notes," little vignettes of courtroom activity and behavior that were printed at the end of each article about the trial in both *EDR* and *EDN*. These, along with the observations of the "Bill Greer" reporter for the *NODP*, provide the best information and insight into public reaction to the testimony. Without a doubt, the two most predominant themes in "Court Notes" were the constant disruptive behavior of children and the unseemly presence of women at the trial. The former issue was brought up almost every day.

2. "A Case of False Pretenses," *EDN*, Oct. 28, 1885.

3. "Minnie Wallace Walkup," *NODP*, Oct. 24, 26, 1885.

4. Ibid.

5. Cutler, *History of the State of Kansas;* "Emporia," *NODP*, Oct. 19, 1885.

6. Cutler, *History of the State of Kansas.*

7. "Calvin Hood," *Emporia Gazette*, Feb. 4, 1910; "The Walkup Case," *EDR*, Nov. 3, 1885; "Court Notes," *EDR*, Oct. 23, 1885.

8. "Minnie Wallace Walkup," *NODP*, Oct. 25, 1885.

9. "Minnie Wallace Walkup," *NODP*, Oct. 14, 1885; "Court Notes," *EDN*, Oct. 20, 1885.

10. Unless otherwise indicated, information on jury selection is in articles titled"The Walkup Case" in both *EDR* and *EDN* Oct. 19, 20, 1885.

11. "The Walkup Case," *NOTD*, Nov. 2, 1885.

12. Unless otherwise indicated, the prosecution's case can be found in *EDR*, Oct. 21–25, 1885, and in *EDN*, Oct. 20–24, 1885. In addition, other newspapers covered it with varying degrees of thoroughness for those dates.

13. "Minnie Wallace Walkup," *NODP*, Oct. 28, 1885.

14. The information in this section is a composite of two separate Sunday reports done by this reporter, at "Minnie Wallace Walkup," *NODP*, Oct. 26, Nov. 2, 1885.

15. "Minnie Wallace Walkup," *NODP*, Oct. 26, 1885.

16. "Minnie Wallace Walkup," *NODP*, Nov. 1, 1885.

17. "Court Notes," *EDN*, Oct. 20, 1885. It cannot be overemphasized how important it is to have an actual transcript. Summaries only give the highlights of a witness's testimony. They do not show hesitancies, contradictions, testiness, defensiveness, sarcasm, arrogance, sincerity—all of which go toward evaluating the reliability of the witness. Unfortunately, despite its good intentions, the *EDR* was unable to come through with complete verbatim testimony for every witness and for the closing arguments. The newspaper, the district court, and the local historical society all have no copies.

7. Defending Minnie Walkup

1. Unless otherwise indicated, the information in this chapter is contained in *EDR*, Oct. 27–Nov. 1, 1885; *EDN*, Oct. 2631, 1885; and *NODP*, Oct. 26–Nov. 1, 1885. For coverage of the "smut" testimony, see "Smut!" *EDN*, Oct. 27, 1885, and "The Walkup Trial," *NOTD*, Oct. 28, 1885.

2. "Minnie Wallace Walkup," *NODP*, Oct. 27, 28, 1885, and "Court Notes," *EDR*, Oct. 27, 1885. For reports of Frankie Morris's crime, see, for example, "Accused of Matricide," *NYT*, July 6, 1885; "Frankie Morris Found Guilty," *Arkansas City Republican*, Aug. 15, 1885; "To Look Again for Poison," *NYT*, Aug. 30, 1885; "The Morris Poisoning Again," *Winfield (Kans.) Courier*, Sept. 3, 1885; and "The Chanute Case," *Arkansas City Republican*," Sept. 19, 1885. Frankie's case was ultimately dismissed for lack of sufficient evidence.

3. "Untitled," *Winfield (Kans.) Courier*, Dec. 24, 1885.

4. "Minnie Wallace Walkup," *NODP*, Oct. 27, 1885.

5. "A Steamer Sunk," *NYT*, Jan. 13, 1883; "Two Negligent River Pilots," *NYT*, Feb. 13, 1883; "Who Is Morton?" *NODP*, Oct. 28, 31, 1885.

6. "Personal Mention," *EDN*, Nov. 5, 1885.

7. "Experience of Ladies Attending the Walkup Trial," *EDN*, Oct. 29, 1885.

8. "Mrs. Walkup's Behavior," *EDN*, Nov. 18, 1885.

9. "Voice of the Press," *EDN*, Nov. 9, 1885.

8. Starring Minnie Walkup

1. The verbatim report of Elizabeth Wallace's testimony is in "The Walkup Case," *EDR*, Oct. 30, 1885.

2. The verbatim report of Minnie Walkup's direct examination is in "The Walkup Case," *EDR*, Oct. 30, 1885.

3. Fred E. Inbau et al., *Criminal Interrogations and Confessions*, 4th ed. (Gaithersburg, Md.: Aspen, 2001), 136–37.

4. The verbatim report of Minnie Walkup's cross-examination is in "The Walkup Case," *EDR*, Oct 30.–Nov. 1, 1885.

5. "Mrs. Walkup's Trial," *Boston Daily Globe*, Nov. 16, 1885.

6. Rebuttal testimony for both sides can be found in "In Rebuttal," *EDN*, Oct. 31, 1885, and "The Walkup Case," *EDR*, Nov. 1, 1885.

9. The Rise and Fall of Minnie Walkup

1. "The Walkup Case," *NOTD*, Nov. 2, 1885.

2. Ibid.

3. "To Improve Their Complexion," *EDN*, Nov. 12, 1885.

4. "Minnie Wallace Walkup," *NODP*, Nov. 2, 1885.

5. For a complete report on the Vinegar case, see Cindy Schott and Kathy Schott Gates, *Boys, Let Me Down Easy* (Lawrence, Kans.: Allen Press, 2005).

6. "The Walkup Case," *EDR*, Nov. 3, 1885.

7. "Minnie Wallace Walkup," *NODP*, Nov. 3, 1885; "Her Face Her Fortune," *EDN*, Nov. 10, 1885.

8. *EDR* covered the closing arguments nearly verbatim (with significant omissions) from Nov. 3–8, 1885, then gave it up because by then the trial was over and Miss Lane's illness was preventing the newspaper from getting complete transcripts.

9. Jury deliberation is covered in *EDN*, Nov. 4, 5, 1885; *NOTD*, Nov. 5, 6, 1885; and *EDR*, Nov. 5, 6, 1885.

10. "Mrs. Walkup's Trial," *Boston Daily Globe,* Nov. 16, 1885.

11. Articles about the verdict can be found in "Mrs. Walkup Acquitted," *NODP,* Nov. 7, 1885; "The Walkup Case," *EDR,* Nov. 6, 7, 1885; "Her Face Her Fortune," *EDN,* Nov. 10, 1885; and "Mrs. Walkup's Behavior," *EDN,* Nov. 18, 1885.

12. Reactions to Mr. Jay's party can be found in "Mrs. Walkup Acquitted," *NODP,* Nov. 7, 1885; "After the Verdict," *EDN,* Nov. 7, 1885; and "Her Face Her Fortune," *EDN,* Nov. 10, 1885.

13. "Dropped Dead," *EDN,* Nov. 11, 1885; "Michael Myers," *EDN,* Nov. 12, 1885.

10. Intermission

1. "Mrs. Walkup's Behavior," *EDN,* Nov. 18, 1885.

2. "Arrival of Mr. Finley [sic], Minnie Wallace Walkup's Brother-in-Law," *NODP,* Nov. 9, 1885.

3. "Minnie Walkup's Return," *NODP,* Nov. 16, 1885.

4. Minnie Wallace Walkup Ketcham, "The Story of a Woman with a Past," *CDT,* Dec. 26, 1897. In 1881 circus promoter Adam Forepaugh held a "$10,000 Beauty" contest, the winner of which would receive the eponymous amount of money and tour with his circus. The contest, thought to be the first American beauty pageant, was won by Louise Montague. Thereafter, the phrase came to connote any high-priced and valued commodity, even baseball players. See "Circus: Adam Forepaugh Circus, 1867–1894," *The Circus in America: 1793–1940,* http://www.circusina-merica.org/public/corporate_bodies/public_show/4; and "Adam Forepaugh," http://en.wikipedia.org/wiki/adam-forepaugh.

5. "Her Life an Eventful One," *CDN,* Nov. 15, 1897.

6. "A Remarkable Interview," *EDN,* Nov. 23, 1885.

7. "Untitled," *Barber County (Kans.) Union,* Dec. 11, 1885. The "dime museum" was a nineteenth-century craze, capitalized on by P. T. Barnum. These museums, which could be part of a traveling circus or carnival, or housed in a building within a city, consisted of man-made oddities and freaks of nature. They provided a wide variety of entertaining exhibits for the admission price of a dime. See Andrea Stulman Dennett, *Weird and Wonderful: The Dime Museum in America* (New York: New York Univ. Press, 1997).

8. Biographical information on William Pitt Kellogg can be found in James Grant Wilson and John Fiske, "William Pitt Kellogg," in *Appleton's Cyclopedia of American Biography, 1887*-1889 (Detroit: Gale, 1968). For details about their traveling together, see "Senator Kellogg and Mrs. Walkup," *Brooklyn Eagle,* Nov. 26, 1886; "Untitled," *Atchison (Kans.) Daily Globe,* Nov. 29, Dec. 3, 1886; "Untitled," *Emporia Daily Globe,* Nov. 30, 1886; and "Why Get Excited," *Emporia Daily Globe,* Dec. 3, 1886.

9. "Walkup's Widow," *EDR,* Dec. 20, 1885; "The Depositions," *EDN,* Dec. 21, 1885; "More of the Walkup Sensation," *Emporia Democrat,* Dec. 23, 1885; "Says It Is Blackmail," *Emporia Democrat,* Dec. 23, 1885; "Walkup's Heir," *Winfield (Kans.) Courier,* Dec. 24, 1885.

10. Inbau et al., *Criminal Interrogations and Confessions,* 136.

11. "An Unpleasant Duty," *EDR,* Dec. 20, 1885; "Minnie Again," *EDN,* Dec. 21, 1885.

12. New Orleans City Directories, 1890–1891; Birth Certificates from New Orleans Vital Statistics; Dora Kirby Findlay declares herself a widow in the federal census in 1900.

13. "Much Mystery about Her," *CDN*, Nov. 16, 1897.

14. "To Go to Coroner," *CDT*, Nov. 16, 1897.

15. "Keller, the Butler, Gone," *CDN*, Nov. 17, 1897.

16. In the 1900 federal census, Dora Kirby Findlay declared that she had borne six children and that only two were living at that time.

17. Death certificate for William D. Willis, New Orleans Vital Statistics.

18. "Untitled," *Arkansas City Republican*, Oct. 16, 1886.

19. "Death Reveals a Coincidence," *CDT*, Aug. 18, 1898.

11. The Levee

1. Julie K. Rose, "A History of the World's Columbian Exposition, 1893," http:// xroads.virginia.edu/~ma96/WCE/history.html (1996).

2. This is the address given in the death certificate of Elizabeth Wallace, from Cook County Vital Statistics.

3. Peter C. Baldwin, "Vice Districts," *Encyclopedia of Chicago*, 2005, http:// www.encyclopedia.chicagohistory.org/pages/1304.html.

4. Timothy Gilfoyle, "If Christ Came to Chicago," *Encyclopedia of Chicago*, http://www.encyclopedia.chicagohistory.org/pages/624.html.

5. Troy Taylor, "Bath House John, Hinky Dink & Others," *Weird and Haunted Chicago*, 2003, http://www.prairieghosts.com/graft.html. For a wonderful look at the inner workings of the Levee in the early 1900s, particularly the most famous brothel (the Everleigh Club), see Karen Abbott, *Sin in the Second City: Madams, Ministers, Playboys, and the Battle for America's Soul* (New York: Random House, 2007).

6. "Writ Ends a Gay Time," *CDT*, Aug. 30, 1902.

7. "Few South Side Saloons Are Open after Midnight," *CDT*, June 13, 1903.

8. The Firehouse Restaurant has the same address, but it is possible that it is not at the same location as Minnie's apartment building; the City of Chicago renumbered its streets around 1901.

9. Federal census for New Orleans, 1870 and 1880; federal census for Chicago, 1910; federal census for New York City, 1930; Passport applications of U.S. Citizens, posted on Ancestry.com; ship's register for the *SS Berengaria*, 1922; Families of Louis Adrian [*sic*] Guillemet, posted on Ancestry.com; Josephine Moffitt's testimony in the *Moffitt v. Pike* case.

10. Information on Josephine Moffitt comes from her direct and cross-examination in the *Moffitt v. Pike* case ("W. W. Pike Suit Is Begun: Jury Is Dispensed With," *CDT*, Nov. 12, 1902; "Pike Case Waxes Warm," *CDT*, Nov. 14, 1902; "Tells Story of Pike and Moffitt," *CDT*, Nov. 15, 1902), as well as from some of the questions she denied on cross-examination. It was obvious the defense had evidence of the information and that she was an inveterate liar about things that did not make her look completely innocent. Therefore, I am surmising that those items are true.

11. "Patrons of Vice Will Be Trapped in Photographs," *CDT*, May 18, 1915.

12. "Hitt Is Asked to Account," *CDT*, Apr. 12, 1898.

13. I plotted a map of Chicago with all of Minnie's addresses and compared them with those of Gladys Forbes and Josephine Moffitt.

14. "A Widow Again," *NODP*, Nov. 16, 1897; "To Go to Coroner," *CDT*, Nov. 16, 1897.

15. Death certificate of Elizabeth Wallace; records of Forest Home Cemetery, Chicago.

16. "Much Mystery about Her," *CDN*, Nov. 16, 1897.

17. "Red Jam Horror in Famous Case," *CDT*, June 13, 1901.

18. "Now Ready for Clients," *CDT*, June 25, 1890.

19. "Interview with Dethlef Hansen," *Chicago Inter Ocean*, Feb. 7, 1893; Tacoma, Washington, City Directories, 1889–1891.

20. Letter to Dethlef C. Hansen, Mar. 26, 1891, *The Writings and Speeches of Grover Cleveland*, ed. by George Y. Parker (New York: Cassell, 1892), 481.

21. "Interview with Dethlef Hansen"; see also Robert Loerzel, *Alchemy of Bones* (Urbana: Univ. of Illinois Press, 2003), 26, 28, on Dethlef Hansen and the Luetgert case.

12. The Death of a Club Man

1. "Third Wife Is Left," *CDT*, Nov. 15, 1897; Clark Waggoner, "First National Bank of Toledo—Ohio 1871," http://www.scripophily.net/finabaofto18.html.

2. Barbara Johnson, "Nettie Poe Ketcham, 1865–1950," *In Search of Our Past: Women of Northwest Ohio*, vol. 2, 1990, available at http://freepages.family.rootsweb.ancentry.com/~gen2/Page40.html.

3. Nelson W. Aldrich Jr., "Death of the Club Man," *Seattle Times*, July 17, 1988.

4. Information on John Ketcham's drinking and debauchery is found in "Divorced in Short Order," *CDT*, Oct. 3, 1896, and "To Go to Coroner," *CDT*, Nov. 16, 1897. Nettie's hiring of detectives is in the Ketcham probate files, Cook County Archives, Chicago.

5. "To Go to Coroner," *CDT*, Nov. 16, 1897.

6. "Christopher Corbett, *Orphans Preferred: The Twisted Truth and Lasting Legend of the Pony Express* (New York: Broadway Books, 2003), 192–95.

7. "To Go to Coroner," *CDT*, Nov. 16, 1897. Since Minnie was seen occasionally at the Auditorium Annex and "attracted much attention" there, I am assuming this is where she met John Ketcham and that she frequented the Annex to catch a rich man.

8. Ibid.

9. "Bridegroom May Have Been Keller," *Atlanta Constitution*, Nov. 18, 1897; "Plot Thickens in the Ketcham Case," *NODP*, Nov. 18, 1897.

10. Dethlef Hansen revealed his dealings with Minnie at the trial of *Hansen v. Ketcham*.

11. Information about the "party flat" is in "To Go to Coroner," *CDT*, Nov. 16, 1897; "Occupied Two Residences," *CDN*, Nov. 16, 1897; and "Keller, the Butler, Gone," *CDN*, Nov. 17, 1897.

12. The Ketcham probate files show the frequency of claret purchases.

13. "To Go to Coroner," *CDT*, Nov. 16, 1897; "Mrs. Ketcham in Court," *CDN*, Nov. 28, 1897.

14. Information on the "marrying parson" is from "How He Ties Knots," *CDT,* Sept. 13, 1895; "Are They Wedded or Only Lovers?" *CDT,* Sept. 18, 1896; and "Marrying Parson Reigns," *CDT,* Mar. 12, 1898.

15. Information on the wedding trip is in "Roberts Married Them," *CDT,* Nov. 16, 1897; "All Eyes on Mrs. Ketcham," *CDN,* Nov. 18, 1897; "Quiz the Valet Joe," *CDT,* Nov. 18, 1897; "Marriage of Mrs. Walkup," *Atlanta Constitution,* Nov. 19, 1897; and "Mrs. Ketcham's Marriage," *NYT,* Nov. 19, 1897.

16. Ketcham marriage certificate, Milwaukee, Wisc., Vital Records.

17. "Widow Lets Body Go," *CDT,* Nov. 17, 1897; "Ketcham Inquest Opened," *NYT,* Nov. 17, 1897; "Attorney Trude Claims Forgery," *CDT,* June 14, 1901.

18. "To Go to Coroner," *CDT,* Nov. 16, 1897.

19. Ibid.

20. "Her Life An Eventful One," *CDN,* Nov. 15, 1897; "Much Mystery about Her," *CDN,* Nov. 16, 1897; "To Go to Coroner," *CDT,* Nov. 16, 1897.

21. "A Widow Again," *NODP,* Nov. 16, 1897.

22. "Much Mystery about Her," *CDN,* Nov. 16, 1897.

23. For an actual demonstration of how this works, see chapter 14, page 162.

24. "Attorney Trude Claims Forgery," *CDT,* June 14, 1901. Dethlef Hansen says Gladys Forbes and another woman of ill repute came to see Minnie after John Ketcham died. I am assuming the other woman was Josephine, as she and Gladys were inseparable at this time and Josephine was a friend of Minnie's. The article "Much Mystery about Her," *CDN,* Nov. 16, 1897, reports, with negative implication, that several women "well known in certain circles of Chicago" were talking about their friendships with Minnie.

25. "A Dramatic Scene," *NODP,* Nov. 17, 1897; "Widow Lets Body Go," *CDT,* Nov. 17, 1897.

26. "A Dramatic Scene," *NODP,* Nov. 17, 1897; "Widow Lets Body Go," *CDT,* Nov. 17, 1897.

27. "Roberts Married Them," *CDT,* Nov. 16, 1897; "All Eyes on Mrs. Ketcham," *CDN,* Nov. 18, 1897; "Quiz the Valet Joe," *CDT,* Nov. 18, 1897; "Marriage of Mrs. Walkup," *Atlanta Constitution,* Nov. 19, 1897; "Mrs. Ketcham's Marriage," *NYT,* Nov. 19, 1897 ;"Keller, the Butler, Gone," *CDN,* Nov. 17, 1897; "Insists Keller Was Groom," *CDT,* Nov. 18, 1897; "Bridegroom May Have Been Keller," *Atlanta Constitution,* Nov. 18, 1897; "Whom Did She Wed?" *Trenton (New Jersey) Evening Times,* Nov. 18, 1897; and "Very Significant Fact," *Newark (Ohio) Daily Advocate,* Nov. 19, 1897.

28. "Ketcham Trial On," *CDT,* Dec. 29, 1897.

29. "Widow Lets Body Go," *CDT,* Nov. 17, 1897.

30. "Mrs. Ketcham in Court," *CDN,* Nov. 28, 1897.

31. Ketcham probate files.

32. Ketcham probate files.

33. Erik Larson, *The Devil in the White City* (New York: Crown, 2003), 382–83.

34. "Mrs. Ketchum [sic] Will Found a Children's Home Here," *CDT,* Feb. 10, 1902; "Mrs. Walkup-Ketcham," *Anaconda (Montana) Standard,* Feb. 19, 1902; "Say Louderback Had Second Home," *CDT,* Apr. 19, 1914.

13. Hansen versus Ketcham

1. Information on the trial in this chapter is from "Ketcham Affair Recalled," *NYT*, Mar. 6, 1898; "Mrs. Ketcham Files Bill," *CDT*, Mar. 6, 1898; "A Peculiar Bill," *Marion (Ohio) Daily Star*, June 13, 1901; "Red Jam Horror in Famous Case," *CDT*, June 13, 1901; "Attorney Trude Claims Forgery," *CDT*, June 14, 1901; "Lawyer Hansen Weeps in Court," *CDT*, June 15, 1901; "Hansen Suit Is Ended by Trude," *CDT*, June 16, 1901.

2. "Cyclist Seeberg Granted a Stay at Desplaines," *CDT*, Aug. 21, 1898.

14. Billy, Baby Jo, and the Prince

1. Unless otherwise indicated, the *Moffitt v. Pike* information is from the following articles, all in *CDT*: "W. W. Pike Suit Is Begun: Jury Is Dispensed With," Nov. 12, 1902; "Pike Case Waxes Warm," Nov. 14, 1902; "Tells Story of Pike and Moffitt," Nov. 15, 1902; "Pike to Take the Stand," Nov. 17, 1902; "Tells Secrets of Mrs. Moffitt," Nov. 18, 1902; "Pike Repudiates Mrs. Moffitt," Nov. 19, 1902; "Finish Evidence in the Pike Case," Nov. 20, 1902; "Pike Case Ends; Ruling Delayed," Nov. 21, 1902; "Finds 'Baby Jo' Not Pike's Wife," Nov. 30, 1902; "William Pike Wins Again," Feb. 26, 1904; "How a Pal's Love Scandal Periled Political Career of 'Big Bill' Thompson," Nov. 14, 1953. Information on Josephine Moffitt comes from her testimony, the 1870 and 1880 federal census for New Orleans, the New Orleans Death Index, and "The Families of Louis Adrian [*sic*] Guillemet," both posted on Ancestry.com.

2. Heidi Pawlowski Carey, "Prairie Avenue," *Encyclopedia of Chicago*, http://www.encyclopedia.chicagohistory.org/pages/1003.html; Janice L. Reiff, "The Worlds of Prairie Avenue," *Encyclopedia of Chicago*, http://www.encyclopedia.chicagohistory.org/pages/10431.html.

3. "Child Outwits the Law," *CDT*, Feb. 6, 1902.

4. *Costa v. Oliven*, 849 NE 2d 122 (2d Dist. 2006).

5. Information on the Prince Victor story is in "Prince Doubts 'Baby Jo's' Story," *CDT*, Mar. 23, 1908; "Prince Refutes Baby Jo's Action," *CDT*, Apr. 2, 1908; "Untitled [front page story]," *NYT*, Mar. 22, 1908; "Miss Moffitt Wanted Cash," *NYT*, Mar. 23, 1908; "Suit against Prince Victor," *NYT*, Apr. 17, 1908; "Prince Victor of Thurn and Taxis," *Washington Post*, Apr. 22, 1908.

15. The Robber Baron's Partner

1. "Coincidence of Ketcham Case," *Washington Post*, Nov. 24, 1897.

2. "Minnie Walkup May Wed Again," *Emporia (Kans.) Weekly Republican*, May 23, 1901.

3. Cathy Joynt Labath, "Chapter 28: Some Old Houses," Scott County, Iowa, USGenWeb Project, http://www.celticcousins.net/scott/chapter28.html.

4. On D. H. Louderback's early years, see "Yerkes' Right-Hand Man," in "Knights of the Key," *Railroad Man's Magazine* 1, no. 1 (Oct. 1906), http://home.mindspring.com/~railroadstories/rrmmv1n1/knights.htm. David Louderback is not in the 1860

census with the rest of the family, when he would have been seventeen, and his half-sister Sallie testified that he had disappeared around 1889 (Louderback probate files, Cook County Archives).

5. The autopsy revealed the shotgun pellets in his skull. See "Poisons in Room of Louderback," *CDT,* Apr. 11, 1914.

6. "Historic Figures: Charles Tyson Yerkes," http://www.chicago-l.org/personnel/figures/yerkes/index.html; Karyn Hodgson, "Charles Tyson Yerkes: Swindler Turned Visionary of the Tubes," *British Heritage* 19, no. 6 (Aug.–Sept. 1998): 16-19. See also John Franch, *Robber Baron: The Life of Charles Tyson Yerkes* (Urbana: Univ. of Illinois Press, 2006). American writer Theodore Dreiser wrote a fictional trilogy based on the life of Charles Tyson Yerkes: *The Financier, The Titan,* and *The Stoic.*

7. "Stations: State/Lake," http://www.chicago-l.org/stations/state-lake.html.

8. "Yerkes' Right-Hand Man."

9. "Chicago Dealers Fear Loss," *NYT,* Nov. 7, 1897; "Chicago Vacant Land Sold," *NYT,* Nov. 29, 1898.

10. Bureau of Land Management, General Land Office Records, http://www.glorecords.blm.gov/PatentSearch (Mixsell and Louderback entries); Tacoma, Washington, City Directories, 1889–1891.

11. "Chicago Traction President," *NYT,* July 14, 1900; "Manager for Yerkes' London Railway," *NYT,* Nov. 1, 1900; "D. H. Louderback Resigns," *NYT,* Dec. 4, 1900.

12. "Chicago Elevated Roads," *NYT,* May 12, 1901; "London Street Railways," *NYT,* June 9, 1901; "Doings of Society in France," *NYT,* Dec. 28, 1902; Passport Applications of U.S. Citizens (for Minnie and the Louderbacks, done the same day, with DeLancey vouching for Minnie), posted on Ancestry.com; Ship's register, *La Lorraine,* 1902.

13. Ship's register, SS *St. Paul,* 1903.

14. "D. H. Louderback Dead," *NYT,* Apr. 10, 1914; "Girl Holds Title to Crystal House," *CDT,* Apr. 23, 1914.

15. Information for the Agnes Sowka incident can be found in "Millionaire's [*sic*] Will Make Bold Affronts," *Lima (Ohio) News,* Oct. 27, 1912; "Girl Sues Realty Man for $25,000, Alleging Attack," *CDT,* Oct. 28, 1912; "Trapped by Girl, Louderback Says," *CDT,* May 6, 1913; "Files in Girl's Case Gone," *CDT,* May 16, 1913.

16. "Boy a Suicide," *CDT,* Mar. 10, 1908.

17. "Poisons in Room of Louderback," *CDT,* Apr. 11, 1914.

16. Death from Afar

1. Federal census, 1910; "Death Notices," *CDT,* Feb. 2, 1913. DeLancey Ritter does not appear in any subsequent census or other record, and, as he was not with his mother in Louderback's home when he would be only thirteen, I am assuming he died between 1910 and 1913.

2. Unless otherwise indicated, information in this section comes from the Louderback probate files and the following articles: "D. H. Louderback Dies; Physician Asks for Inquest," *CDT,* Apr. 10, 1914; "D. H. Louderback Dead," *NYT,* Apr. 10, 1914; "Says Poison Found in Louderback's Body," *CDN,* Apr. 10, 1914; "New

Mystery Is Seen in Louderback Death," *CDN,* Apr. 11, 1914; "Poisons in Room of Louderback," *CDT,* Apr. 11, 1914; "Louderback Drug Search Blocked," *CDT,* April 12, 1914; "Defends Silence on Death," *CDT,* Apr. 13, 1914; "Overdose of Poison Killed Louderback," *CDN,* Apr. 17, 1914; "Poison Verdict on Louderback," *CDT,* Apr. 18, 1914; "Gift to Mrs. Ketcham Louderback Puzzle," *CDN,* Apr. 18, 1914; "Say Louderback Had Second Home," *CDT,* Apr. 19, 1914; "Both Known Here," *New Orleans Times-Picayune,* Apr. 20, 1914; "Rich Widow Shares Louderback Estate," *Indianapolis Star,* Apr. 20, 1914; "Mrs. Walkup Inherits Another Fortune," *Emporia Times,* Apr. 23, 1914; "Girl Holds Title to Crystal House," *CDT,* Apr. 23,1914; "Corporation Owner of Louderback Home," *CDN,* Apr. 23, 1914; "D. H. Louderback Left Only $10,000," *NYT,* Apr. 29, 1914; "Mrs. Ketcham Sues Estate of Louderback for $2,550," *CDT,* Mar. 20, 1915.

3. Emporia, Kansas, researcher Robert Hodge distinctly remembers seeing this article but, unfortunately, did not write down the source. I did not come across it in my own research.

4. *Online Medical Dictionary,* http://www.online-medical-dictionary.org/omd. asp?q=cyanamide.

5. D. H. Louderback Death Certificate, Cook County Vital Statistics.

6. Ship's register, RMS *Lusitania,* 1915; Passport applications of U.S. Citizens, posted on Ancestry.com.

17. Where Are They Now

1. Information in this section comes from federal census records, 1900–1930; New Orleans Death Index; Cook County Vital Statistics; World War I Draft Registrations; Social Security Administration, Washington, D.C.

2. Information in this section comes from "The Social Career of 'Silent' James Henry Smith," *NYT,* Sept. 16, 1906; "James Henry Smith Is Dead in Japan," *NYT,* Mar. 28, 1907; "No Smith Heir, LeRoy Says," *NYT,* June 18, 1907; "Arrest in Will Contest," *Washington Post,* Mar. 8, 1910; "W.T. Houston's Will Filed," *Washington Post,* Aug. 17, 1918.

3. Information in this section comes from "A Long Funeral Line," *NYT,* Jan. 3, 1888; "The Bigger Brute Won," *NYT,* July 9, 1889; "Anti-Italian Mood Led to 1891 Lynchings," *New Orleans Times-Picayune,* Mar. 14, 1991; Joseph E. Persico, "Vendetta in New Orleans," *American Heritage* 24, no. 4 (June 1973); "James D. Houston Ill," *NYT,* Sept. 14, 1893; "The Obituary Record," *NYT,* Jan. 30, 1894; Houston Death Certificate, New Orleans Vital Statistics.

4. "$1,200,000 Estate Left by Kellogg," *Washington Post,* Aug. 15, 1918.

5. Information in this section comes from federal census records, 1900–1930; William E. Connelly, "John Elmore Martin," in *A Standard History of Kansas and Kansans* (Chicago: Lewis, 1918); "Calvin Hood," *Emporia Gazette,* Feb. 4, 1910.

6. Information in this section comes from *Portraits and Biographical Record of Leavenworth, Douglas, and Franklin Counties, Kansas* (Chicago: Chapman, 1899), 323–24; personal correspondence from the Baldwin family.

7. Information in this section comes from Ancestry World Tree Project: Thomas Baily, Ancestry.com; Illinois Death Index, http://deathindexes.com/illinois/index. html.

8. This story is recounted in David Traxel's *1898: The Birth of the American Century* (New York: Knopf, 1998), 23–24.

9. Information in this section comes from "Calvin Hood," *Emporia Gazette,* Feb. 4, 1910; federal census, 1900–1930; personal correspondence from the Wilhite family.

10. Information in this section comes from the federal census, 1900–1930.

11. Information about Feighan comes from "Feighan Chosen," *Atchison (Kans.) Daily Globe,* Feb. 24, 1888; Rev. H. K. Hines, *An Illustrated History of the State of Washington* (Chicago: Lewis, 1893), 442–43; Civil War Pension records, Ancestry. com. For Sterry information, see "A Legislative Scandal [subtitle; main title is illegible]," *Arizona Republican,* Mar. 21, 1901; federal census, 1900–1910. Fenlon information was taken from federal census, 1900; Western Life Newspaper Name Index, 1900–1902 (Feb. 7, 1901), Ancestry.com. The Dodds details come from *Joplin v. Chachere,* 192 US 94 (1904).

12. Information in this section comes from "Untitled," *Newark (Ohio) Advocate,* May 18, 1908; "Former S. F. Doctor Released on Bonds," *Placerville (Calif.) Mountain Democrat,* Sept. 25, 1915; Howard L. Conard, *Encyclopedia of the History of Missouri:* Vol. 4, *Medical Journals in St. Louis* (New York: Haldeman, Conard, 1901), 292; federal census, 1900–1910; Florida Death Index, Ancestry.com.

13. Information on Hansen comes from "Court Calls Dethlef Hansen," *CDT,* July 17, 1901; "Lawyer Reveals Suits against Thos. F. Walsh," *NYT,* July 12, 1905; "T. F. Walsh Fights Back," *NYT,* July 13, 1905; "Walsh Silent on Suits," *NYT,* June 17, 1907; "D. C. Hansen Suspended," *NYT,* June 22, 1907; "Walsh's Counsel Heard," *Washington Post,* June 28, 1907; "To Head Off Miss Watson," *NYT,* June 28, 1907; "Victory for T. F. Walsh," *NYT,* July 2, 1907; "Walsh Sued for $250,000," *NYT,* Mar. 25, 1910; "Calls Arrest of Girl as Bond Thief 'Frameup,'" *CDT,* July 13, 1919; "Bond Protects Holdings of Girl Held as Thief," *CDT,* July 16, 1919; "Funeral Rites Held for Attorney Dethlef Hansen," *CDT,* May 7, 1932.

14. "William W. Pike's Death Revealed by Filing of Will," *CDT,* Apr. 28, 1932; federal census, Chicago, Ill., 1910.

15. Information on Forbes comes from "Patrons of Vice Will Be Trapped in Photographs," *CDT,* May 18, 1915; "Was There a Horsewhip?" *CDT,* May 21, 1915; "Police Ignored by Prosecutor on Nymph Raid," *CDT,* Nov. 22, 1915.

16. Information on Josephine Moffitt comes from "Princess's Case Has New Defendant," *NYT,* Apr. 19, 1914; "Says Prince Married Her," *NYT,* July 10, 1914; Passport applications of U.S. Citizens (1921), posted on Ancestry.com; Ship's register of the SS *Berengaria* (July 29, 1922); Clarke's Galleries ad, *NYT,* Jan. 17, 1926; federal census for New York City, 1930; "'Princess' Is Arrested," *NYT,* May 21, 1915. Information on Lida Nicolls comes from "'Count' Asks $50,000 of Princess Victor," *NYT,* May 9, 1920, and personal correspondence with Nicolls family connection; "Count" Gregory: "'Count' Gregory Arrested as Thief," *NYT,* Sept. 9, 1915; "'Count' Gregory in Crooks' Lineup," *NYT,* Sept. 10, 1915; "Send Count to Jail," *NYT,* Sept. 16, 1915; "Career of Dapper 'Count' Hits a Snag," *NYT,* June 21, 1921.

17. For an analysis of William Hale Thompson's administration as mayor of Chicago, see Douglas Bukowski, "Big Bill Thompson," in *The Mayors: The Chicago Political Tradition,* ed. by Paul M. Green and Melvin G. Holli (Carbondale: Southern Illinois Univ. Press, 1995), 61–81.

18. On Pam, see "Judge Hugo Pam," *NYT,* May 31, 1930. On Trude, see Jim Abbs, "The Royal Trude and Its Cousins: A Midwesterner's Gift to the West," *FFF Fly of the Month,* Aug. 2000, http://www.fedflyfishers.org/FlyofMonth/trude. htm; Terry Hellekson, "The Trude," http://www.flyanglersonline.com/flytying/fotw/050100fotw.html.

19. Corbett, *Orphans Preferred,* 198–99.

20. Federal census, 1920–1930; Illinois Death Index; World War I Draft Registrations; "Marriages," *CDT,* Sept. 9, 1917; "Death Notices," *CDT,* Oct. 12, 1936 .

21. On Agnes, see federal census, 1920–1930; On Harvey, see federal census 1930; "Banker Rejects Plea of Son in Cabareter's Cell," *CDT,* Oct. 5, 1916; "Harvey Hill Is in Again," *CDT,* Oct. 18, 1916; "Yessir, Hill's in Bad Again," *CDT,* Oct. 21, 1916; "Harvey Hill in Jail in South; Bigamy Charged," *CDT,* Feb. 13, 1920; "Death Notices," *CDT,* Dec. 19, 1937.

22. Information in this section is taken from "Seek to Find $468,000 Missing from Bank," *NYT,* Apr. 19, 1922; "Investigate Methods of New Ponzi," *Wisconsin Rapids Daily Tribune,* Apr. 19, 1922; "Say Peacock Holds Missing Bank Funds," *NYT,* Apr. 20, 1922; "Flowers Grew as Bank Faded, Charge at Trial," *CDT,* Jan. 15 1924; "Link Juror in Peacock to Two Mistrials," *CDT,* Feb. 2, 1924; "Charges a Plot to Drop Suit against Mayor," *CDT,* Aug. 31, 1928; "Everett R. Peacock," *NYT,* Oct. 21, 1949; "Death Notices," *CDT,* Oct. 21, 1949; database of Deaths in World War II, Ancestry.com.

23. Information on the rest of Minnie's life comes from Forest Home Cemetery Records; federal census, 1930; death certificate, San Diego County Vital Records; Mt. Hope Cemetery Records.

Bibliography

Abbott, Karen. *Sin in the Second City: Madams, Ministers, Playboys, and the Battle for America's Soul.* New York: Random House, 2007.

Abbs, Jim. "The Royal Trude and Its Cousins: A Midwesterner's Gift to the West." *FFF Fly of the Month* (August 2000), http://www.fedflyfishers.org/FlyofMonth/trude.htm.

"Adam Forepaugh ($10,000 Beauty)." http://en.wikipedia.org/wiki/adam-fourepaugh.

Aldrich, Nelson W., Jr. "Death of the Club Man." *Seattle Times,* July 17, 1988.

"Circus: Adam Forepaugh Circus, 1867–1894." *The Circus in America: 1793–1940.* http://www.circusinamerica.org/public/corporate_bodies/public_show/4.

Connelly, William E. "John Elmore Martin." *A Standard History of Kansas and Kansans.* Chicago: Lewis, 1918.

Corbett, Christopher. *Orphans Preferred: The Twisted Truth and Lasting Legend of the Pony Express.* New York: Broadway Books, 2003.

Cutler, William G. *History of the State of Kansas.* Chicago: A. T. Andreas, 1883.

Dennett, Andrea Stulman. *Weird and Wonderful: The Dime Museum in America.* New York: New York Univ. Press, 1997.

Fairall, Herbert S. "New Orleans: Gateway to the Americas." *Industrial Cotton and The World's Exposition, New Orleans, 1884–1885.* Iowa City: N.p., 1885.

Foner, Eric. *Reconstruction: America's Unfinished Revolution, 1863–1877.* New York: Harper & Row, 1988.

Franch, John. *Robber Baron: The Life of Charles Tyson Yerkes.* Urbana: Univ. of Illinois Press, 2006.

Green, Paul M., and Melvin G. Holli, eds. *The Mayors: The Chicago Political Tradition* (rev. ed.). Carbondale: Southern Illinois Univ. Press, 1995.

Hellekson, Terry. "The Trude." http://www.flyanglersonline.com/flytying/fotw/050100fotw.html.

Hodgson, Karyn. "Charles Tyson Yerkes: Swindler Turned Visionary of the Tubes." *British Heritage* 19, no. 6 (August–September 1998): 16–19.

Inbau, Fred E., et al. *Criminal Interrogation and Confessions* (4th ed.) Gaithersburg, Md.: Aspen, 2001.

Johnson, Barbara. "Nettie Poe Ketcham, 1865–1950." *In Search of Our Past: Women of Northwest Ohio,* Vol. 2 (1990). Available at http://freepages.family. rootsweb.ancentry.com/~gen2/Page40.html.

Labath, Cathy Joynt. "Chapter 28: Some Old Houses." Scott County, Iowa, USGen-Web Project. http://www.celticcousins.net/scott/chapter28.html.

Larson, Erik. *The Devil in the White City.* New York: Crown, 2003.

Loerzel, Robert. *Alchemy of Bones: Chicago's Luetgert Murder Case of 1897.* Urbana: Univ. of Illinois Press, 2003.

Martyr, Philippa, "When Doctors Fail: Ludwig Bruck's List of Unregistered Practitioners (1886)." *Electronic Journal of Australian and New Zealand History* (1997). Available at http://www.jcu.edu/au/aff/history/articles/bruck.htm.

Medical Online Dictionary. http://www.online-medical-dictionary.org/omd.asp?q=cyanamide.

Officer, Lawrence H., and Samuel H. Williamson, "Purchasing Power of Money in the United States from 1774 to 2008." MeasuringWorth.com (2009), http://www.measuringworth.com/ppowerus/.

Persico, Joseph E. "Vendetta in New Orleans." *American Heritage* 24, no. 4 (June 1973).

Rose, Al. *Storyville, New Orleans: Being an Authentic Illustrated Account of the Notorious Red-Light District.* Tuscaloosa: Univ. of Alabama Press, 1974.

Schott, Cindy, and Kathy Schott Gates. *Boys, Let Me Down Easy.* Lawrence, Kans.: Allen Press, 2005.

Speth, Kenneth R. "The World's Industrial and Cotton Exposition, New Orleans, Louisiana, December 16th, 1884—June 1st, 1885." *Kenblog* (November 17, 2008), http://expoguy2.blogspot.com/2008/11/new-orleans-exposition-of-1885.html.

Taylor, Troy. "Bath House John, Hinky Dink & Others." *Weird and Haunted Chicago* (2003), http://www.prairieghosts.com/graft.html.

Traxel, David. *1898: The Birth of the American Century.* New York: Knopf, 1998.

Waggoner, Clark. "First National Bank of Toledo—Ohio 1871." http://www.scripophily.net/finabaofto18.html.

Wilson, James Grant, and John Fiske. *Appleton's Cyclopedia of American Biography, 1887–1889.* Detroit: Gale, 1968.

"Yerkes' Right-Hand Man." In "Knights of the Key," *Railroad Man's Magazine* 1, no. 1 (Oct. 1906). Available at http://home.mindspring.com/~railroadstories/rrmmv1n1/knights.htm.

Index

Alger, Frances Aura, 164
Ancient Order of United Workmen (AOUW), 12, 203
Anderson, William, 101, 103
AOUW. *See* Ancient Order of United Workmen (AOUW)
Arkansas City Republican, 124
Armour, Phillip, 159
arsenic: anecdote for, 68; behavior of eaters of, 68–69; calculation required to use for murder, 107; for the complexion, 35, 38, 43, 92, 98–99, 103, 111, 119; copycats, 103; eaten by Walkup, 52, 53–55, 55–56; and Ketcham's death, 148; lethal dose, 72; and male sexual powers, 83, 86; Minnie's purchases of, 35, 38, 41–43, 51, 56, 72, 93, 97, 98, 99, 111, 119; symptoms of poisoning, 39; and syphilis, 78, 83; Walkup as alleged eater of, 76, 81, 82, 83, 83–85, 106, 107, 108, 117, 119; and Walkup's death, 43–44, 51, 68, 71–73
Atchison, Topeka, & Santa Fe Railroad, 12, 13, 21, 33, 41, 63, 204
Atlanta Constitution, 75

Baldwin, Eben: further career and death of, 204; photograph, *12;* testimony, 76, 78, 90, 92, 95, 101, 112; Walkup accompanied to World's Fair by, 13; Walkup described by, 11; and Walkup's illness, 13–14; and Walkup's interest in Minnie, 15–16

Barnum, P. T., 77
Bates, Betsey Maddock, 26, 32
Bates, Moses, 67, 93, 97, 98, 112
Bates, Moses H., 32, 33, 35, 36, 42
Baton Rouge, 13, 14
Baudelaire, Charles, 134
Berman, William F., 166, 167, 170
Bill, Dwight, 38, 39, 40–41, 42, 51–52, 81, 118
Bill & Walkup Company, 28
Bishop, Elmer, 168, 169, 172
bismuth powders, 41, 73
Born, William, 50
Boston Daily Globe, 108
Bostrom, Charles, 189
Bowers, Dora, 31
Braun, Charles, 190
Braun, Claribel Louderback, 190, 193
Brewster, Robert, 4, *5,* 5, 6
Brown, H. V., 27
Buchanan, "Dr.," 55
Buck, J. Jay, 64, 107–8; sketch of, *107*
Buffalo Bill's Wild West Show, 136
Burke, James Lee, 3
Burnett, Lina, 11, 77, 112
Burnham, Daniel, 159
Butler, T. H., 101–2
Butterfield, Mr., 78

calomel, 31, 92, 96–97
Capone, Al, 128, 211
Capote, Truman, 45
Carleton, Josephine Carrel, 129

Cattlemen's Convention, 78, 101, 102
Chicago, IL: bribery in, 183; elevated lines, 183–84; Lake Forest, 160; Levee area, 127–28, 160, 172; Minnie's move to, 121, 124; Prairie Avenue area, 159, 160
Chicago Athletic Club, 135, 159, 160, 161, 166, 170
Chicago Daily Tribune, 140
Chief Justice Waite, 156
Cincinnati, OH, 16, 17, 23
Cinnamon Pete, 109
City of Greenville, 79
Civil War, 9, 12, 22
Clarke, William, 137
Cleveland, Grover, 6, 133
Clifford, Judge, 168, 171, 172, 174, 175
Cody, "Buffalo Bill," 136, 212
Collard, James, 28
Columbian Exposition. *See* World's Columbian Exposition
common-law marriage, 146, 175, 176
Concordia Sentinel, 78, 79
Connaway, A. N., 83
Cotton Exposition. *See* World's Fair
Coughlin, "Bathhouse John," 128
County Union, 119
Covington, KY, 23
Crushers, "Handsome Charlie," 9, 90
Crysler, Charles, 63
Cummings, John, 195
cyanamide: and Louderback's death, 192, 193, 194, 195, 196; symptoms of ingestion of, 191, 196
cyanide, 148

Daily Pacayune, 4, 6, 117–19
Dalton, Willie, 214
Daugherty, Mae, 142
Davey, Robert, 133
David, Jefferson, 10
DeJonghe Restaurant, 170
Democracy of the State of Washington, 133
DeVeny, Stephen, 143, 144, 147
Dodds, George S., 65, 106–7, 117, 119, 206
Dreyfus, Gus, 174

Emerson, Ralph Waldo, 188
Emporia, KS: drugstores of, frequented by Minnie, 31–34; and Minnie, 16, 24–25, 26, 27, 45, 50, 115, 195; photograph, *36, 37;* population, 21; Walkup in, 11, 12, 13
Emporia Daily News, 74; and the Gutekunst-Wilhite affair, 123; Jay's let-

ter to the editor, 58; Minnie portrayed in, 123; poem on the Walkup trial published by, 87–88; Walkup trial covered by, 74, 77–78, 80, 103; Wilhite in, 82
Emporia Daily Republican, 45, 73; and the Gutekunst-Wilhite affair, 123; Judge Graves' jury instructions printed by, 105; Minnie portrayed in, 123; transcript of Walkup trial published by, 63–64, 73–74, 77–78, 94, 105–6; Wilhite in, 82
Evans, Maggie, 26
"Experience of Ladies Attending the Walkup Trial" (Nottingham), 87–88

Faherty, Michael J., 192, 193
Feighan, John W., 62; attorney for Lyon County, 64; closing arguments, 105, 108, 109; Elizabeth Wallace cross-examined by, 89; and the experiment with Squibb bismuth, 51; further career and death of, 205; and the prosecution, 67, 81, 82, 85, 117, 118; and the rebuttal, 101; on Sunday during the trial, 73; and the verdict, 110
Fenlon, Thomas P.: banter with Sterry, 87; closing arguments, 108; death of, 205; and Elizabeth Wallace's testimony, 89; Minnie defended by, 59, 65, 117; Minnie introduced to Frankie Morris by, 77; and Minnie's direct examination, 90–91, 94, 96, 97; strategic savvy, 108
Field, Marshall, 160
Filkins, John, 82
Findlay, Dora Kirby (half sister): appearance of, 3, 7; children of, 4, 57; contacted by Morton, 79–80; death of, 215; education of, 8; entertaining at the Wallace House, 9, 14; and Judge Houston, 3–4, 7; marriages, 4, 9, 215; mentioned, 46, 95; move to New Mexico, 120; in New York, 124, 201; World's Fair visited by, 16
Findlay, Edward George: businesses offered by Walkup to, 25–26; death of, 123, 201; marriage, 9; mentioned, 16, 17, 91, 106; Minnie supported by, 116–17; move to New Mexico, 120; post-trial claims, 117
Findlay, Edward Kirby George "Edwin" (nephew), 9, 123, 124, 201–2
Findlay, Milton Howard (nephew), 9, 16, 17, 56, 76, 123; death of, 124, 201

Findlay, Minnie Jay (niece), 60, 123, 124, 202
Fisher, Nettie, 16
Fitzgerald, Edward, 209
Fitzgerald, Lord Gerald Purcell, 209
Fleetwood, H. R., 80
Foley, Ann, 173
Forbes, Gladys, *131;* child raised by, 173; falling out with Josephine Moffitt, 173–74; further career of, 208–9; and Gale Thompson's bachelor party, 159, 160; mentioned, 132, 163, 168; and Minnie, 129, 130, 131, 139, 146, 197; procuress of women, 130; testimony in *Moffitt v. Pike,* 172, 173–74
Forbes, Margaret. *See* Thorpe, Margaret
Forepaugh, Adam, 119
Forest Home Cemetery, 131, 146, 202, 215
Fowler's Solution, 78

G. W. Newman's Department Store, 26, 27, 36, 37–38, 47, 49, 105, 113
Gardiner, Charles, 68–69, 101
gonorrhea, 85, 112, 113
Goodchild, Ella, 212
Graham, J. R., 45, 73
Graves, Charles B., 64, 73, 88, 110, 117; instructions to the jury, 104–5, 106, 117; and laughter in the courtroom, 63, 87, 206; photograph, *65*
Greenbaum, Bernard, 210
Greer, Bill: on the defense, 70, 80; on Dodds' closing arguments, 106; Jay described by, 57; Judge Graves viewed by, 64; Kansas law researched by, 103–4; on post-trial Emporia, 115; reporting on Minnie Walkup, 47, 61, 89, 100; reporting on the Walkup case, 45–46, 64, 73; and the verdict, 110; on the Walkup trial's physicians and experts, 55, 70–71
Gregory, Bernard Francis, 210
Guillemet, Adrien, 129
Gutekunst, Edward, 121, 122–23, 205
Gutekunst-Wilhite affair, 121–23, 205

Hall, Mary Turnbull, 212
Hamilton, John, 150
Hansen, Dethlef C.: attempts to scam Minnie, 152–54, 158, 168 (see also *Hansen v. Ketcham*); breakdown in lawsuit against Minnie, 157, 166, 170; further career of, 206–8; and Ketcham's estate, 138, 146, 151, 152–54; and Ketcham's will, 142, 143, 144, 155; law practice of, 132, 133; in Minnie's house, 149, 152; and Minnie's marriage to Ketcham, 139–40, 142; revenge against Josephine Moffitt, 166; revenge against Minnie, 166; sketch of, *132*
Hansen v. Ketcham, 154–58, 166, 168, 181, 206, 208
Harrison, Carter, II, 211
Harrison, Carter, Sr., 151
Haslam, Robert "Pony Bob," 136, 137, 139, 212
Head's Toxicology, 53, 54
Hennessy, David, 203
Hill, Alonzo H., 185–86, 212–13
Hill, Elizabeth McMillan, 212, 213
Hill, Elmer, 186
Hill, Harvey, 186–87, 212
History of Kansas (Cutler), 65
Hitt, Homer, 130, 131
Holmes, Oliver Wendell, 116
Hood, Calvin, 22, 117, 204; and Minnie's house arrest, 59, 60
Hood, Henry "Harry" Platt: and the Gutekunst-Wilhite affair, 123; mentioned, 204, 205; and the prosecution, 64–65, 75, 106, 117, 118, 122–23; and Walkup's marriage to Minnie, 22, 23
Hood, Mattie Walkup, 13, 16, 39, 40, 41, 204; and the Gutekunst-Wilhite affair, 123; relationship with her father, 21; and Walkup's funeral, 49; and Walkup's marriage to Minnie, 22, 23, 27, 37, 68; and the wedding/welcome party in Emporia, 24; wrongful death suit considered by, 115
Houston, James D., 4, 5, *5,* 47, 203
Houston, Judge William T., 17; death of, 202; defended by brother James, 4, 5, 6; depicted by Minnie, 119; further career of, 202; relationship with Dora Kirby, 3–4, 7; relationship with Minnie, 3, 8, 48, 95, 112, 119, 120; and the Walkup case, 47, 48, 56–57
Hunsberger, Mrs. Wesley, 141, 142
Hunsberger, Wesley A., 140, 141, 142, 149, 170

If Christ Came to Chicago (Stead), 128
In Cold Blood (Capote), 45
Ingersoll, Robert, 65, 119
Ireland, William, 42

Irwin, William, 32, 33, 68
Irwin's Drugstore, 32, 33

Jacobs, Luther D., 118; and the antidote,
68, 70; arsenic poisoning suspected
by, 39, 42, 43–44; and Born's poisoning, 50; cross-examined by Scott, 68;
death of, 204; and the experiment with
Squibb bismuth, 51; and the inquest,
51, 52; Minnie's demeanor viewed by,
44; Walkup treated by, 33, 37, 68, 73,
92, 111
James, Frank, 63
James, Jesse, 63
Jay, Mary, 66, 73, 113, 114, 205
Jay, William, 61; appearance and character of, 57; death of, 124; and the
deliberation, 108–9; denounced
in the *County Union,* 119; and the
Gutekunst-Wilhite affair, 121; during
jury selection, 66–67; and Minnie's
departure from Emporia, 115; Minnie
viewed by, 57, 58, 83, 85, 205; and
Minnie Walkup's defense, 58–59, 64,
108, 117; in Nottingham's poem, 88;
post-trial behavior, 113, 114; sketch of,
84; on Sunday during the trial, 73; and
Walkup as arsenic eater, 83, 86, 110;
and Walkup's estate, 116
Jefferson, Thomas, 133
John A. Moore's Drugstore, 31
Jones, Stanhope, 5
Jones, William, 70

Kansas: and Minnie's post-trial behavior,
115; murder in, 66, 103–4; notoriety
of, 45; widow's estate in, 29
Kansas City Journal, 52
Kansas City Times, 73, 88, 103, 115, 116
Keating, Estelle. *See* Ketcham, Minnie
Wallace Walkup
Keller, Joe: employed by Minnie, 132, 137,
155; and Ketcham's death, 196; and
Ketcham's will, 143, 150; and Minnie's
marriage to Ketcham, 140, 142, 144,
148–49; and Minnie's party house,
139; sketch of, *141*
Kellogg, William Pitt, 120–21, 132, 203;
photograph, *120*
Kelly, Paul, 191, 192
Kelly, R. B., 31, 32, 35, 43, 92, 93, 97
Kenna, Michael "Hinky Dink," 128
Kern, Jacob, 153

Ketcham, George, 138, 142–43, 146, 147,
148; and John's death, 144, 150
Ketcham, John Berdan, 133; and alcohol,
135, 136, 137, 139, 148; autopsy, 145,
146–47; background of, 134; behavior
in Chicago, 136; burial rights, 144–45,
147; common-law wives, 146; death
of, 144, 148, 153, 181, 195; illness of,
139, 140, 142, 143, 147, 148, 153; im-
prisoned in Minnie's home, 136–37,
147–48; inquest, 144–48; marriage
to Minnie, 140–42, 143, 144, 148–50;
murder, 147, 148; sketch of, *135;* social
life of, 134, 135–36, 161; will made by,
142, 143–44, *144,* 148, 150, 195
Ketcham, Mary Granger, 134
Ketcham, Minnie Wallace Walkup: advice
given to Josephine Moffitt by, 162, 167,
175; after Ketcham's death, 181; death
of, 215–16; and Ketcham's estate, 152;
and Louderback's death, 195–97; and
Louderback's estate, 190, 193, 194, 195;
names used by, 193, 215; relationship
with Louderback, 181, 182, 185; subtlety
of, 165
Ketcham, Nettie Poe, 134, 135, 137, 138
Ketcham, Rachel Berdan, 134, 138, 144
Ketcham, Valentine Hicks, 134
Kierkegaard, Søren, 201
Kilrain, Jake, 203
Kirby, Dora (half sister). *See* Findlay,
Dora Kirby (half sister)
Kirby, Patrick, 7
Knights of Honor, 12
Krick, Helen, 212

Lambert, Isaac E., 65, 81, 82, 107, 117
Landry, Mr., 67
Lane, Miss, 64, 73, 88, 106
Lanphear, S. Emory, 71, 86–87, 206
Laura Lee, 79
Liberty Bell, 10
Louderback, Albert, Jr., 193
Louderback, Alfred, 182
Louderback, David, 183
Louderback, DeLancey Horton: back-
ground of, 182–85; and the Crystal
House, 185, 188–89, 194; cyanamide
taken by, 191, 192, 193–94, 196, 197;
death due to cyanamide poisoning,
192, 193–94, 195–97, 213; estate, 192–
93, 194, 195; at *Hansen v. Ketcham,*
154, 181, 182, 185; ill health, 187, 190,

Louderback, DeLancey Horton (cont.)
191; photograph, *182;* relationship
with Minnie, 185, 195–96, 197; sleeping potions taken by, 190, 191, 192,
194, 196; will made by, 189–90, 191,
192, 194, 195, 197; and Yerkes, 183–85;
and younger women, 185–87, 190–91,
192, 197
Louderback, Sarah, 182
Louderback, Susan, 182
Louderback, Virginia Mixsell, 182, 185,
192, 195, 197
Luetgert, Adolph, 133
Lusitania, 194–95
lynch law, 104

Mann Act, 206
Martin, Governor, 12
Martin, J. G. . *See* Morton, Nathaniel
Benjamin
Martin, John, 124
Martin, John Elmore, 203
Maximilian, Prince, 176
Mayer, Isaac, 168
Mayer, Levy, 168
McCulloch, Frank, 68
McEnery, Samuel, 6
McKinley, William, 164
McKinney, Sallie, 34, 47, 51, 101
Mealey, Patrick, 203
mercury, 53, 56, 70, 112
Miersch, Annie, 142
Missouri & Pacific Railroad, 12, 13
Mixsell, Philip, 184
Moffitt, J. Westley, 130
Moffitt, Josephine, 129–30; advised by
Minnie, 162, 167, 175; and Billy Pike's
money, 162, 163, 166, 167–68, 172,
173–74 (see also *Moffitt v. Pike*); direct
examination, 170; end of story about,
210–11; falling out with Gladys Forbes,
173–74; and Gale Thompson's bachelor party, 160, 161, 162; lies told by,
170–71; mentioned, 132, 139, 208; and
Minnie, 129, 138, 146, 197; names used
by, 129, 130, 172, 210, 211; photograph,
129, 169; and Prince Victor, 176–77,
209; procuress of women, 130; sketch
of, *163;* station in life, 165
Moffitt v. Pike, 168–75; entertainment for
court crowd, 168, 171, 172, 174; Gladys
Forbes' testimony, 172, 173–74; Josephine's direct examination, 170; and

the Ketcham case, 175; men attendees,
169; verdict, 175
Monroe Restaurant, 130, 159, 160, 161,
163, 172
Moore, John A., 31, 32, 37, 68, 92
morphine, 33, 93, 97
Morris, Alice, 160, 161, 170
Morris, Frances (Frankie), 77
Morton, Nathaniel Benjamin, 78–80, 81,
101, 102, 109, 110
Moss, Mary, 25, 38, 39, 40, 42, 118; and
Minnie's drugstore purchases, 33, 34,
93, 98; testimony, 67–68; and Walk-
up's murder, 42, 60, 107
murder, 107; a hanging offense, 66, 103–4
Murphy, Joseph, 68
Myers, Michael, 115

Newman's. *See* G. W. Newman's Depart-
ment Store
New Mexico, 120, 121, 123
New Orleans, LA, 3, 13, 14
New Orleans Cotton Exposition. *See*
World's Fair
New Orleans Daily Picayune, 45, 47, 61;
on the women attendees of the trial, 80
New Orleans Mascot, 4, 9, 48; and James
Houston's attack on editor, *5,* 6–7,
21–22, 47, 95
New Orleans Times-Democrat, 46, 49
New York City, NY, 124, 154, 176
New York Herald, 47
Nicolls, Princess Lida, 209–10
Nottingham, Naomi, 87

Osmond, George, 4, 5, *5,* 47
oxalic acid, 46

Paiute Indians, 136
Pam, Hugo, 155, 156, 157, 167, 211
Parkman, 80–81
Payne, John Barton, 168, 172, 175
Peacock, Everett, 213–15
Pike, Charles "Charley" Burrall, 161, 162,
164
Pike, Eugene "Gene" Rockwell, 161, 162,
166–67, 170, 173, 174, 211, 214
Pike, Eugene S., 159
Pike, William "Billy" Wallace: and alcohol,
161, 165; and Gale Thompson's bach-
elor party, 159, 161–62; marriage and
death of, 208; photograph, *169;* rela-
tionship with Josephine Moffitt, 162,

163–64, 165, 167, 176; sketch of, *161, 169;* testimony in *Moffitt v. Pike,* 174
Plumb, Preston B., 110
Poe, Edgar Allan, 134
Poe, Isaac, 134
Poinsette, Nancy, 77
poison. *See* arsenic; cyanamide; cyanide; strychnine
Pony Express, 136
Prendergast, Patrick, 151
Pullman, George, 160
Purnell, James, 150, 153
purple prose, 46

quinine, 31, 32, 68, 93, 97

Reid, John E., 94, 123
Reutlinger, Arthur, 139
Rich, Delia, 114
Richards, Mary, 205
Rigley, G. W. *See* Morton, Nathaniel Benjamin
Riley, Tom, 149
Ritter, Henry App, 188
Ritter, Henry, Jr., 188–89, 193, 194, 196, 197, 212
Ritter, Sarah "Sallie" Eckert Louderback, 188–89, 191, 193, 194, 196, 197, 212
Roberts, I. P., 141, 142, 148, 149
Ruley, Jim, 9
Ryder, Charles, 32, 44, 51, 73
Ryder's Drugstore, 32

Samuel, Johnnie, 38
Schneider, Bertha, 191, 192, 194, 195, 196, 213, 215
Scott, Charles W., 52, 53–55, 56, 78, 110, 111
Scott, Dred, 182
Scott, William W.: and Dr. Scott's arsenic story, 52, 54, 55; encystment theory of, 69, 86; Gardiner cross-examined by, 68–69; Jacobs cross-examined by, 68; Mary Moss cross-examined by, 67–68; Minnie defended by, 59, 65, 75, 76, 82, 113, 117, 119; sketch of, *53;* Sterry described by, 76; Stover cross-examined by, 86; on Sunday during the trial, 73; and the verdict, 110
Seeberg, Frederick, 156
Severy, Luther, 41, 42, 43–44, 51, 68, 204
Shannon, Thomas P., 173–74, 209
Sherman, John B., 159

Shope, Judge, 157
Smith, Asa, 80
Smith, "Silent" James Henry, 202
Snodgrass, Winfield, 34–35, 36, 49, 68, 112
snowflake, 92, 96–97
Sommers, Julia, 34, 47, 98–99, 101
Sowka, Agnes, 185–87, 190, 212
Squibb's bismuth, 39, 51
St. Louis Post-Dispatch, 45
State of Kansas v. Minnie Wallace Walkup. See Walkup trial
Stead, William, 128
Sterry, Clinton N.: banter with Fenlon, 87; closing arguments, 92, 105, 106; described by Scott, 76; further career and death of, 205; gross error made by, 106; Jay cross-examined by, 84–85; Lanphear cross-examined by, 87; lies told by Minnie about, 118; Minnie cross-examined by, 94–100; Morton cross-examined by, 78–79; Parkman cross-examined by, 81; portrayed by Dodds, 106; and the prosecution, 65, 106, 117; and the rebuttal, 101–2; Scott cross-examined by, 78; and Scott's cross-examination of Mary Moss, 67–68; Van Holmes cross-examined by, 76; viewed by the courtroom audience, 100
Stewart, Rhinelander, 202
Stover, H. W., 85–86
strychnine: calculation required to use for murder, 107; and the inquest, 51; and Ketcham's death, 147, 148; Minnie's purchases of, 31, 32–33, 34, 35, 36, 41, 42, 46–47, 68, 72, 93, 97–98, 111–12, 113; recovery from, 35; and stain removal, 33, 41, 42, 43, 97; symptoms of poisoning, 33, 92
Stuart, William, 190
Sullivan, John L., 203
syphilis: and arsenic, 76, 81, 82; and Walkup, 70, 87, 112; woman treated for, at Walkup's request, 82, 85–86

Thiel Detective Agency, 137
Thompson, Gale, 159
Thompson, Mrs. William Hale, 209
Thompson, Percy, 161, 162, 163, 172
Thompson, William "Big Bill" Hale, 159, 161, 162, 171, 172; photograph, *160, 171*
Thompson, William Hale, 211, 214
Thorpe, Margaret, 173, 209
Times-Democrat, 4

Times-Picayune, 4
Tolleston Club, 161
Toomey, Michael, 165
Topeka Daily Capital, 45
Torrey, Sena, 132, 139, 143, 149, 150, 154
Torrio, Johnny, 128
Trude, Alfred S.: Billy defended by, in
    Moffitt v. Pike, 168, 169–70, 172,
    174–75; fishing lure named after,
    211; in *Hansen v. Ketcham,* 151, 153,
    154–56, 157
Trude, George, 151, 168
Tuthill, Judge, 155
Twain, Mark, 29, 127
Twombly, Hamilton M., 183

Ursuline Academy, 8, 48, 129

Vanderbilt, Cornelius, 183
Vanderbilt, Grace, 207
Van Holmes, 76
Vickery, Fannie, 47, 68
Victor, Prince, 176, 209
Vinegar, Sis, 104

Walkup, Annie (first wife), 13
Walkup, Elizabeth Ann "Libbie" or
    "Lizzie," 13, 15, 16, 17, 40, 67; diamond
    ring purchased by Walkup for, 91–92;
    and the fire incident, 39–40, 68, 94;
    and the Gutekunst-Wilhite affair, 123;
    marriage, 124, 203; Minnie's attempts
    to implicate, 42, 47–48; relationship
    with Minnie, 16, 23, 25, 39, 49; sketch
    of, *24;* and Walkup's death, 41, 44, 49,
    51, 60k, 107, 115
Walkup, Hannah Maddock (second wife),
    13, 22; mentioned, 32
Walkup, James Reeves: age of, 11, 24; al-
    leged arsenic eating, 52, 53–56, 60, 76,
    78, 81, 82, 83–85, 92–93, 111, 117, 119;
    alleged illness in Topeka, 68, 80–81,
    82, 92, 99; alleged suicide attempt, 36,
    37, 68, 76, 112; appearance of, 11; arse-
    nic poisoning, 37, 38–39, 48; author's
    views on death of, 111–13; autopsy,
    46, 55–56, 68, 70–71, 87; death of, 44,
    47, 55, 124, 195, 204; depicted by the
    defense, 76; estate, 113, 114, 116, 121,
    122, 123–24, 127, 151; funeral, 49–50,
    147; interest in getting better, 54–55;
    kidney stone ailment, 13–14, 52, 55;
    marriage to Minnie, 14–15, 16, 23, 24,

29, 30, 48; mentioned, 34, 120, 203;
    and Minnie's shopping, 27–28, 29,
    113; Minnie suspected by, 40–41, 42;
    money given to Wallace family, 16,
    25–26; in New Orleans, 15; niece of,
    in Chicago, 181; oysters eaten by, 38;
    political and financial success of, 11,
    12–13; prescription medication taken
    by, 13–14; previous marriages, 11, 13;
    reaction of family and friends to Min-
    nie, 21–23; and sexually transmitted
    diseases, 11, 56; sexual proclivities of,
    11, 26, 29, 36, 37, 76, 78–79, 80, 88,
    112, 113; sketch of, *23;* strychnine poi-
    soning, 33, 35; will made by, 195; and
    the World's Fair, 10, 13
Walkup, Martha "Mattie". *See* Hood, Mat-
    tie Walkup
Walkup, Minnie Wallace: appearance of,
    3, 7, 35, 46, 66, 114, 117–18, 123, 150;
    arsenic purchased by, 35, 38, 41–43,
    51, 56, 72, 93, 97, 98, 99, 111, 112, 119;
    birth of, 7, 8; in Chicago, 124, 127, 129,
    130, 131; contacted by Morton, 79–80;
    copycats, 103; demeanor after Ket-
    cham's death, 145, 146; demeanor after
    Walkup's death, 46, 47; education of, 8;
    in Emporia, 16, 24–25, 115; entertain-
    ing at the Wallace House, 9, 14; and
    Frankie Morris, 77; under house arrest,
    46, 59; innocence protested by, 41–42;
    in jail, 59, 60, 121–23; and Judge
    Houston, 3, 8, 48, 95, 112, 119, 120; and
    Ketcham's estate, 138, 150–51; lies told
    by, 26, 30–31, 46–47, 51–52, 60–61,
    68, 118, 119; marriage to Walkup, 16,
    17, 23, 24, 29, 48, 94–95; names used
    by, 8, 131; notoriety of, 59, 114; party
    house rented by, 138–39, 143, 146,
    154; photograph, *114,* 114; poems and
    songs about, 88, 100–101; post-trial
    behavior, 113, 114–15; post-trial plans,
    109, 119; pregnancy hinted at, 60, 121,
    122; quoted, 45; relationship with Lib-
    bie Walkup, 23, 25, 68; relationship
    with Walkukp, 11, 15, 16, 17; shopping
    in Emporia, 26, 27–28; signature, *145;*
    sketch of, *23, 27, 30, 34, 138;* stories
    told by, 68; strychnine purchased by,
    31, 32–33, 34, 35, 36, 41, 42, 46–47, 68,
    72, 93, 97, 98, 111–12, 113; suspected
    in Walkup's illness and death, 40–44,
    47, 61; unprepared for housework and

marriage, 24–25; viewed as innocent, 52, 54, 60, 61, 73, 75, 88, 100–101, 109, 118; viewed by Greer, 47; viewed by Jay, 83, 85; and Walkup's estate, 113, 114, 116, 121, 122, 123–24, 127, 151; Walkup's friends' background check on, 21–22; and Walkup's funeral, 49–50; and Walkup's murder, 29, 31, 112–13 (*see also* Walkup trial)

Walkup, William, 61

Walkup trial: attendance at, 62–63, 66, 75, 80, 89, 105; attorneys for, 64, 65, 117; author's views on, 111–13; and the autopsy, 70–71; closing arguments, 105–8; and the defense, 74, 76, 77–83; deliberation, 108–9, 110; Elizabeth Wallace's testimony, 88, 89–90; hypothetical questions, 71–73, 86; inquest, 51–52; judge, 64; jury instructions, 104–5, 106; jury selection for, 63, 66–67; Minnie's complaints about, 103, 109; Minnie's cross-examination, 94–100; Minnie's demeanor during, 76–77, 90, 100, 106; Minnie's direct examination, 90–94; Minnie's testimony, 88; newspaper coverage, 45, 59, 73–74; notoriety of, 45, 50, 61; preparing for, 62–64; prosecution's case, 67–71, 71–73; rebuttal, 101–2; reporters of, partial to Minnie, 73; song sung about, 100–101; Sunday during, 73–74; transcript of, 63–64, 73–74; verdict, 109–11, 118–19; women attending, 62–63, 80

Wallace, Elizabeth (mother): boarders taken in by (*see* Wallace House); buried in Forest Home Cemetery, 131, 146; in Chicago, 124, 127; children of, 7; and Cincinnati, 17; death of, 131, 201, 202; departure from Emporia, 115; and Houston's relationship with Minnie, 3, 57; marriage and divorce of, 7, 8; and Minnie's financial future, 8; and Minnie's relationship with Walkup, 14, 15, 16, 17, 22, 25, 48–49; reactions to Walkup's death, 48–49; testimony, 88, 89–90, 100; as unlikely coconspirator with Minnie, 29, 48, 89; and the Walkup case, 60–61, 66, 110, 112, 113; Walkup's friends' background check on, 21–22; World's Fair visited by, 16

Wallace, James (father), 22; concerns for daughter, 6, 8, 48; death of, 201; divorce, 7, 8; and Minnie's paternity, 48; and the Walkup case, 48, 65, 117

Wallace, Mabel Estelle. *See* Walkup, Minnie Wallace

Wallace, Minnie. *See* Ketcham, Minnie Wallace Walkup; Walkup, Minnie Wallace

Wallace House, 7, 9–10, 14, 22, 90; sketch of, *8*

Walsh, Thomas F., 206–8

Ward, Edward C., 65, 117

Warren, S. S., 102

Watson, Violette, 206–8

Wells Fargo Express, 27, 28, 93

Wheldon, Ben, 38, 39, 41–42, 43, 54

White, Margaret, 170

White, William Allen, 204

Whittlesey, Nelson, 12, 24

Wilde, Oscar, 159

Wilhite, Jefferson, 62, 82–83, 110, 205; and Minnie's house arrest, 49–50, 59; photograph, *122*

Wilhite, Oscar Milton "Mit," 121, 122–23, 205; photograph, *122*

Willis, William "Willie" (cousin): character of, 25; death of, 124; and the fire incident, 40; mentioned, 3, 15, 17, 28, 34; relationship with Minnie, 7; and Walkup, 25, 30, 36, 196; and Walkup's death, 46, 47, 49, 59, 196; warning against oysters given by, 38, 39

Wilson, Mrs. Augustus, 65, 117

Wilson, Woodrow, 168

Winfield Courier, 56, 77

Wing, Frank, 128, 159, 162, 174, 186

Wing, Thomas, 150

Wooster, Waldo, 59, 66, 96

World's Columbian Exposition, 124, 127

World's Fair, 9–10, 16, 21, 65, 124, 150

World's Industrial and Cotton Centennial Exposition. *See* World's Fair

Yerkes, Charles Tyson, 154, 181, 182, 183–85

Zennecke, Adolph, 4, 5; sketch of, *5*